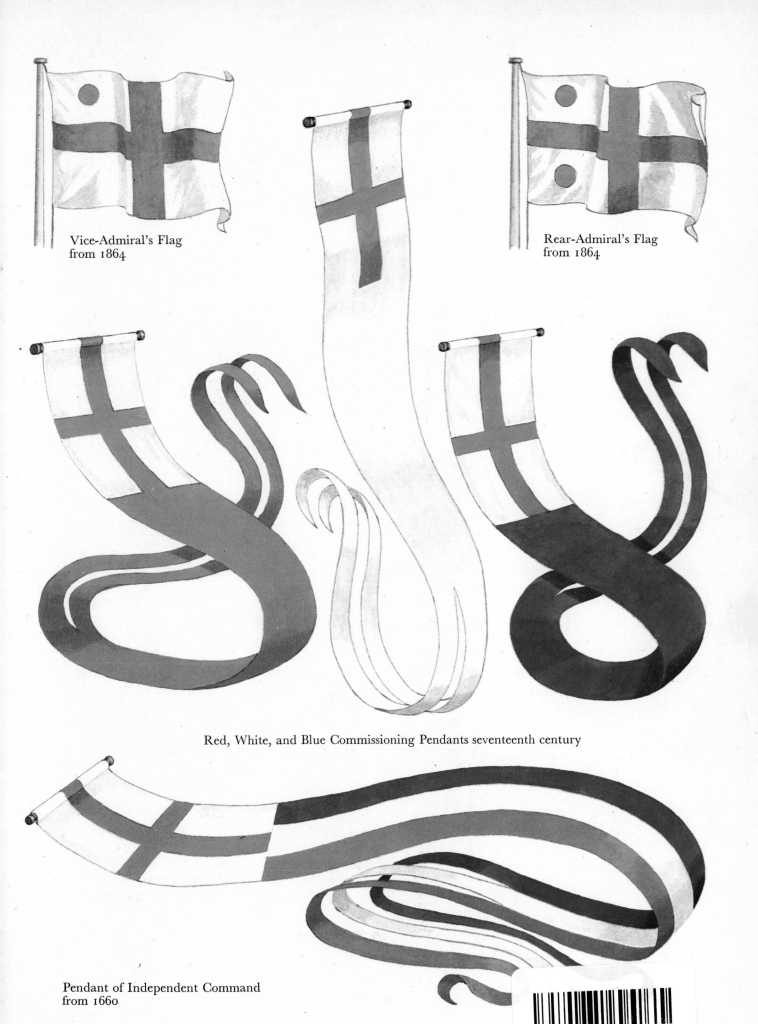

Vice-Admiral's Flag
from 1864

Rear-Admiral's Flag
from 1864

Red, White, and Blue Commissioning Pendants seventeenth century

Pendant of Independent Command
from 1660

The Wooden Fighting Ship

The Wooden

in the Royal Navy AD 897–1860

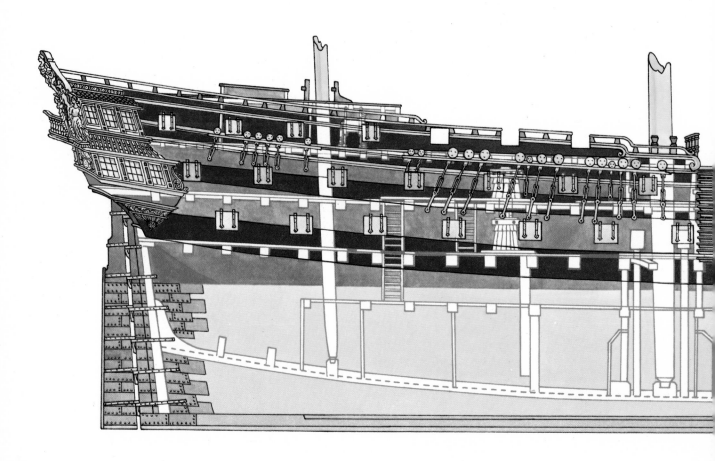

The classic ship of the line, a British seventy-four. This drawing was made from the draught of the Berwick of 1775. She fought the French at the Battle of Ushant in 1778, the Dutch at Doggerbank in 1781, and was in Lord Howe's fleet that finally relieved Gibraltar in 1782. In 1793 she was in fleet at the capture of Toulon. Eighteen months later, still in the Mediterranean, she had the rare experience for a

British ship of the line to be captured by the French. She was sailing under a jury rig, having been dismasted, when she was found by Admiral Martin's fleet and taken by three of his frigates. She fought for the French at Calder's action of Ferrol in 1805, and at Trafalgar in the same year was recaptured by the Achilles 74, but was wrecked in the storm that followed the battle.

Fighting Ship

By E.H.H. Archibald

Illustrated by Ray Woodward

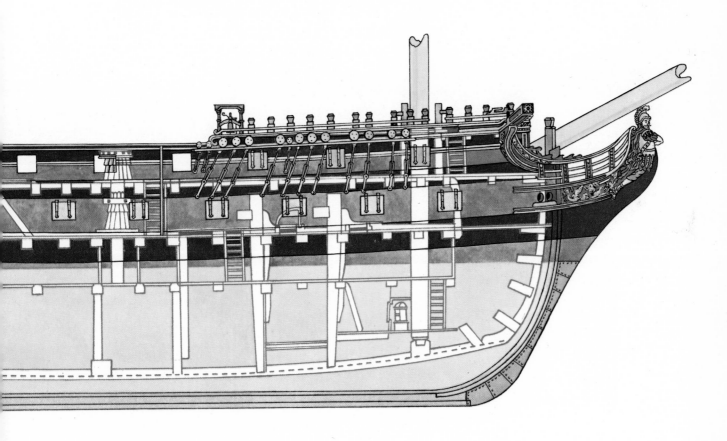

ARCO PUBLISHING COMPANY, INC., NEW YORK

Published by ARCO PUBLISHING COMPANY, INC.
219 Park Avenue South, New York, N.Y. 10003
Copyright © Blandford Press Ltd, 1968
All Rights Reserved
First American Edition 1970
Reprinted 1976
Library of Congress Catalog Card Number 75-124422
ISBN 0-668-02369-4
Printed in Great Britain

Preface

The original conception was for a single volume in pocket format on the history of English fighting ships. As the months went by, the conception grew, like Jack's beanstalk. We decided at the outset that the best way to depict the ships and their details was by original illustrations, rather than by prints and reproductions. This gave better continuity and flexibility. The meticulous quality of Ray Woodward's illustrations, working from the original architect's plans and sketches, was too good to cram into the small format, and we feel that this more ample page does justice not only to the drawings but to the magnificent ships which they depict. We also realised that it would be necessary to split the book into two volumes; this one to deal with the wooden armament and the following one to cover the iron and steel fighting ship up to the present time.

Nearly all the material for this work is to be found in the National Maritime Museum at Greenwich, and I am grateful to my colleagues for their assistance in making it available to me as I required it. Especially I would like to thank George Osbon for letting me use his copious private notes on the early steam navy. Grateful thanks too to Ian Rowan for typing most of the draft from my not very legible manuscript. Finally I take it most kindly that Charles Rickitt should have suggested to Blandford Press that I could write this book, which has been a most enjoyable and informative experience. It has been a particular pleasure to work with an artist of Ray Woodward's standards, whose speed in grasping the technicalities of an unfamiliar subject made my work so much easier. Indeed apart from putting a live cow in the bilge of a frigate, quickly rescued, his has been a near-perfect performance.

EDWARD H. H. ARCHIBALD

Contents

To attack with greater numbers from a larger, higher platform: King Alfred's lesson in tactics to the Danes.

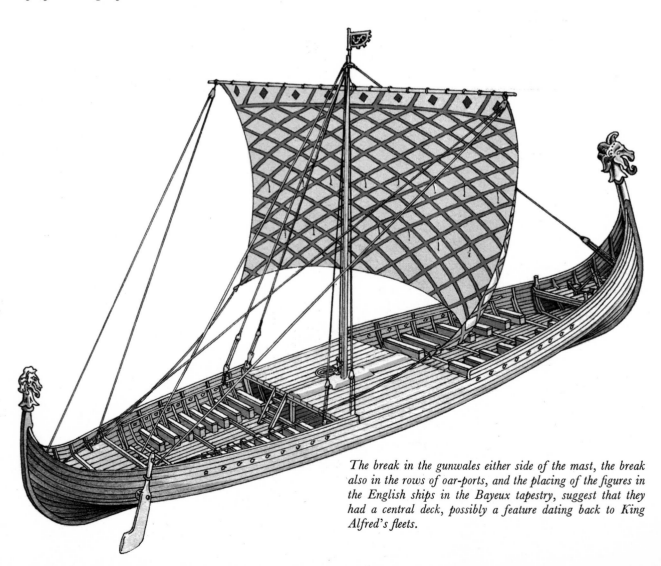

The break in the gunwales either side of the mast, the break also in the rows of oar-ports, and the placing of the figures in the English ships in the Bayeux tapestry, suggest that they had a central deck, possibly a feature dating back to King Alfred's fleets.

1

Alfred the Great to William the Conqueror

The purpose of warship design is now and has always been to procure some advantage over the known qualities of the vessels of one's enemies, or potential enemies, or friends. The first conscious expression of this principle in England that we know of occurred in the year 897, when King Alfred ordered ships to be built to particular specifications which he believed would enable his navy to beat the squadrons of the marauding Danes. The new ships that the king ordered were to be larger and higher than the Danish ships, so that when they met in combat the English had the advantage of fighting from a higher platform in greater numbers, and the Danes were defeated. To keep their advantage the English would decline to land and fight on shore if they found the Danes already disembarked, but would stand off shore and wait for the Danes to put to sea and fight them. Alfred thus created a formidable navy and used it as an effective weapon against his enemies, but there was to be no continuity of organisation or service, nor could there have been in those chaotic times. As soon as the danger receded the ships were laid aside, and a new navy had to be created to meet a new threat. As for the Danes, many settled in the lands they had come to pillage and became respectable, so that this nuisance abated.

We do not know what Alfred's ships looked like, but the Saxon Chronicle does say that they were different in appearance from those of the Danes. Even so, apart from their size, it seems unlikely that they differed in more than styling and proportions, and their higher freeboard would give them a contrasting profile to the sleek Danish ships. But if we do not know the form or details of the English ships we do know something about the ships of the Danes and the other Scandinavian tribes. Two beautiful ships of this period have been discovered in Norway and restored, but they are both merchant ships, both shorter and proportionately broader in the beam than the long ships. The bigger of the two, the Gokstad ship, is 76 feet long and 17 feet broad amidships, clinker-built and decked close to her floor. There is provision for a single mast which carried a large square sail, and being a merchant ship she would have depended more on this than on her oars. There are sixteen oar ports a side, since her crew would normally be small. The long-boats which were the fighting ships, or drakkans, were enormous open rowing boats which, even allowing for poetic exaggeration, must have been up to 150 feet long, twice as long as the largest pleasure boats now plying on the Thames in the London area.

The size and shape of these ships were conditioned to their purpose, which in the ninth century was to transport a strong body of men as quickly as possible to the places that were to be attacked. The large crews made possible the manning of powerful banks of oars, thirty or forty a side, and these, unlike in a merchant ship, were the principal means of propulsion. They were especially important in the rivers which were the high roads through the lands they sailed to, and on whose banks were to be found the richest communities. There was a large square sail as well as the oars and the ships must have run well before the wind or on a broad reach. The long ships, though built for war, were not themselves weapons, like the ram-bowed Mediterranean galleys, nor did they carry weapons heavier than hand arms. Their armament was their men and they provided the transport and on occasion a platform to fight from. The crew had the comfort and amenities of an open rowing boat, though it seems reasonable to assume that they could rig an awning if they wanted to. But the men were used to hardships, both ashore and afloat; they were vigorous and mostly young, and there was the expectation of adventure, the chance of coming on a rich town, to fight and kill, to take what they wanted and destroy what they did not, and afterwards to celebrate with the wine and women of the place.

As a result of the Danish invasions in the late tenth and early eleventh centuries they gained political control in England, and the raids largely ceased. From this time on the role of the oared fighting ship became less and less important in northern waters, and the need for a bluffer cargo carrier increased.

There is no reason to believe, however, that the English and Norman ships in 1066 differed substantially from Alfred's. The Bayeux Tapestry, which records the Norman invasion and the events leading up to it, confirms this, but also makes a clear distinction between the Norman and English ships. In the former there is a continuous row of oar ports which indicates that their decks were flush from bow to stern. The English ships, on the other hand, have a break in the gunwale amidships where there are no oar ports, and the men standing in that area near the mast can be seen from their ankles up, while those behind the oar ports stand lower. This can surely only mean that the English ships had a deck amidships with a 6- to 8-foot clearance between the floor and deckhead. This must have been useful as a covered place for cargo or shelter, and in a fight the high deck would have been a useful vantage point. It is to be noted also that both Normans and Saxons lined the inside of the gunwales of their ships with their long oval topped shields, which protruded to give added protection against wind and spray. In the Saxon ships the shields amidships are outside the gunwales, which is evidence that there was something to prevent their going inside, such as a raised deck.

2

The Normans to the Tudors

This is the period in England when the fighting ship as a separate design disappeared for over four hundred years in the largest type of vessel. These all came to be designed to the needs of commerce, and if they also had sometimes to be modified to take an army to war, this could be done. This does not mean that the oared warship entirely disappeared. Large double-ended rowing boats called balyngers were used in peace to fend off raids by the pirates who came to infest the Channel and other coastal waters; and in wartime they accompanied the fleet, which consisted mostly of sailing cogs, though also of some large-oared vessels.

If the English had abandoned the building of large specialised fighting ships it did not mean that they had abandoned fighting; far from it. It is, therefore, within the scope of this book to look at the merchant ships in which they fought and see how their design affected tactics. In any case, it was this type of ship that was to become the vehicle for Britain's naval supremacy over the world, though much modified, and much later. The chief pressure which forced a change in design was the need for the big double-ended ships to carry more cargo, but so long as they kept their banks of oars the deck could not be too high above the water-line or the oarsman could not work, nor could the ships be too broad in the beam as they would be too clumsy to row. Once, however, the oars were abandoned in the twelfth century the deck and sides of the ships could be raised to make room for a proper hold inside. The raising of the ships' centres of gravity meant that their beams had to be increased as well for stability and to keep their draught shallow for river work. At the same time their length had to be reduced, for long, wide, high ships with a single sail and a steering oar would have been too unhandy. They were still double-ended and clinker-built like the Viking ships, but they would not sail to weather as a replica of the Gokstad ship was able to do. They were called cogs.

By the thirteenth century, ships of this type that were impressed by the king in time of war began to be modified if they were expected to have to fight. This took the form of raised platforms with protective sides fore and aft called forecastles and sterncastles from which the bowmen could shoot down into the waist of an enemy ship, and these were followed by a topcastle at the head of the mast, which, however, could only have held a couple of warriors. These structures served no other purpose and were dismantled at the end of the charter. The ships were fought by soldiers as if they were little floating forts, which was really what they were. On the whole the men relied on their hand

The cog, a double ended sailing ship with a steering oar, developed in the twelfth and thirteenth centuries for trading, but here shown with a temporary forecastle, aftercastle and topcastle, as modified for war.

The nef, being fitted with a rudder, was no longer double-ended, and here, as in the detail, the old high sternpost is retained which gave the chief support to the aftercastle, so that the tiller had to bow round it. This is an early type of the first half of the fourteenth century.

arms, as the use of the great siege engines for throwing rocks would not have been practical; though some of the smaller catapults and slings were used on occasion. In 1217 when a French fleet under Eustace the Monk threatened Kent, the English purposely manœuvred to have the weather gauge, bore down on them and threw bags of quicklime over them. Under cover of this cloud of blinding powder they grappled, boarded and entered the French ships, winning a brilliant victory, with great slaughter.

This was a real naval battle of ships and movement, more so than the better remembered Battle of Sluys in 1340, which was Edward III's curtain-raiser to the Hundred Years War. The French fleet of about two hundred ships was drawn up in four lines, the ships of the first line at least were chained together side to side, a most unwieldy arrangement, reflecting an attitude of mind adapted only to land warfare on the part of the French commander. The English with a similar force attacked them from to windward and destroyed nearly all of them.

In this nef, slightly later than the one on page 5, the stern post is cut short below the rudder-head, so that support for the aftercastle comes from the raised gunwales, which soon become permanent structures for shelter and accommodation.

By this time the English cog type ships were being built with rudders instead of using steering oars and were called nefs. This made a considerable difference in their appearance since they had now a distinctive bow and stern, but it made no material difference to their qualities as fighting ships. Another development was that the temporary castles, which had been growing in size, began in the mid-fourteenth century to become permanent structures, boarded in all round for cabins. This began with the sterncastle and was followed in the fifteenth century by the forecastle. When this happened the difference between a ship prepared for war and a merchant ship disappeared; they were equally fitted to play both roles as built. Indeed they had to fight to trade, for pirates were plentiful, and many merchants, who would not have thought of themselves as pirates were close to Chaucer's Shipman:

> *who of nyce conscience took no keep*
> *If that he faught, and hadde the hyer hond,*
> *By water he sent hem hoom to every lond.*

An early fifteenth-century nef with solid castles, but as yet only one sail.
These ships were suitable without alteration for warlike or peaceful purposes.

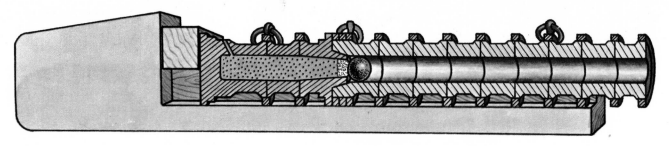

3

The Tudor Navy and the Gun

It was the use on shipboard of the heavy gun that forced the shipwrights to modify the design of ships intended for war, with the result that they could only be of practical use as fighting ships, being uneconomical if put to trade. By the same token, ships built for trade could no longer satisfactorily be adapted for war. This is a generalisation which was not true of all classes of ships, but it was true of ships of the largest size and force afloat at the end of the Tudor period, and it marks the end of the medieval dual purpose ship. Guns had been carried aboard ships since the fourteenth century, but they were at first of small size and only meant as man killing adjuncts to the hand arms. The opportunity for a change came with the rapid developments in the size and rig of the northern round ship, which at the beginning of the fifteenth century had one mast, one sail and one deck; and at the end of it had perhaps as many as three masts and a bowsprit, five sails and two decks, and these ships could bear guns heavy enough to cause damage to an opposing ship's structure and not just to her crew.

There were two types of large gun available, the cast bronze or brass muzzle-loader or the iron breech-loader, and before they invented a suitable gun-carriage and tackle for overcoming the loading problems of muzzle-loaders on board ship, the early naval guns of any size were iron breech-loaders. Because of the difficulty of heating iron to a sufficient temperature to pour into a mould, it had proved impossible for the medieval gun founders to cast them in iron. They therefore made them exactly as a cooper makes a barrel, with a faggot of wrought-iron bars fitting together to form a tube; this was the earliest and worst kind of iron gun. The bars were held in place by iron hoops sweated on round the outside, the joins between the bars being sealed with lead. The resulting

A wrought-iron breech-loader with a bar-barrel, fifteenth to mid-sixteenth centuries.

Preparing a breech-loading bobbin-barrelled gun for firing. The block and tackle shown are hypothetical, but the guns must have been secured in some way.

barrel was open at both ends, so a separate chamber was attached to one end to hold the powder. The whole contrivance had to be set in a stout timber cradle with a solid piece of timber behind the powder chamber which took the recoil and held the wedge, which in turn held the breech shut. The bar gun type of bombard was followed by an improved design at the end of the fifteenth century, whereby instead of a barrel of iron bars, a core of short lengths of wrought-iron tube was made, the ends of each being lipped like a cotton bobbin. As with the bar guns, the tubes were held together by broad iron bars, beaten round the barrel where the lips met. These guns were breech-loaded as before, but a big improvement on the bar guns though still a very rough instrument. Indeed the bar guns must have belched fire from other places than the barrel mouth and touchhole. The gun at Greenwich, which was salved from the king's ship *Mary Rose*, is of this type, and that ship sank off Portsmouth in 1545. It is 7 feet 6 inches long and has a bore of about 5 inches; there are rings on the barrel for moving it, but maybe also for a rope tackle to be attached to it as its wooden cradle was not solid on the deck. The gun at Woolwich on the other hand is of the bar type, as are those at the Tower of London. Both types used stone shot. In Madrid there are iron guns which combine the bar and bobbin techniques.

The size of ships' guns was partly governed by their weight; the really heavy guns had to be carried lower in the ship than the upper deck, and these took the form of large brass or bronze muzzle-loaders on wheeled carriages, carried on the lower deck. In order to get the big guns working between decks it was necessary to pierce the ship's sides for gun-ports, and to devise a carriage and tackle so that the barrel mouth could be run in and out of the port for firing and loading. These guns might be 10 or 12 feet long and threw a stone or iron ball of up to 30 pounds. In design they differed hardly at all from the guns of the mid-nineteenth century, but they were lighter and thinner for their bore since the powder was then so bad that the barrels need be no more than eighty times the weight of the shot as against about four hundred times a century later. From the mid-sixteenth century the improvement in smelting processes made possible by the blast furnace made the casting of guns in iron possible. To their credit they were cheaper than bronze ones and the metal being harder they did not bruise themselves with their own shot, nor did their vents so easily wear out. On the other hand, when the barrel failed, it shattered like a bomb without warning, while the bronze barrels usually just gave a warning bulge; both the iron and bronze guns suffered too from honey-combing, making the inside of the barrels look like lump sugar. The iron guns were also despised by the gunners because they were of a coarse metal which could not be enriched by the elaborate decoration which embellished so many sixteenth- and seventeenth-century bronze pieces.

By the middle of the century all the larger units belonging to King Henry VIII had two tiers of heavy guns, with the old breech-loaders still continuing to be the main part of the upper-deck armament. The ships themselves were modelled on the most admired type of northern round ship, the carrack; the ships were up to 1000 tons, only twice as long as they were broad. Henry either built them in England or bought them from abroad, and although they were exactly similar to the largest merchant ships, they were too large and valuable, and too much modified, for gun platforms to be chartered out for trading in the summer, as the fifteenth-century English kings had done with their ships. In the winter they were laid up; so that the 'great ships' of the Tudor navy, because they were used exclusively for war, became separate and specialised fighting ships. The king was anxious to make his fleet an effective fighting force to beat the French, and was not only receptive to new ideas, but also designed some of the ships himself.

The Venetians had been trading with their galleys to England and the north European ports for many years, and it was they who developed from them a type of

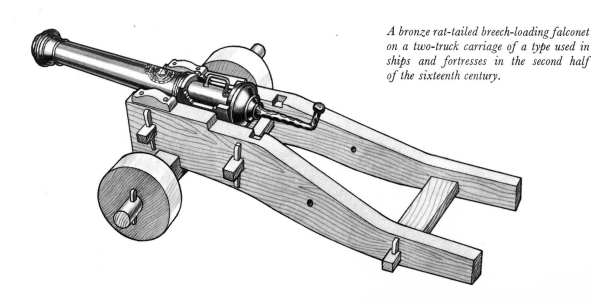

A bronze rat-tailed breech-loading falconet on a two-truck carriage of a type used in ships and fortresses in the second half of the sixteenth century.

sailing ship which the English were to adopt and turn into a world-beating warship. In these ships, the race-built galleons, the hull proportions lengthened to two and a half to three times the beam, and the towering superstructures, especially the forecastles, were reduced in size; all this in the interest of creating a faster and more weatherly ship. The Venetian ships appeared when Henry was enlarging his fleet in the first quarter of the century, and were admired and copied. Even so, it was to be many years before a full-scale maritime war was to prove or disprove the various schools of thought that existed on the effective composition of a fleet and how it should be used, so that the possibilities of the new race-built galleons were not generally appreciated at first, and indeed they were probably built to work with the galleys and galleasses, as they were in the Venetian navy.

The result was a mixture of types which reflected the conflict of ideas, for Henry's early experiences with the French convinced him that he should have in his fleet several large vessels of free movement, which at that time meant oared, as well as the smaller-oared vessels that traditionally accompanied the fleet. These were called galleasses, but according to the Anthony Anthony Rolls they did not much resemble their Mediterranean namesakes. They had square tucks, and English type superstructures, though much lower than the great ships; they also had beaks, a tier of guns along their upper decks and tiers of oars below, they were presumably long and lean in proportion. Apart from their ability to move without a wind, they were in all other respects inferior to

a great ship. They lacked the loftiness for boarding and their lower decks, instead of housing the heaviest tiers of guns, were full of oarsmen who could not fight and who, so far as the English were concerned, were extremely hard to recruit, since the English did not employ slaves, or send felons to the galleys as the French did. By the middle of the century, however, the large-oared warship was fast disappearing from the English service, probably because of the great improvement in sailing rigs, which would especially have benefited the galleon and galleass type of hull, so that the galleasses were probably rebuilt as sailing ships. By Queen Elizabeth's time the navy had only one left, and that seldom employed.

The argument as to what constituted the most effective sort of capital ship resolved itself into two main lines of thought. The first, supported by the traditionalists, the military-minded and the very able Sir Richard Hawkins, favoured the old type of carrack-built great ship. The second, passionately advocated by the hard core of seamen such as Drake, Raleigh and Sir Richard's father, Sir John Hawkins, were in favour of the race-built galleon. There is no doubt that in a close fight, and for boarding, the former type had all the advantages. From their high musket-proof superstructures her people could fire their light breech-loading pivot guns, hand guns and crossbows down on to the unprotected deck of the galleon, and even if the galleon's crews managed to swarm into her waist and clear it, the great ship's company could retire into the fore-castle and steerage and continue to harry them from there. These ships were even armed with light truck-mounted cannon of the murderer type, pointing across the waist

An English great ship of the time of Henry VIII. She is of the floating fortress type which lost favour in the Elizabethan navy, but which the Spanish continued to build.

for this purpose. The great ship needed a broad beam to carry her superstructure, and so be able also to carry more men and ordinance for her length. It was Alfred's theory again, more men on a higher platform; and in this case the enemy was the Spanish infantry, then the best in the world, who ran their ships on military lines and strongly favoured the great ship principle. The galleon, on the other hand, by her greatly superior sailing qualities, did not have to close, but could sit to weather of the great ship or off her quarter, knocking her about at a distance on her own terms. Admittedly, gunnery was a most inexact art and the bigger ship could take a lot of punishment, as well as serve it out. There was, however, one overriding disadvantage to the great ship types in an age of exploration and deep-water seafaring. They had been given a rig that should have let them sail on a wind, but their great superstructures baulked them, and their bluff bowed beamy hulls would not bite the water. They were leewardly, crank and unhandy; not at all the sort of ships in which the seamen of England cared to take the war to Spain and her empire. They therefore evolved the fast, handy big-gun warship, which lasted in principle entirely, and largely in form, until the coming of armour in the middle of the nineteenth century.

In the English galleass of the time of Henry VIII, the broadside guns are carried above the banks of oars. The type disappears from the English lists early in Queen Elizabeth's reign, but they were the precursors of the race-built galleons.

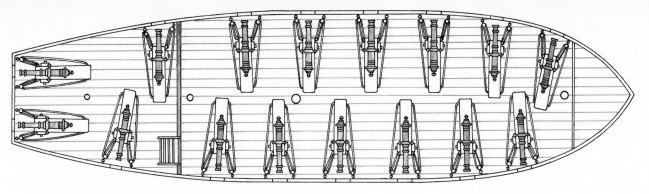

Owing to the length of the guns and their carriages, it is suggested here that the tiers were staggered on the gun-deck and falls.

4

The Elizabethan Galleon

The high-water mark of Tudor ship design was the building of the queen's ships of the galleon type, of which the most admired model was the *Revenge*, Drake's favourite ship and the one that Raleigh held up as a shining example against the great ships of 'marvellous charge and fearefull cumber'. Indeed, she and her near sisters were very small for capital ships by the standards of even fifty years after he wrote. She was 100 feet on the gun-deck, with an overall length from beakhead to taffrail of about 120 feet, or roughly the same overall length as a present-day motor gunboat. Her beam was 32 feet, a bluffer proportion than was usual later, but not far from the 100-foot gun-deck and 30-foot beam of the average eighteen-gun brig-sloop in the Nelsonic period. The Elizabethan galleons had a main armament of about twenty large truck-mounted muzzle-loading culverins, which were about 12 feet long and fired a ball weighing about 18 pounds. These were carried on the lower deck and a further battery of demi-cannon and demi-culverins were on the upper deck; these fired ball of about 10 pounds. In addition to all this, room was found to mount a further fifteen or so smaller carriage guns; all of them muzzle-loaders of bronze or brass. There was always a tendency for the English to over-gun their ships, but nothing afterwards approached this.

Elizabethan gunnery was cursed with a great variety of guns. In the same ship might be found the demi-cannon, cannon-perier, whole-culverin, demi-culverin, saker, minion and falcon, as well as a variety of lighter pivot guns. The result was that it was difficult to have a sufficient store of every type of shot when it was wanted so that by the end of the week's fighting with the Spanish Armada in the Channel in 1588, too many guns in the English ships stood around like scarecrows for want of shot. It must be supposed that the lower-deck batteries were staggered, otherwise with an internal beam of only about 28 feet and gun plus carriage lengths of about 14 feet, the guns must have recoiled on to each other. The deckhead must also have been very low for working such large pieces.

Unlike the older carrack-built ships, the galleons had a rather pronounced sheer, so to keep the weight low they had their lower gun-deck stepped down aft for the two sternmost broadside guns, which also served as stern-chasers. This enabled all the decks above to be stepped down as well, which reduced the top weight aft and also gave the opportunity for higher deckheads in the officers' quarters. The men were quartered on the lower or gun-decks, and below that there was at least a partial orlop-deck. This was a platform in the hold about 8 feet above the floor which held the cable and cabins for the boatswain, master gunner, carpenter, surgeon and storekeeper. In Elizabethan ships it would not have extended aft of the step in the deck above, and probably stopped short of the galley which was in the hold amidships. This awkward arrangement was a relic of medieval times, but in merchant ships it had been sensibly moved to the fo'c'sle; the navy followed suit in the seventeenth century. The total company of a galleon was about one hundred and fifty sailors, thirty gunners and seventy soldiers. The soldiers manned the guns as well as fought as infantry, and the sailors manned the guns and fought and sailed the ship as well. This was a flexible system which meant that the maximum fighting power was to be had from the crew; whereas in a Spanish ship the sailors were not armed and did not fight, the gunners only served the guns, and the soldiers did nothing but keep watch and ward and clean their equipment. In the fight their ship was turned into a fortress; not a nimble one, nor on the whole so powerfully gunned as the English galleons, but formidable all the same.

The moment of truth in the great ship versus galleon controversy came in 1591, when the *Revenge,* for reasons that need not concern us here, was trapped in the Azores

How open are the decks of an Elizabethan race-built galleon. This one is as close as one can get to the Ark Royal, *built privately to Sir Walter Raleigh's ideas, but bought from him by the State.*

by a fleet of fifty-three Spanish warships and fought them for fifteen hours before she surrendered. It might have been supposed that she must have fought the action by keeping her enemies at a distance, but the accounts say that she was boarded a number of times and once by the Spanish flagship the *San Felipe*, a vessel three times her size. It must have been a desperate moment for the English and the enemy should have triumphed, but the terrible havoc that the *Revenge*'s lower guns continued to make in the hull of the Spaniard caused her to haul off. It is amazing that the *Revenge*'s crew, and through sickness less than a third of them were fit to even begin the action, could sustain their morale so long in the circumstances. In the end they had used up all their powder, which was another reason for not following up her commander's famous order to 'split me the ship Master Gunner'. During the action at least two, possibly four, Spanish ships were sunk by the *Revenge*'s guns, and in the storm that blew up after it sixteen more as well as the *Revenge* foundered, presumably because of gun damage.

This action took place three years after the great confrontation with the Spanish Armada. But indeed in the week's fighting up the Channel the English fleet made little impression on the Spanish, who kept excellent order while the English banged away at their heels. Only three ships were taken, and these because they became disabled and fell behind, and none were sunk. It was at the Battle of Gravelines, after the Spanish had been driven out of Calais Roads in disorder by the fireships, that they really suffered severely from the Anglo-Dutch guns, and after that the weather took over to destroy them. In 1602 the final lesson on the uselessness of the Mediterranean-type galley in northern waters was given to Frederigo Spinola, when he tried to bring his galleys to Flanders and lost eight out of a fleet of nine to Sir Robert Mansell's galleons, assisted by the Dutch. The galleys were not only smashed by the guns, but were rammed and sailed over.

The Sovereign of the Seas of 1637. The biggest ship in the world at that date (see page 22), she was the first ship to mount 100 guns, have three flush decks, rig topgallant sails at her fore and mizzen, and a royal sail at the main.

5

Enlargements and Improvements under James 1 and Charles 1

During the last years of Elizabeth's reign the English fighting ship was supreme in northern waters, both for itself and because of the people who handled it. The Spanish had fallen behind for backing the wrong set of ideas; the Dutch were only just beginning to find their sea legs and build warships on the lines of the English galleons, and the French were too busy with civil wars to attempt anything on the sea. For the English the first fifty years of the seventeenth century were comparatively uneventful at sea. Peace was made with Spain in 1604 and apart from two abortive expeditions to La Rochelle against the French, which were more military than naval, and a skirmish or two in the Civil War, the English ships had little to do. It was the increase in foreign trade in England and the Low Countries that set the straws in the wind for a commercial war between them, and it was the massacre in 1623 of the English traders by the Dutch at Amboyna that made this certain. But England's domestic affairs and the Civil War delayed an open clash for nearly thirty years, and when it came, in 1652–53, the Dutch were badly beaten.

All this was far away when James I came to the throne in 1603. He inherited a fine navy of forty-two ships, thirty of them of great or considerable force. James had nothing particularly in mind to do with them, but he was interested in his navy and conscious of the dignity it gave to his crown; so that when the idea of a super-ship was put to him, he was delighted. She was the brainchild of a master shipwright in the royal service called Phineas Pett, a member of an old shipbuilding family which continued to be famous throughout the century. He built a model in 1607 which he showed to his patron, old Nottingham, the lord admiral, who arranged for the king to see it, and James ordered Pett to put the ship in hand. She was to be 115 feet on the keel, which would mean about 135 feet on the gun-deck, and 43 feet in the beam and was the first English ship to be double planked. She was to be twice as big as the *Revenge*, and mount fifty-five carriage guns weighing in all over 83 tons, carried on three decks. She was built to the accompaniment of three courts of inquiry, the last presided over by the king himself, at which every informed opinion roundly condemned the design of the ship, the competence of the builder, as well as his honesty in choosing his materials. In spite of this Pett survived, for he was an inner member of the dishonest little clique that ran the navy; the Lord Admiral was his patron, and he was a retainer of Henry, Prince of Wales, who was enthusiastic about the ship.

The *Prince Royal*, as she was called, was floated out at Woolwich in 1610, after one failure to do so had humbled Phineas Pett before his king. Success came with the following tide at two o'clock in the morning, and Phineas was comforted by the cheerful presence of Prince Henry, who rode over from Greenwich to be aboard for it. There are no draughts of her to show her internal arrangements; but there are a number of paintings of her, of which the authoritative ones are the two by Hendrik Cornelisz Vroom who painted her as she appeared on a visit to Flushing in 1613, and again in 1623. In the 1613 painting there are also two other large English warships which show the design trend of the time, and how the *Prince* was evolved. There had been a swing back from the extreme race-built galleon of the 1570s and 1580s, towards the great ship type. Not in the hull proportions, but in the lofty superstructures that towered fore and aft, made possible by the larger hulls. Sir Walter Raleigh, writing at this time, acknowledges the trend, and puts it down to a desire to improve the accommodation, 'The high charging of ships is it that brings them all ill qualities . . . for men may not expect the ease of many cabins and safety at once in sea-service . . . and albeit the marriners doe covet store of cabins, yet indeed they are but sluttish dens, that breed sickness in peace, serving to cover stealths, and in fight are dangerous to teare men with their splinters.'

To return to the two warships with the *Prince* at Flushing; the larger of the two has two decks with full tiers of guns on each. These have falls aft, and over the upper tier there is a third deck which forms the waist, and which bears no ordnance, but two guns aside are mounted on the same deck aft under the half-deck. What is remarkable is that the break of the half-deck and fo'c'sle is two decks high, and there is a quarter-deck abaft and above the half-deck. The other ship is similar except that the breaks of the half-decks and fo'c'sle are only one deck high and there are no guns on the third deck.

When Phineas Pett came to build the *Prince*, he gave her nearly 10 feet more beam than existing English warships, and length in proportion, so that he could increase the top weight without a dangerous loss of stability. She was built with all the decks and superstructures described in the larger of her two consorts at Flushing, but in addition the third deck was given complete tiers of guns, and another deck, presumably a light one, was built over the guns in the waist, joining the lower decks of the two superstructures. It is just possible, for we cannot see it clearly, that this deck did not cover the entire waist, but took the form of two platforms along the gunwales, as became the practice in the eighteenth century, but if this was so it was out of keeping with contemporary practice, and the full deck is the more likely. She thus had four decks, and, incredible as it may seem, she had gratings above this as a spar-deck. This was a light platform supported on stanchions, which was level with the half-deck and fo'c'sle deck, but as these also had gratings their height was raised also. The other English ships lack this, so the *Prince* may have started the fashion in the English navy.

It is not surprising that her rig was light by later standards, for she must have been top heavy and crank. She was rigged as a four-master, which was a little old fashioned by that date, and is shown at Flushing with the recent additions of topgallant sails at the main and fore, and square topsails at the mizzen and bonaventure-mizzen. These last required crossjack yards, to which the riggers had felt obliged to bend sails, a

'A ship to fight for a Kingdom', the Prince Royal, *55 guns of 1610.*
The first three-decker, she was the greatest ship of her time (see page 21).

practice soon dropped. The picture of her in 1623 shows her in her winter rig; no
topmasts on the mizzen and bonaventure-mizzen, and no topgallant masts on the main
and fore. There is provision for a sprit topmast, which was not in the 1613 picture, but
the mast is not stepped, and her spar-deck on the fo'c'sle has been removed; all of which
is evidence of a very tender sided ship. One other alteration is that her channels have
been brought down a deck in the case of main and fore from the upper to middle
gun-deck level. This was presumably because the tumblehome of the sides would give
the shrouds a better leverage from the middle deck, and this practice continued until
they went up again in the 1740s, and up again, in three-deckers to quarter-deck level
in 1794.

She was, of course, a prestige ship, a mighty galleon with the potential of a great
ship; indeed a 'ship to fight for a kingdom', as they said at the time, and she had no
sisters and no peers until Phineas Pett and his son Peter built the great *Sovereign of the
Seas* in 1637.

As the *Prince* was built to be the prestige ship of James I's navy, so the *Sovereign* was
to be of Charles I's. She was a good deal bigger again than the *Prince* and triple planked,

with a keel length of 127 feet and with a beam of 48 feet. In the 1670s her gun-deck was 167 feet 9 inches, but her keel had by then been lengthened to 135 feet 6 inches. Her total length from beakhead to taffrail was 234 feet, and it was 63 feet from the bottom of her keel to the top of her huge lantern, in which twelve men might stand together. It is interesting to compare these figures with the measurements of the last wooden three-decker to serve in a British fleet as a sea-going flagship, the *Victoria* of 1859. She was 289 feet from figurehead to taffrail, had a beam of 60 feet, and it was 72 feet from the base of her keel to her poop rail, a vastly larger ship.

The *Sovereign* had a lower profile than the *Prince* with, according to her portraits, only a single deck to the break of the fo'c'sle and half-decks, though she did have a roundhouse at the after end of the quarter-deck. As built she was given the gratings such as the *Prince* had and, surprisingly, light carriage guns (murderers) were mounted to fire across the waist from the half-deck, and down the half-deck from the quarter-deck. This was old-fashioned thinking of the great ship school, which advocated close action and boarding. She carried a hundred guns on three decks which were flush throughout the length of the ship without falls. These consisted on the gun-deck of twenty cannon drakes on the broadsides and eight demi-cannon drakes as stern- and bow-chasers; twenty-four culverin drakes with six culverins as chasers formed the middle-deck tiers, and on the upper broadsides were twenty-four demi-culverin drakes and four demi-culverins as chasers. The word drakes implies cannon of a lighter type than the full cannon. There were eight demi-culverin drakes in the fo'c'sle, six on the half-deck and two in the quarter-deck. Broadside guns were also carried for the first time on the half-deck, and there was even one aside on the quarter-deck. The long low

The building of these little cruisers was probably the first instance of the building of a class of vessel to one draught, and certainly the first to have a class name; they were called The 1st to the 10th Whelps.

beak permitted a battery of eight bow-chasers in the fo'c'sle. The rig was remarkable for including royal sails at the main and fore, and a topgallant sail at the mizzen. She was the only ship in the fleet to have these sails, and although the mizzen topgallant was revived in the second quarter of the eighteenth century, it was not until the 1780s that English naval ships began to use royals again. The sprit topmast is in evidence, which carried the jack and a small square sail. Its position at the end of the bowsprit was precarious, but before the fitting of fore stay-sails it was useful in getting the ship's head about when tacking.

Unlike the *Prince*, which was, in her first building, something of a freak, the *Sovereign* was the prototype for every English capital ship to be built until 1860, two hundred and forty-three years later. To study her is to understand in all but detail the ships that fought at Trafalgar in 1805, and served at the Crimea in 1854–55. The *Sovereign* would have looked a bit odd at Trafalgar, with her long beak, her partially open quarter-galleries and old-fashioned rig; but she still would have carried a hundred truck-mounted muzzle-loaders on three decks, just like the other three-deckers, and would have been a force to reckon with. In 1651 some of her superstructure was removed to improve her performance. In the shipwrights' recommendation to the Commissioners they say:

> 'First as to the Soveraigne wee conceive that to make her more serviceable than now shee is, the gratings and the upper-decke in the midshippe bee taken downe that the side lored to the upper edge of the ports in the midshippe, the upper state room to bee taken away, the forecastle to be lored to six foote high and the works abaft be taken down proportionably to the waist and answerable to the sheere of the worke fore and after, the halfe deck to be shortened as shall bee convenient, as alsoe the head to bee made shorter and soe fitted for the sea. And the galleryes to bee altered as may be comely and most convenient for service.'

She thus assumed her modern image. The one puzzling reference in this is to the 'upper-decke in the midshippe' and the 'side lored to the upper edge of the ports'. In the *Prince* this would be perfectly understandable, but neither the drawing by the elder Van de Velde, nor the contemporary Payne engraving, from which admittedly the former may wholly derive, really suggest that there was room for a deck over the guns and under the gratings as with the *Prince*. But it does seem that she had such a deck, so either Payne was wrong or perhaps it was added in the fourteen years before she was cut down. Whatever the answer it was certainly not true, as is still sometimes suggested, that it was the upper gun-deck that was taken down and that she was made into a two-decker. Other new buildings in Charles I's reign were, in the late 1620s, ten fourteen-gun ships obviously conceived as a class as they were named the *First* to the *Tenth Whelp* and were built to deal with the Dunkirk privateers which played havoc with English trade in the Channel during the French war. The name whelp might have become a famous generic name for a type of warship, but it did not come to pass, and foreign names like frigate, corvette and sloop were adopted. In the 1630s Charles also built ten two-deckers, besides the *Sovereign* and the rebuilding of the *Prince*, the Ship Money fleet.

6

The Rates

From the time of Charles I until the 1850s the force of an English fighting ship was graded into six rates. Originally the rating was based on the number of men carried per ton, until 1677 when Pepys changed it to the number of men needed per gun. The number of men, and therefore a ship's rating depended on the number and weight of her guns, which in turn determined the size of her crew. Once a proper gun establishment had been defined (see page 134), it was no longer necessary to consider the number of men but merely rate the ships by the number of their guns. There is also a theory that in early days the word rate meant the rate at which a captain was paid, and this makes sense if one considers that captains of royal yachts were given a second-rate's pay. There were six rates in 1652, on the eve of the First Dutch War; ships with crews of over three hundred were called first-rates, over two hundred second-rates, over a hundred and fifty third-rates, and over a hundred fourth-rates, over fifty fifth-rates, and below that was the sixth-rate. The effective part of the fleet that was going to meet the Dutch, in what proved to be furious action, consisted on paper of three first-rates, of one hundred, eighty-five and sixty guns; seven third-rates of forty-six to forty guns and thirty-one fourth-rates of forty to thirty guns, but not all of these would have been fit for service. As a whole they were ship for ship larger and more powerfully armed than the Dutch ships, which proved a decisive factor in the war. The Dutch throughout the three wars built nothing larger than two-deckers, though the biggest carried over eighty guns. They were built full-bellied by English standards, so that they drew less in their shallow home waters, but it enabled them to place the ports of their lower tier over 4 feet above the water, whereas it might be as little as 3 feet in the English ships, whose fine underwater lines made them more inclined to plunge in a sea. The Dutch ships could carry provisions for four months instead of only ten weeks as for the English, which was to be important in the Third Dutch War when the English and French were blockading the Dutch coast. Because the Dutch ships had the lines and sailing performance of merchantmen, a fair proportion of their fleet consisted of temporarily converted Indiamen and large merchantmen, a practice to which the English did not resort. As the Dutch had been fighting the Spanish more continuously and much more recently than the English, they started the war more experienced in naval warfare; they also had a slight superiority in numbers of ships. Against this England had been engaged in a bloody civil war which had bequeathed to her a generation of unusually hardy and able soldiers whose Model Army was indeed a model of order and discipline to the world. When it came to a war at sea some of them exchanged their tents for a quarter-deck and brought their ideas with them. It took them a season to settle down, and the battles of 1652 were indecisive, but in 1653 the Dutch were routed at the Battle of Scheveningen and their great commander, Marten Tromp, was killed. The English success against the world's greatest maritime power owed much to a central and comparatively efficient administration, whereas the Dutch provinces each had their own administration, which supplied the ships and men for the common cause, but not often in common accord.

Cromwell as Lord Protector squeezed far more money out of the country for the navy than ever poor Charles had tried to do, besides cutting down the royal forests for his ships, with the result that by 1658 the Ship Money fleet of forty-two had risen to a Commonwealth fleet of one hundred and fifty-seven, seventy-three of these being fourth-rates and above.

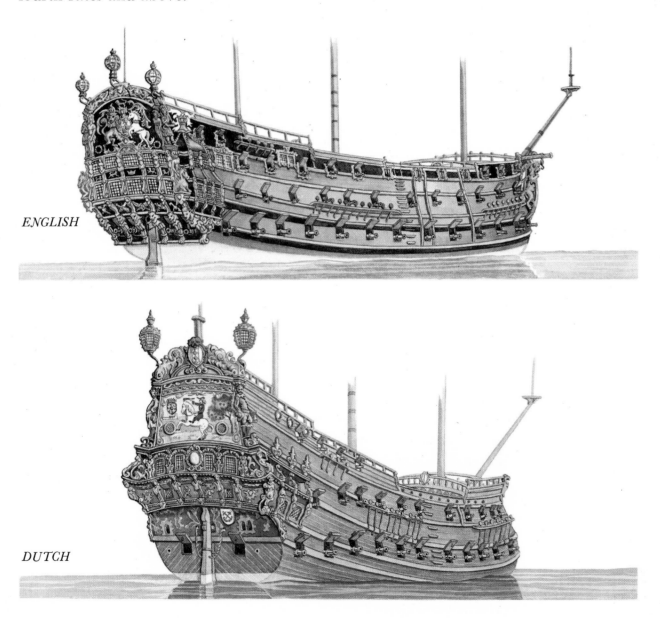

ENGLISH

DUTCH

26

7

The Restoration

Charles II, on his return as king in 1660, became master of the finest fleet in Europe, which proceeded to underline its success in the First Dutch War by giving the same enemy fleet a shattering defeat in the first action of the second, the Battle of Lowestoft, 30 May 1665. The Dutch were driven off the North Sea for the rest of the year, and in those days fleets only commissioned for the summer. Their precious East India fleet was bottled up in Bergen and would have fallen a prize to the English squadron sent to take it, for they had unscrupulously bought the co-operation of the neutral king of Denmark, had not the governor of Bergen taken the Dutchmen's part, and between them the English were driven off.

The following year a new factor emerged which nearly led to England's undoing. The French by a heavy building programme in 1663–64 now appeared as a competing sea power, and it was thought that they were going to join the Dutch for the 1666 fighting season, which began in May. Charles foolishly split his fleet, sending two-thirds under Albemarle to watch for the Dutch, who had spent the year frantically enlarging their fleet, and a third under Prince Rupert to watch for the French. In fact, the French made no move, and when Albemarle met the Dutch on 1 June he was heavily out-numbered. It was the one big chance the Dutch had of inflicting a decisive defeat on

FRENCH

The sterns of the English, Dutch and French ships of the seventeenth century were quite distinctive as those of about 1670 plainly shown. This did not apply only to the galleries, but also in the case of the English to a round, instead of a square, tuck below them.

the English fleet. After two days of fighting, in which Albemarle did most of the attacking, he decided to run west to join Rupert, and putting his damaged ships before him he set off in that admirable order that had saved him in the first two days.

It was now, however, that English losses occurred, for any crippled ship that fell behind was doomed. The most serious loss was the *Prince*, the rebuilt giant of 1610; she ran on the Galloper Sand, and Sir George Ayscue was given the sad distinction of being the only British flag officer ever to be captured in action. On the fourth day of this marathon of all fleet actions, Albemarle and Rupert, now together, and de Ruyter, fought each other to a standstill. It was a Dutch victory, but they were not elated: 'If we cannot defeat them divided, how will we fare with them united?' Six weeks later, on St James's Day, they had their answer in a severe defeat which left the English masters once again. Indeed the war would have ended with the Dutch in eclipse had not the English committed the crowning folly of at once demanding harsh peace terms at Breda in the spring of 1667, and at the same time deciding to save money and leave the fleet in ordinary. So de Ruyter sailed up the Medway on 9 June and stayed in Sheerness nearly a fortnight. The disaster to the English was more to their pride than to the fleet, which only lost six destroyed and the principal flagship captured, but the Dutch got better terms at Breda.

The battles of the Third Dutch War were fought in the same manner as the other two, but with more credit to the Dutch than to the Allies; for the French had joined the English. Though the four hard-fought fleet actions of 1672–73 were tactically drawn, they were a strategic defeat for the Allies who were trying to clear the way for an invasion; so that de Ruyter, outnumbered, won the war by denying the Allies the victory they needed, and by keeping the Dutch fleet in being.

The presence of the new French fleet in the Thames gave the English naval architects the opportunity to study their new ships, and they liked what they saw. French influence was nothing new, for Pepys regarded the Restoration fleet as 'Dunkirk built', i.e. with very fine underwater lines; yet the French two-deckers of 1663–64 were over 3 or 4 feet broader in the beam as well as being deeper in the hold than their English counterparts which made them better gun platforms and gave their lower ports 4 feet 6 inches clearance from the water. Sir Anthony Deane, the naval architect, instigated the building of similar two-deckers in the middle 1660s, his own *Resolution* 70 being the best remembered. Now again, in 1673, the French fashion proved a strong influence on English building. Charles II and his brother James visited a fine seventy-four called the *Superbe*, Deane measured her, and for some years her dimensions were the pattern for all English second- and third-rates. The end of Charles II's reign saw the navy in a sad state of neglect due to the meanness of Parliament, and an inquiry of 1684 stated that:

'The greatest part of the 30 new ships, without having ever been out of harbour, were let to sink into decay; and even their exterior appearance was rendered worse than had been usually seen upon the coming in of the Fleet after a battle. And several of the said Ships had been recently reported by the Navy Board to be in danger of sinking at their moorings. Some ships were become altogether irreparable.'

Charles himself had been the keenest sailor the country had ever had for a monarch, delighting in his yachts with his brother James, who had been a conscientious Lord High Admiral and a brave commander, and who knew as much about the fleet as any man in England. At Charles's death in February 1685 the fleet consisted of one hundred and seventy-nine vessels, one hundred and eight of them of the fourth-rate and above, and fifty-five of these of seventy guns and above.

It is from this time that the first ships' draughts exist. There are seven of them, drawn by William Keltridge and dated 1684, though one has James II's cypher on it, showing that it was finished later. The first is of a fourth-rate of the largest size, and is 124 feet 6 inches on the gun-deck with a beam of 35 feet. She is a two-decker with eleven guns on each tier, and three aside on the quarter-deck. The height between decks 'planke to planke' is 5 feet 9 inches forward and 6 feet 6 inches aft. This does not take into account the beams which make her true deckheads very low indeed; she drew over 15 feet. The second is of a slightly smaller fourth-rate, similarly laid out, and the third of a fifth-rate of the largest dimensions. She is also a two-decker, mounting twenty guns on the gun-deck which is 103 feet 9 inches ('frome ye rabbit of the stem to ye rabbit of the sternpost'). On the upper-deck she mounts five guns aside under the quarter-deck and two aside under the fo'c'sle, but none in the waist; there are also two aside on the quarter-deck. The last four draughts are of sixth-rates. These all have one deck, of from 70 to 90 feet long to carry the guns (eight to ten a side), a quarter-deck with two to three aside, and a fo'c'sle; below the gun-deck is the hold. In the case of the fourth-rates the guns are specified as culverins on the gun-deck (12-pounders), 6-pounders on the upper-deck, and sakers on the quarter-deck ($5\frac{1}{2}$-pounders), which shows that the old names still held, but that the new ones based on the weight of ball were coming in.

Fireships

The sixth-rates were also of the size suitable for adapting into fireships. These instruments of destruction were an idea as old as naval warfare, and though most alarming to see as they approached, those captains who kept cool heads usually saved their ships. As we have seen, Drake had a great success against the Spanish with his fireships, not for the destruction they did, but because the Spanish were panicked into leaving their anchorage, and drove out on the open sea never to return and some to destruction. Admiral Saunder's fleet, on the other hand, anchored in the confined waters of the St Lawrence off Quebec in 1759, survived two dangerous attacks by fireships and fire rafts from upstream, by the resolute action of the crews of his ships' boats in guiding the flaming vessels safely past.

The Dutch were fond of them and used them with some success in their wars with England. At Scheveningen in 1653 one of the best English ships, the *Andrew*, was nearly destroyed by one, and the *Henry* was grappled by two and had her sails set alight on the first day of the Four Days Fight in 1666, but survived. Their greatest success was the destruction of the *Royal James*, a first-rate and a flagship at the Battle of Solebay in 1672. The English did not seem to bother much with them during the Dutch wars, though Pepys mentions being very touched at Myngs's funeral when some of the dead admiral's seamen stopped Sir William Coventry, who was walking with Pepys, and

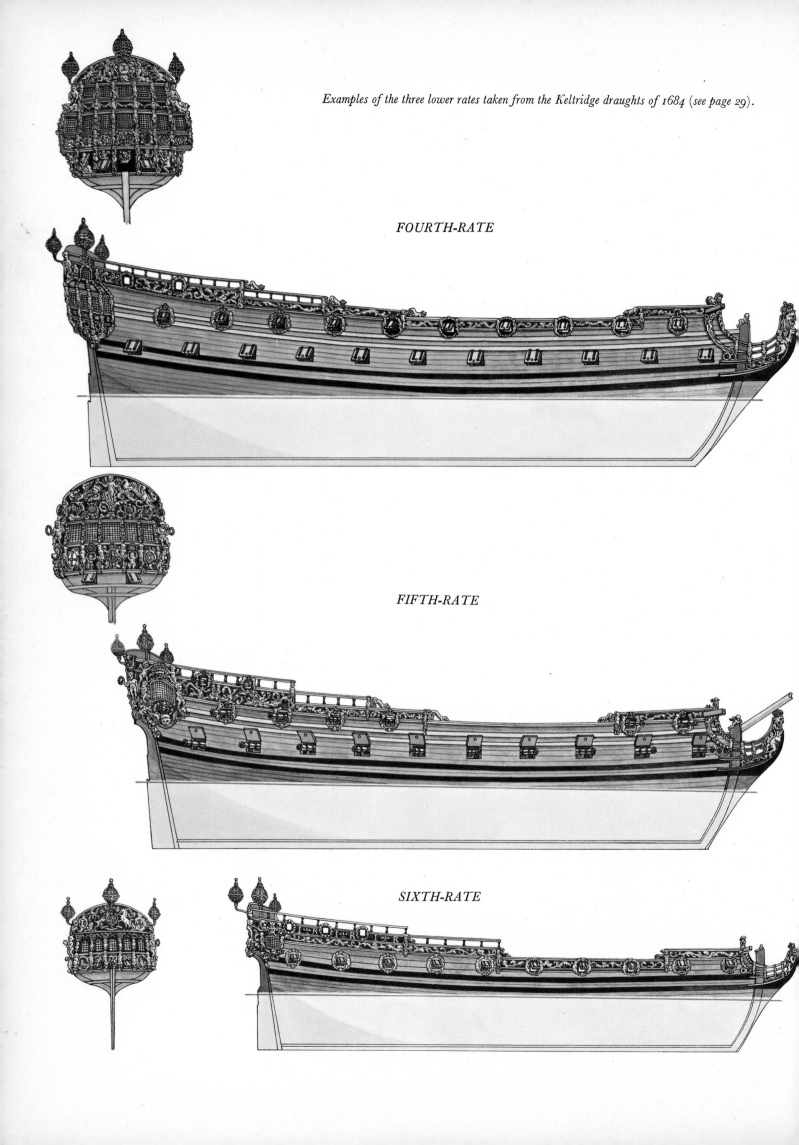

Examples of the three lower rates taken from the Keltridge draughts of 1684 (see page 29).

FOURTH-RATE

FIFTH-RATE

SIXTH-RATE

A fireship: note how the ports hinge downwards, lest they closed while she burned.

asked 'if you will please to get His Royal Highness to give us a fireship among us all . . . (to) do what shall show our memory of our dead commander and of our revenge'.

In 1675 the English only had three fireships, but in 1688 the number had risen to twenty-six, and they were used successfully to destroy a large part of the French fleet which had taken refuge at La Hogue and near Cherbourg after the Battle of Barfleur in 1692. This sudden enthusiasm did not last, and the number had sunk to one in 1712 and remained around three until 1780, when there was a sudden jump to eighteen. After that war the number was halved and declined to nothing in the Napoleonic Wars.

31

How a fireship was fitted out depended on the type of vessel used, but they were basically small vessels filled with combustibles and explosive materials. The English eighteenth-century sixth-rates which were built or converted as fireships had a complete row of ports cut in their lower decks, where before there were only two or four for guns. These were hinged at the bottom so that they would stay open and serve to let air in to speed the burning rate, and also to let the flames out to do their worst. Their upper decks had their planking removed forward of the accommodation and altered to square sectioning that kept the barrels from moving in bad weather. Over this the quarter-deck and fo'c'sle were joined to keep out the wet. Large fireships built as such might have three decks, but the middle deck was again of square sections of timber and very close to the lower deck. More common were the smaller vessels built with two decks.

In fact, outside of attacks on anchorages, they were not very effective. The technique in a fleet action was to attack the enemy ship from to windward when she was either holding her wind or, better, disabled. As only large and important ships were worth the expenditure of a fireship, there was a good chance of being sunk by the enemy guns before she could grapple. If she was fired too soon she would burn out harmlessly, and if too late the crew of the target might ungrapple her and probably free themselves of her. It took a cool nerve and good judgment on the part of the fireship captain, who at the last moment escaped with his devoted crew in a small boat that they were towing, if it was still afloat.

A sectioned drawing of a fireship showing the stowage for the combustibles.

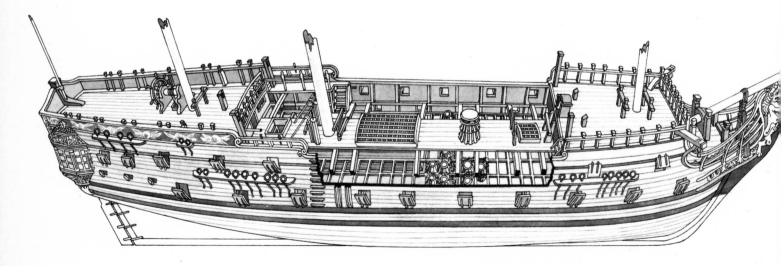

8

The Fighting Ship
in the Eighteenth Century

During the wars of the English and Spanish Successions, which covered the period 1689 to 1713, the English fleet emerged as the largest in the world with one hundred and thirty-one ships of the line on the books in 1714 which, combined with the Dutch, were too much for the French and Spanish, even though at the drawn Battle of Malaga of 1704 the opposing fleets had a parity of fifty-one ships of the line each. The expression 'ship of the line' first appears at this time because of the evolution of fighting tactics which involved manœuvring in the line of battle. The strength of the English fleet, which had a grand total of two hundred and forty-seven vessels in 1714 of all kinds, sank a little after the war, until it rose again in the mid-eighteenth century to three hundred and thirty-nine in 1748, though the increase was mainly in the smaller rates. The Seven Years War, 1756 to 1763, showed a marked increase. Of the line the number remained almost the same as in 1748 at one hundred and forty-one, but by now the fifty-gun ships were excluded, and there were twenty-four of them. The total of all vessels was four hundred and thirty-two. The struggles with France and Spain and Holland which started with the revolt in the American colonies required a further increase, so that by 1783 there were a hundred and seventy-four ships of the line on the list, which, with the rest totalled the huge figure of six hundred and seventeen vessels. It should be remembered that a fairly large proportion of the fleet was in various states of unfitness for sea, depending on time of peace and war and other factors; but in the late 1780s great efforts were made to put the fleet in order so that in 1790 ninety-three ships of the line were in the first state of repair out of a total of a hundred and forty-six, a proportion considered extremely high, though many of the older ships had been scrapped. Such a great armada required a great organisation, and the eighteenth-century navy provided the country with its largest industry and was the biggest employer of manpower, which was spread over the great dockyards at Deptford, Woolwich and Chatham on the Thames, and Portsmouth and Plymouth on the Channel.

Eighteenth-century First-rates
The first-rate men-of-war were the biggest ships in the world from the early seventeenth century until the building of iron merchantmen in the second quarter of the nineteenth century, and were rightly regarded as one of the great marvels of their age. They were reserved almost exclusively for wearing the flags of the commanders-in-chief of the main

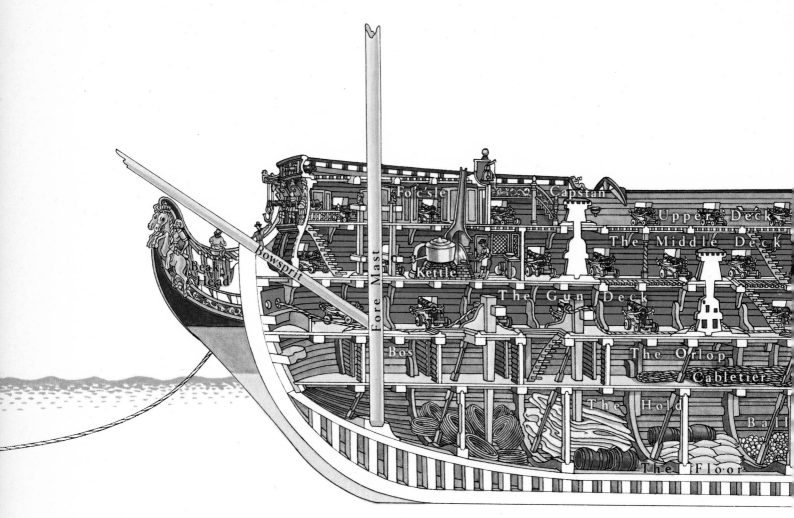

Fo'c'sle   Capstan   Upper Deck
                        The Middle Deck
Beak
Head   Bowsprit   Fore Mast   Kettle   The Gun Deck
                    Bo's   The Orlop
                            Cabletier
                        The Hold
                                Ball
                        The Floor

A profile section of a first-rate of 1701. The layout
remained almost unchanged for over 200 years.

fleets in home waters in wartime, and there was seldom more than one in commission
out of a possible half-dozen in existence. Admittedly, when old Sir John Norris commanded the Channel Fleet in 1741 there were three in commission, two as private ships,
and in 1795 both the *Queen Charlotte* and, for a time, the *Victory* also served as private
ships; but this was exceptional, and they all, right up to the very end in the 1860s,
confined their activities to European waters, never straying farther than the Baltic and
the Black Sea. In 1701 the first of the eighteenth-century first-rates, the *Royal Sovereign*,
was built by Fisher Harding. She showed an increase in size on the old *Royal Sovereign*,
originally Pett's *Sovereign of the Seas* of 1637, but not a great one; 174 feet 6 inches against
167 feet 9 inches on the gun-deck, and 50 feet in the beam against 48 feet in the older
ship.

There were two obvious differences between the first-rates built between 1700 and
1750 and the other three-deckers of the second- and third-rates, apart from their size.
They had a topgallant poop, or poop royal, which was divided into two little cabins for
the master and another officer. Previous first-rates usually had large flag lockers at the

34

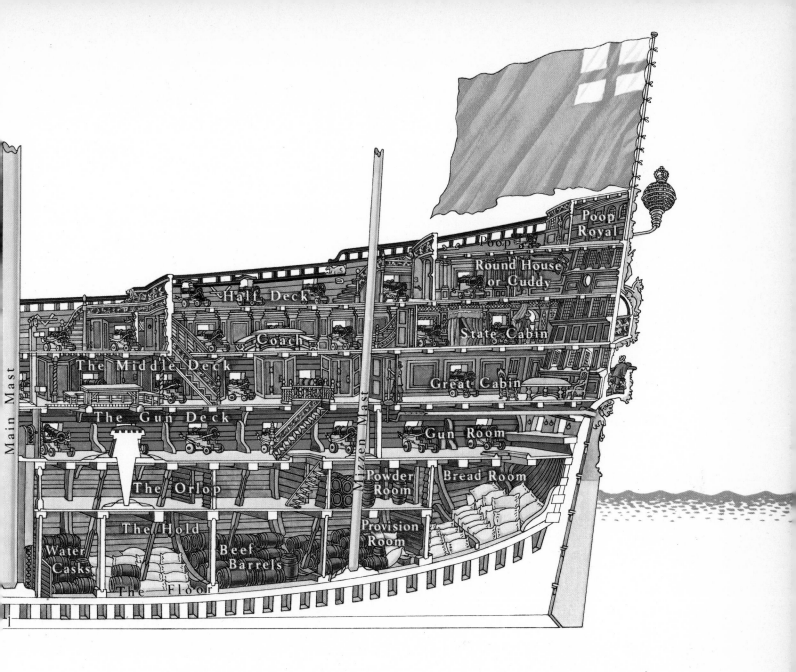

after end of the quarter-deck which also provided cramped quarters for the trumpeters. The cabins in the topgallant poop started as a modest structure, with their stern lights peeping through the carvings, but by 1737, when the *Victory* was built, it had grown to a full coach, with a stern-walk and galleries. She had a gun-deck and four tiers of stern galleries above the water-line, a formidable sight. In 1744 this ship was lost on the Casquets of Guernsey in a storm at night with all hands, apparently due to a navigational error; the only first-rate ever to be lost in this sort of accident. The only other losses in this class of ship were the *Royal George* which sank at anchor at Spithead in 1782, and the *Queen Charlotte* which accidentally burnt off Leghorn in 1800. The *Royal George* was lost under the most extraordinary circumstances. She had been listed to port by running out her guns on that side and shifting weights so that she could repair a small damage under the water-line on the starboard side; in addition she was taking on stores from a hoy, naturally also on the port side. Crowded with visitors, many of them women and children, it was not noticed that the sills of the lower ports were getting dangerously close to the water as the stores piled up on the port side of her upper deck. In any case

THE WOODEN FIGHTING SHIP

it would have been a difficult business to drag the 42-pounders up the canting-deck. As soon as the water began to lap in and add to the weight it was too late, and down she went with the loss of about nine hundred people.

The other noticeable distinction of early eighteenth-century first-rates was the profusion of decoration, which was natural for prestige ships of their importance. The amount of carving in the seventeenth century had steadily increased to include almost every visible deck fitting on and above the upper deck, as well as the beak and the stern galleries. This reached its apogee in the *Royal Sovereign* of 1701, which at the same time resulted in a large cut in the carving of future ships; for the scandal of the expense of her decorations, which included an allegorical scene, painted on panels set into the deckhead of the state cabin, induced their lordships to order that in future carving was to be confined to the beakhead and stern galleries, and anything further must be carried out in paint. This created considerable unemployment in the dockyards, and the wood-carvers sought employment where they could find it, which is why so many interiors of houses and churches decorated in the first thirty years of the eighteenth century show a wealth of fine baroque carving.

A less obvious feature of the first-rates which made them much more powerful than the other three-deckers was their armament. The difference of one hundred guns against ninety, or later ninety-eight, between the first- and second-rates may not seem much until it is realised that the mid-eighteenth-century first-rates, such as the *Royal George* of 1756, mounted 42-pounders on the lower gun-deck against a second-rate's 32s; 24-pounders on the middle deck against 18s, and 12-pounders apiece on the upper deck, though some second-rates had only 9s; late eighteenth-century ships of both classes had 18s. This is why the crew ratio had to be eight hundred and fifty men for first-rates against seven hundred and fifty for second-rates, and why the first-rates were not so often employed. The ordnance establishment of 1715 gives a choice of 32-pounders or 42-pounders for the gun-deck, but in fact the extra weight of the 42-pounder ball did not compensate for the slower rate of fire due to the greater weight of the guns. These were therefore exchanged in all ships about 1800, and a ship such as the present *Victory*, which had fought the Battle of St Vincent in 1797 with a lower battery of 42-pounders, fought at Trafalgar with 32-pounders. Ships rearmed in this way were rearmed with 18-pounders on the upper deck. The *Victory* is the biggest and the latest of the three first-rates built between 1756 and 1765, being 186 feet long on the gun-deck and 51 feet 10 inches in the beam, a considerable increase on the *Royal Sovereign* of 1701.

A further increase in size was on the way. The draught of the *Ville de Paris* (named after the French flagship captured at the Saints in 1782) of 1788, is for a ship of one hundred and ten guns, and she is 190 feet on the gun-deck, with a beam of 53 feet. It is interesting that this same draught was used for the *Hibernia* ten years later, but with 16 feet inserted in the centre section which gave her a gun-deck of 206 feet, and she was to mount one hundred and twenty guns. This lengthening, it was estimated, would raise her freeboard by 1½ feet, so that the sills of her lower gun-ports would be a clear 6½ feet above the water, or about twice the clearance of an equivalent ship of 1660. This was about the limit in size that wood alone and the traditional methods of construction could stand without the danger of serious hogging of the hull. To build bigger ships,

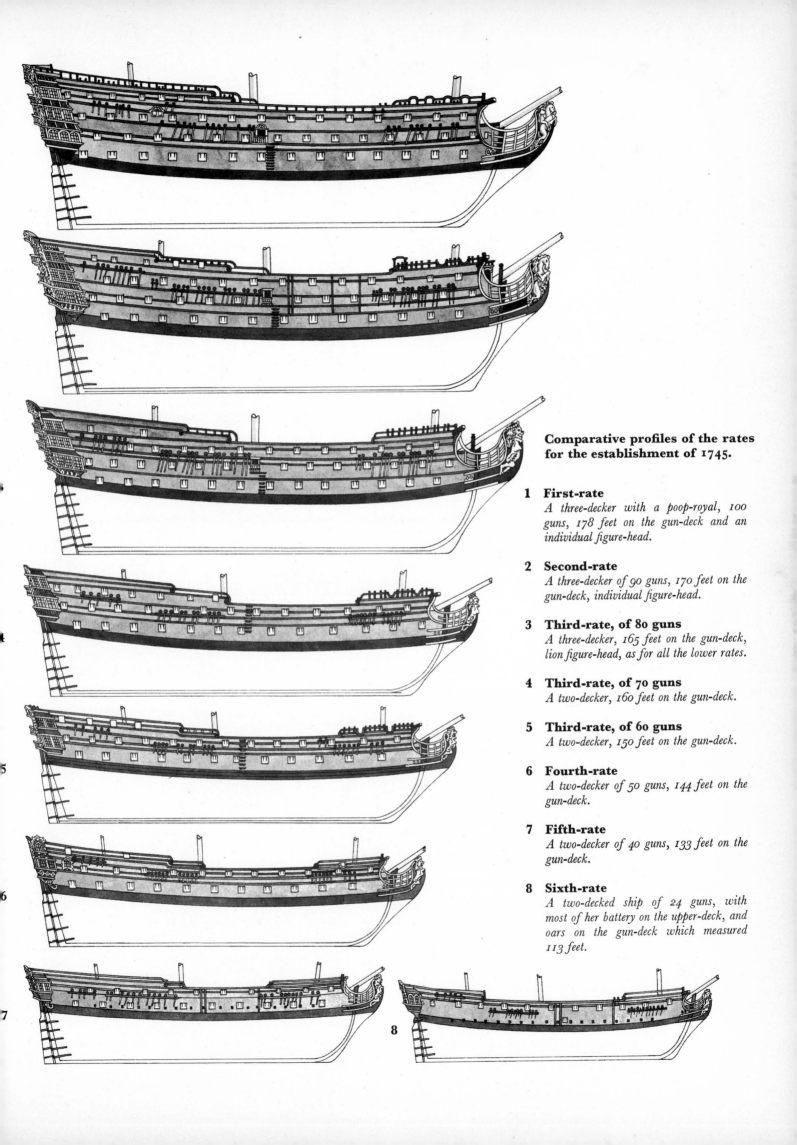

Comparative profiles of the rates for the establishment of 1745.

1 First-rate
A three-decker with a poop-royal, 100 guns, 178 feet on the gun-deck and an individual figure-head.

2 Second-rate
A three-decker of 90 guns, 170 feet on the gun-deck, individual figure-head.

3 Third-rate, of 80 guns
A three-decker, 165 feet on the gun-deck, lion figure-head, as for all the lower rates.

4 Third-rate, of 70 guns
A two-decker, 160 feet on the gun-deck.

5 Third-rate, of 60 guns
A two-decker, 150 feet on the gun-deck.

6 Fourth-rate
A two-decker of 50 guns, 144 feet on the gun-deck.

7 Fifth-rate
A two-decker of 40 guns, 133 feet on the gun-deck.

8 Sixth-rate
A two-decked ship of 24 guns, with most of her battery on the upper-deck, and oars on the gun-deck which measured 113 feet.

The Victory *of 1737, known as Balchen's* Victory *because she was wearing his flag when she was lost with all hands in 1744. In her short day she was the biggest ship in the world and the only English first-rate to have an open gallery to her poop-royal.*

A first-rate of the Establishment of 1741. The chief improvement over the seventeenth-century ships is in the rigging. Reef-points and stay-sails have appeared, and the awkward sprit-topmast, though officially still retained for the first-rates, had all but disappeared.

new ideas had to be introduced to stiffen the hulls which were the problems of the nineteenth-century surveyors. Nevertheless the degree to which design had frozen was remarkable, and shows how excellent it was. Not only was the *Victory* forty years old when she fought at Trafalgar as the principal flagship, but nearly fifty when she retired from active service; her draught, slightly amended in the upper works, was used for the proposed building of four second-rates in 1801. Two of them were completed; one was the *London* in 1810 and she served as Sir Edward Pellew's flagship in the Mediterranean in 1815; the other, the *Princess Charlotte*, was not launched until 1825, though admittedly she had collected the new round bow and stern over the years, and she was Sir Robert Stopford's flagship in the Mediterranean as late as the Syrian operations of 1840.

39

Eighteenth-century Second-rates

The ninety-gun three-deckers which comprised the second-rate, until the increase to ninety-eight guns in the late 1770s, were the work-horse fleet flagships of the eighteenth century. They were cheaper to operate than the first-rates but very powerful, and at all the important fleet actions in the Mediterranean, the West Indies and off North America up to the French Revolutionary Wars, the flag was in a second-rate.

Something of the difference between their armament and a first-rate's has already been mentioned previously, and there was also the difference in size. They were generally about 165 feet on the gun-deck, or a little less for the first half of the century, and around 45 feet to a maximum of 48 feet in the beam. This was close to the seventeenth-century first-rates, some of which had survived into the eighteenth century to serve in the lower rate. By the third quarter of the century lengths had increased by 10 feet and beams by 2 feet. It needed the increase to ninety-eight guns to make a large increase in size necessary to take the extra two or four guns per deck. Indeed a late eighteenth-century ninety-eight gun ship, such as the *Ocean* with a 195-foot gun-deck, was over 10 feet longer than the *Victory*, and differed in armament from her, at the time of Trafalgar, only in having 18-pounders on the middle deck instead of 24-pounders.

In Queen Anne's navy there were thirteen second-rates, and the number remained fairly constant until the wars connected with the revolution in America, by the end of which, in 1783 there were nineteen, and this increased to twenty-one by the end of the century. Of this number only a few would be in commission even in wartime, and at the beginning of the Revolutionary Wars in 1793 the number was eight. In appearance and layout they closely resembled the first-rates except that they were never given topgallant poops, and the ones built in the early part of the century often had only quite modest coaches.

Eighteenth-century Third-rates, the Three-decker Eighties

The notorious three-decker eighties are always held up as the example of how English warship design lagged behind the Continental. This was mainly due to a bellicose determination on the part of the English to fill their ships full of guns, and certainly the effect of putting three decks of too closely fitted guns into the smallest three-decker built proved unfortunate. Their narrow beam made them crank, and their lower tiers lay too near to the water. There is a famous letter from Admiral Mathews to the Duke of Newcastle, written after the drawn Battle of Toulon in February 1744, when the English had been unable to achieve more against the combined Franco-Spanish fleet than the capture of one Spanish sixty-four, in which he complains of his equipment: 'I have now but two ships of 90 and three of 80 guns that can make use of the lower tiers of guns if it blow a cap full of wind.' This meant that they could not fight with their heaviest batteries, the 32-pounders, and in the case of the eighties were reduced to the 12-pounders on their middle deck, 6-pounders on the upper and quarter-decks. In comparison the French two-decker seventy-fours had no such difficulty, and some carried 40-pounders on the gun-deck and 18-pounders on the upper. On the day of the battle there was a 'cap full of wind', so that the lower ports on the leeside of many English ships had to be kept shut, though some commanders contrived by desperate

The framing of a two-decker ship of the line in the eighteenth century.

measures to keep them open. Rear-Admiral Rowley, the third in command, in the *Barfleur*, a ninety gun second-rate, Mathew's letter continues, 'was obliged to run out his weather guns, to lash thirty tuns of water to windward, and to cut away his lee anchor before he could do it, the *Princess Caroline* (an eighty) took in water so fast, that her captain, whose conduct and behaviour proves him to be a very good officer, was obliged to skuttle the deck to vent the water; she took it in so fast'. That is to say, he tore up some of his lee-deck planking on the lower deck so that the water coming in through the ports could escape down into the bilge and be taken out by the pumps. 'As for the rest of them, they can scarce haul up a port; the *Chichester* hauled up but her two aftermost, but was obliged soon to lower them; as for the rest of her ports they were caulked in when she was fitted out, and have never been opened since, nor will they ever be, except in a Mill Pond.'

The dimensions of the *Chichester* show her to be 155 feet 6 inches on the gun-deck, and 43 feet 5 inches in the beam; almost the same as the old *Prince Royal* of 1610, but without her towering superstructures. The model of the *Chichester* shows her to have had no fo'c'sle at all, though there is a quarter-deck, and apparently no coach. In the model she mounts no guns in her waist, so that she was armed like a two-decker but with a deck joining the quarter-deck and fo'c'sle. The draughts of other three-decker eighties show them to have had at least a tiny coach, and though some have fo'c'sles, in others it is reduced to the forward bulkhead and a small platform. The *Chichester* was one of the early ones of 1706, which were originally designed as two-decker eighties, but were decked over the waist to strengthen them.

At the time that Mathews was writing there were seventeen on the list, but his words and the criticism of other naval officers such as Vernon had their effect, for after the war ended in 1748 most of these ships were scrapped or reduced to two-decker sixty-fours. The new three-decker eighties that were built up to 1757 were bigger and presumably better. The last, the *Princess Amelia*, was 165 feet on the gun-deck and 47 feet 3 inches in the beam. Like all those built after the gun establishment of 1740 she had 18-pounders on her middle deck and 9-pounders on her upper, her gun-deck continued to carry 32-pounders.

41

Eighteenth-century Third-rates, the Two-decker Eighties

Eighty guns was the limit a wooden two-decker, built on traditional lines, could mount without hogging or straining. The Dutch had built them successfully in the seventeenth century, and in the 1690s the English built thirteen of their own. The principle was good, but unfortunately they were built too light in their upper works and strained. In three further ships laid down the difficulty was dealt with by decking over the waist, so that they became three-deckers, but with their armament disposed like a two-decker; and this is really why the English began on their long and unlucky attachment to the eighty gun three-decker. Indeed, although the latter type ceased to be built in the late 1750s, the resumption of the building of two-decker eighties did not begin until the late 1780s.

In the meantime the navy had to rely on foreign prizes. The best-known of these was the *Foudroyant*, a magnificent French eighty which in 1758, as M. Duquesne's flagship, was fought to a standstill in a four and a half hours action with the *Monmouth* 64; which was very creditable since, apart from the disparity in the number of guns, the *Foudroyant* mounted 42- and 24-pounders against the *Monmouth*'s 24- and 12-pounders. The *Foudroyant* was added under her own name and became Rodney's flagship in the West Indies, and in the following war, from 1775 to 1782, was commanded by Captain John Jervis, who was knighted for capturing with her the brand-new French seventy-four *Pegase*. He was later to become one of our greatest naval officers, and Lord St Vincent. The ship was 180 feet 5 inches on the gun-deck and 50 feet 3 inches in the beam, and was considered all her active life to be the finest two-decker in the service.

The *Caesar* was the first of the new English two-decker eighties and was launched in 1793. The dimensions were much the same as the old *Foudroyant*'s, 181 feet on the gun-deck by 50 feet in the beam. A new *Foudroyant* was another built at the same time, and

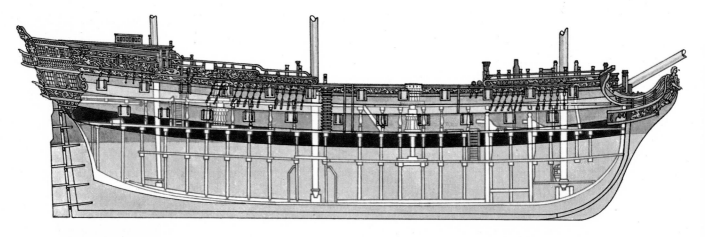

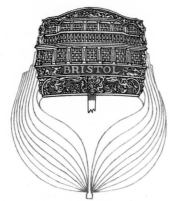

A profile section and stern of a 50-gun ship of 1775, taken from the draught of the Bristol *(see page 45).*

she became Nelson's flagship after the Battle of the Nile in 1798. On this occasion the *Franklin*, a new French eighty and their vice-admiral, was captured and turned out to be so notable a performer under sail that eight ships were built to her lines, one of them, the *Asia*, built in Bombay of teak and launched as late as 1824, was Codrington's flagship at the Battle of Navarino in 1827, when an Anglo-Franco-Russian fleet destroyed the Turkish-Egyptian one. The *Franklin* was added as the *Canopus* and became a great favourite in the service for half a century. Almost at the end of her active career, in 1847, she took part in a sailing trial off Lisbon in a squadron including some of the newest English liners, and beat them all, to the delight of nearly everybody present. One feature of the new eighties was that they carried their lower tier of guns high enough, and were deep enough in the hold, for the orlop-deck to become a proper deck instead of three platforms as before. The number of eighties built at the end of the eighteenth century and during the Revolutionary Wars was quite small, since building policy continued to concentrate on the seventy-four.

Eighteenth-century Third-rates, the Seventies and Seventy-fours

The standard large two-decker until the middle of the eighteenth century was the seventy, of which at the end of Queen Anne's reign there were twenty-six, ten more than of the eighties. The 1716 gun establishment shows that they mounted 24-pounders on the gun-deck and 12-pounders on the upper. They sailed better than the three-decker eighties and could work their lower tiers in weather when the others had to close their lower ports. A typical seventy would be 151 feet on the gun-deck and 43 feet in the beam. In the late 1740s ships with that odd number of guns, seventy-four, began to appear in the lists. These ships, the seventy-fours, became the type of ship of the line, that was to endure the longest, of which by far the most were built, and which, in English hands, proved indeed to be 'the ship to fight for a kingdom'.

Those on the list in 1750 were there for several reasons; three were French, captured in 1747, and the largest of them the *Monarch* was no less than 174 feet 10 inches on the gun-deck and 47 feet 2 inches in the beam. One was an old ninety, the *Torbay* (ex *Neptune*), cut down a deck; she had been the second flagship at Mathew's action off Toulon in 1744. (Mathew's own ship, the *Namur*, was similarly treated, but was lost in the East Indies in 1749.) One only, the *Culloden*, had been built, at Deptford, and launched in 1747. She was quite small, only 161 feet 4 inches on the gun-deck with a 46 foot 4 inch beam; but she does prove, especially as another, the *Somerset*, was launched in 1748, that the English did not build seventy-fours just to copy the captured Frenchmen, though the increase was probably prompted by the urge to keep up with French policy; nor were those built in the late fifties up to the dimensions of the Frenchmen: it was the middle sixties before they approached a gun-deck of 170 feet. Around this figure it remained until a general lengthening was ordered for new ships in 1793, about 10 feet in the gun-deck and a foot in the beam. Of the great armada of these ships, the navy at the beginning of the Seven Years War in 1755 possessed only six, but seven fought at the Battle of Quiberon Bay in 1759, the largest number of any class of ship present, and by the end of the war in 1763 the number built was around forty. This figure was doubled by the end of the American Revolutionary War in 1783, when they nearly equalled the total number of ships in other rates of the line listed, and when it came to ships in commission the proportion was far higher. In 1800 the fleets in home waters contained of the line, three first-rates, fourteen second-rates, six third-rate eighties, a seventy-eight, a sixty-eight, fifteen sixty-fours and forty-one seventy-fours, five of them flagships. In the Mediterranean there were sixteen more and six in the West Indies.

The popularity and prestige of the large two-decker reached its peak during the French Revolutionary War when the British found that not only did they sail better than the stately three-decker, which they knew already, but that by superior gunnery and training their two-deckers could be a match for any enemy warship, even three-deckers of over one hundred guns. In the long Franco-Spanish wars that stretch from 1689 to 1815 the British never lost a three-decker in action, but the French lost three in battle and one, the *Commerce de Marseille* 120, taken at Toulon in 1793. The Spanish lost seven, all in action, and it is interesting to see that six of them fell to English two-deckers.

To take them in order: in 1782 the French *Ville de Paris* 104, their flagship at the Battle of the Saints, struck to the English three-decker *Barfleur* 98. At the Battle of St Vincent in 1797, two Spanish three-deckers, both flagships, were captured, the *Salvadore del Mundo* 112, by the *Victory* 100, and the *San Josef* 112, by the *Captain* 74, though other ships contributed. There was nothing above a seventy-four in Nelson's fleet at the Battle of the Nile when the great French flagship *L'Orient* 120 was destroyed. In 1801 a squadron under de Saumarez defeated a much stronger Spanish squadron, destroying two one-hundred-and-twelve-gun three-deckers, the *San Hermenegildo* and the *Real Carlos*, all the British ships were two-deckers. Three more enemy three-deckers, all Spanish, struck at Trafalgar. The *Santissima Trinidad* 136, the biggest ship in the world and a four-decker, struck to the *Prince* 98, but earlier in the action the captain of the *Africa* 74, seeing the great ship silent and apparently beaten, sent aboard a lieutenant to take the surrender. When this officer, Lieutenant John Smith, appeared on her quarter-deck he found that she had not struck; he therefore withdrew, unmolested. The *Santa Anna* 112 was taken by the *Royal Sovereign* 100, but was recaptured with her prize crew two days later. The third one, the *Rayo* 100, escaped from the main battle but was captured at anchor off Lucar by the *Donegal* 74 three days later. In 1806 during Duckworth's action the *Canopus* 80 drove ashore the *Imperial*, a French one-hundred-and-twenty-gun ship which became a total loss. Finally, Napoleon Bonaparte was sent to St Helena in the *Northumberland* 74 after he had surrendered to the captain of *Bellerophon* 74. For years the very words seventy-four were synonymous to the British public with an invincible naval supremacy.

The Eighteenth-century Third-rates, the Sixties and Sixty-fours

The sixty-gun ships became sixty-fours in the 1740s which was made possible by the increase in size that allowed them to bear the extra two guns per deck. The sixty of the beginning of the century was 145 feet on the gun-deck and 38 feet in the beam, while one of the later sixty-fours of the 1780s measured 159 feet by 44 feet 4 inches. They remained ships of the line throughout their service in their original form, and were certainly fit to stand in it for the first half of the eighteenth century. There were sixty-two of them on the list in 1762 against forty-seven seventies and seventy-fours. The older sixties carried 24-pounders on the lower deck, 9-pounders on the upper, and 6-pounders on the quarter-deck and fo'c'sle; the sixty-fours mounted 24s, 18s, and 9s. By the end of the century they had come to be thought rather light for the line and found employment as flagships on distant stations, convoy work, or even, after conversion, as troopers.

The most famous sixty was the *Centurion* of 1732. She was Commodore Anson's ship when he set out with a squadron to circumnavigate the world in 1740, and only she completed the journey, after wonderful adventures which included capturing the Spanish treasure ship *Nuestra Senora de Covadonga*. It took thirty carts to carry the treasure from Plymouth to London. The *Centurion* was reduced to a fifty-gun ship in 1746. In 1749 Commodore Augustus Keppel hoisted his broad pendant in her at the tender age of twenty-four to take a squadron to the Mediterranean where he was chiefly concerned with the Barbary pirates. Two years later the commodore called on the Dey of Algiers over some breach of treaty. The Dey asked him why his master had had the insolence to send an insignificant beardless youth to be his representative. 'Had my master supposed that wisdom was measured by the length of one's beard,' said Keppel, 'he would have sent your deyship a he goat.' This, however, was not well received, and Keppel had to remind the Dey that Algiers would be destroyed by his ships if anything happened to him.

The most famous sixty-four was the *Agamemnon*, Nelson's favourite command, in which he fought in the Mediterranean in the early years of the French Revolutionary Wars; it was a commission characteristically full of incident.

Eighteenth-century Fourth-rates, the Fifties

The prestige of the fifty-gun ship remained high from the early seventeenth century when the *Prince Royal* 55 was the greatest ship in the world, until the 1860s saw the last of the great fifty-gun frigates. The dimensions of the ships serving at the beginning of the eighteenth century have already been described from Keltridge's draughts, and in the 1716 gun establishment they mounted 18-pounders on the lower deck, 9-pounders on the upper deck and 6-pounders on the quarter-deck and fo'c'sle. Although still listed as ships of the line, this was obviously insupportable, and by 1760 they had been dropped. Their usefulness remained particularly as flagships on foreign stations where large enemy vessels were unlikely to be met with and the fifty was the ideal size. At 146 feet on the gun-deck, with a 40-foot beam and a complement of 350, they were small enough to be reasonably inexpensive to maintain, yet big enough to carry a coach on the quarter-deck to accommodate the admiral and his secretaries. They also had, as two-deckers, the required presence for a flagship. They were in fact warships built more for peace than for war, and on the eve of the French Revolutionary Wars in 1790 six out of the seven flagships on foreign stations were fifties.

There are two stories about individual fifties which are worth retelling. Early in 1778 Vice-Admiral Clark Gayton was preparing to give up his post as commander-in-chief at Jamaica and return to England in his flagship, the *Antelope* 50. Two circumstances were causing comment. One was that the very large sum that the admiral had amassed from the sale of American prizes he had turned into the form of gold dollars which he was preparing to take with him, not trusting bills, for as he said, 'he knew nothing so valuable as money'. The second circumstance was the extreme age and rottenness of the *Antelope* which made it doubtful if either the admiral or his gold would ever reach England. But when it was suggested that he sent the money home in a frigate he said, 'No, my money and myself will take our passage in the same bottom, and if we are lost there will be an end of two bad things at once.' On the passage home they sighted a large ship and beat to quarters. The stranger would have been much the stronger even if the *Antelope*'s lower-deck guns had not been taken out before she sailed, to ease her. The admiral, who was unwell, took a chair on the quarter-deck, saying to his men that, 'he could not stand by them, but that he would sit and see them fight for as long as they pleased'. Fortunately the stranger turned out to be English and the *Antelope* reached home safely, collecting one more American prize on the way.

The other story is of a sterner occasion. At the Battle of the Nile in 1798 the *Leander* was the only fifty present and was the last one to play a full part with the liners in a fleet action. The French were anchored in line, but the *Peuple Souverain* had parted her cable and fallen out of the line. The *Leander* moved into the gap and her raking fire into the bows of the *Franklin* 80 on her port side and the stern of the *Aquilon* 74 greatly contributed to their surrender. After the victory Captain Thompson was publicly kissed by Nelson on the quarter-deck of the *Vanguard*, this being before the days of British phlegm, and the *Leander* was sent home with the dispatches. These were entrusted to Captain Berry who had been Nelson's flag captain during the campaign. Unfortunately she fell in with one of the two French ships of the line that had escaped from the battle, the *Genereux* 74, and was captured after a furious action lasting six and a half hours, at the end of which all the *Leander*'s masts had gone and she had lost ninety-two men killed and wounded. The *Genereux*'s casualties were two hundred and eighty-eight, and considering that her broadside weighed over twice that of the *Leander*'s, and that she carried over three times the crew, the British ship's performance was very creditable. The French captain made the most of this crumb of success from the French disasters in Egypt by promoting his prize to a seventy-four in his report to his superiors. He pillaged his prisoners and made the wounded seamen help refit the ship, and in general behaved rather worse than was usual; but when he tried to get the British to join the French navy, George Bannister, a seaman, gave him this reply: 'No, you damned French rascal; give us back our little ship and we'll fight you again till we sink.'

Fifth-rates, the Forties and Forty-fours and Large Frigates

Just as the smallest class of three-decker was considered a failure, so the smallest of the two-deckers was equally unsuccessful. These suffered from the same defects, which were that they could not work their lower-deck guns in blowy weather and were heavy sailers compared to ships of similar force which carried their main batteries on one deck. In the early years of the century when the French and Spanish were still building small two-deckers the shortcomings of ours were not so apparent, but when they began to meet the large frigates that the French had in service during the War of Jenkins' Ear in the 1740s, which could out-sail them, and in rough weather out-gun them too, it was clearly time to make a change in the design of our large cruisers.

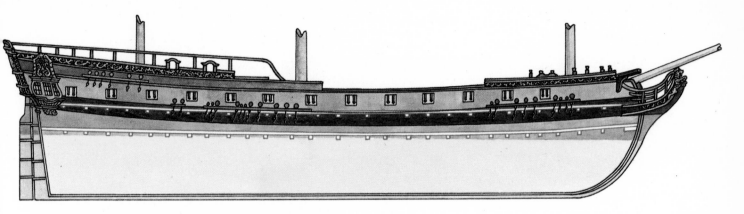

The Renommée, *one of the French frigates captured in 1747, and which set a trend in cruiser design.*

The early eighteenth-century forties were only about 115 feet on the gun-deck and 31 feet in the beam. They carried 12-pounders on the gun-deck and 6-pounders on the upper deck. In the second quarter of the century they increased in length to around 124 feet on the gun-deck and were rated up to forty-fours by the addition of guns on the fo'c'sle. The weight of the metal was also increased in the 1743 gun establishment to 18-pounders on the gun-deck and 9-pounders on the upper; the fo'c'sle guns were 6-pounders.

By 1760 no more ships of this type were being built, and the dockyards were beginning to build frigates of the type we had captured from the French in the previous war. The word frigate has been bandied about in so many contexts that it must be made clear that the word here means only a ship of two decks which carried a main armament of twenty to fifty guns on her upper deck, quarter-deck and fo'c'sle, there being no ports of any kind at gun-deck level.

The *Embuscade*, a French forty-gun frigate which was captured in 1746, was a fine example. She carried twenty-eight 12-pounders on her upper deck, ten 6-pounders on the quarter-deck and two on the fo'c'sle. She was able to do this since, by having no gun-ports on her lower deck, the deck itself could be lowered to the level of, or just below, the water-line. The upper deck in turn was lowered so that though there was a fine freeboard to the gun-ports of about 8 feet, the deck was still low enough for the ship to carry reasonably heavy guns on it, and more guns and spar-decks over it, without making her crank. She was 132 feet 6 inches on the gun-deck (lower deck) and 36 feet in the beam.

The first large English-built frigates were the *Pallas* and *Brilliant*, both thirty-sixes

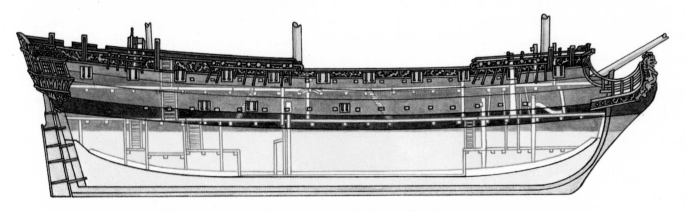

The Queenborough, *an example of the type of sixth-rate of the Establishments of 1733, 1741, and 1745, which was to be superseded by the frigate.*

and launched in 1757, so that the English were in no rush to build the new type; but some were ready in time for the Seven Years' War. They were 128 feet 4 inches on the gun-deck and 35 feet 11 inches in the beam. They went on calling the lower deck in frigates the gun-deck for another fifty years even though it carried no guns at all. The frigates were a great success, and one would have thought the discredited two-decker forty-fours would have vanished for ever; but in 1774 Their Lordships rediscovered some forgotten virtue in the type and ordered a whole new class of them, some twenty-five of which were built. The new two-decker forty-fours were a good deal larger than the previous ones of a generation before, about 140 feet on the gun-deck and 38 feet in the beam, and their guns were 18-pounders, 12-pounders, and a couple of 6-pounders on the fo'c'sle. They served at home and on the American station during the war of 1775 to 1783, but by the eve of the French Revolutionary Wars all thought of using them as fighting ships had gone, and those that were in commission operated as troop-ships, storeships or hospital ships. The one selected to become the hospital ship for the Channel Fleet was, naturally, the *Charon*.

The large frigate caught on rather slowly in England and there were only four thirty-sixes at the end of the Seven Years' War, and they carried a light armament of 12-pounders on the upper-deck and 6-pounders on the quarter-deck and fo'c'sle. Even at the end of the following war in 1783, the number was only seventeen thirty-sixes and seven thirty-eights, but the guns were now 18-pounders and 9-pounders. The French were by this time building forties with heavier guns than the *Embuscade*, and were soon to build forty-fours. The British followed suit in the Napoleonic Wars, but only in small numbers. A typical thirty-eight-gun frigate of 1795 was 148 feet on the lower deck and 40 feet in the beam; this was an increase of over 20 feet in length and these ships proved magnificently seaworthy and efficient instruments of naval warfare.

The Smaller Fifth-rates
These were the thirties, and at the beginning of the eighteenth century were of two types: those as drawn and previously described in the Keltridge draughts with their main battery on the gun-deck, and a few small guns on the upper deck, but with the waist kept clear, and the newer ones with a main battery of 6-pounders on the upper deck and eight 9-pounders on the lower or gun-deck, the other ports being row-ports and two loading ports. However, the building of the thirties ceased by the 1719 establishment, and until after the middle of the century there was no class of ships built for the navy between the twenties and the forties. The return of the small fifth-rate began with the building of a class of thirty-two-gun frigates similar to the *Renommée*, captured in 1747, though the draught for the first one, dated 1756, following the layout rather than the lines of the Frenchman, and was called the *Southampton*. They became the standard and most successful class of English frigates until the end of the French wars in 1815. At the height of the Revolutionary Wars there were sixty of them. At first they mounted 12-pounders on their upper-deck and 6-pounders on the quarter-deck and fo'c'sle, but the larger and later ones mounted 18-pounders instead of 12s, and from the 1770s onwards the 6-pounders tended to be replaced by the short-barrelled, heavy-shotted carronades. The *Southampton*'s lower-deck was 124 feet 4 inches long and

48

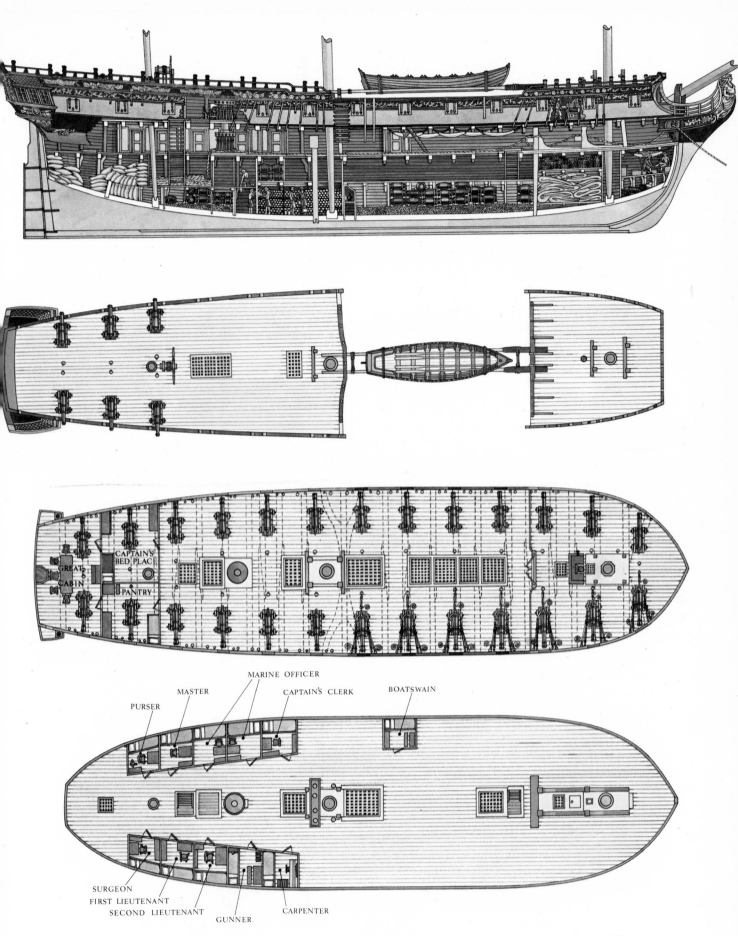

PURSER   MASTER   MARINE OFFICER   CAPTAIN'S CLERK   BOATSWAIN

GREAT CABIN   CAPTAIN'S BED PLACE   PANTRY

SURGEON
FIRST LIEUTENANT
SECOND LIEUTENANT   GUNNER   CARPENTER

The first English frigate, the Southampton, *launched in 1757.*

49

her beam 34 feet. By the middle 1790s the thirty-twos were being built 144 feet on the lower-deck and 39 feet in the beam.

There is no doubt that the thirty-twos and the larger frigates were the most popular commands. Properly handled they could take on any sort of merchantman, and foreign frigates of similar force. The smaller thirty-twos had a complement of two hundred and twenty, and the big forty-fours nearly three hundred. With such crews, and being handy under sail, they were found to be ideal for the harrying of enemy coasts, with cutting-out parties and raids. A good and lucky frigate captain could make himself rich on prize-money and the crew had their share too, so that he would not usually have to resort to the press gang like the captains of the liners, and might even pick and choose his crew.

Eighteenth-century Sixth-rates
The smaller the vessel the cheaper it is as a subject for experiments, so that there is some variety of type in this rate. The old type still in service in the early years of the eighteenth century was a single-decked ship of between twenty and thirty guns with plat-forms low in her hold and a quarter-deck and fo'c'sle. It was a layout that, without the quarter-deck and fo'c'sle, was to reappear in the last quarter of the century. A few were two-deckers with all their battery on the gun-deck and neither guns nor spar-decks on or above the upper deck; but the sixth-rate of the Establishments which they continued to build into the late 1750s was a two-decker with her main battery on her upper deck and the lower deck pierced for seventeen or eighteen row-ports a side. According to the Establishment there might be two, four or no gun-ports on the lower deck and there was always a loading-port a side. The guns were 9-pounders, and a late-built ship would be 107 feet on the lower deck and 29 feet in the beam.

The advantages of being able to manoeuvre under oars was the same as offered by the outboard motor in a sailing yacht today, particularly in getting in and out of harbours in conditions adverse to sailing. On the other hand, the ports were close to the water, which made things uncomfortable by leaking, unless they were caulked. When it was decided to do away with the lower-deck ports in the middle fifties, lower the decks and generally conform to the frigate type, the row-ports were moved up a deck and appear between the guns on the upper deck. This meant much longer sweeps at an awkward angle, but quite a few vessels up to the twenty guns and some even larger continued to have row-ports well into the nineteenth century and, for instance, at least one Spanish two-decker fifty. With this type of sixth-rate came in the twenty-eight-gun frigate, only 107 feet on the gun-deck and with a 30 foot 4 inch beam; a useful cruiser with 9-pounders, whose number in the lists for the last quarter of the century fluctuated around thirty. The twenties and twenty-twos of the last half of the century were small frigates with 9-pounders, or carronades, but were only built in small numbers.

Eighteenth-century Sloops, Gun-vessels and Corvettes
The general term for a man-of-war, excluding cutters, of a force less than twenty guns was a sloop-of-war; the largest ones were ship-rigged and frigate-built, if not below

eighteens. Draughts of the first half of the eighteenth century show a reversion to the stepped deck in ships and brig-rigged sloops, with a fall aft for the commander's cabin, and a low poop. This fashion did not persist, and those that were not fully frigate-built were designed without spar-decks, carrying their guns on an open deck, with platforms in the hold where everyone and most things had to find a place. Some vessels of this type, which were called gun-vessels, were as long as twenty-gun frigates, say 118 feet, and might carry as many as twenty or more guns or carronades, but were not classed as sixth-rates because of their shallow build and poor accommodation; a sixth-rate being a captain's command. As stated the accommodation in the open-decked sloops was all below, with a 5-foot deckhead to the beams and even less below the platforms to the floor. These vessels appeared during the Revolutionary Wars at the end of the century and could carry a heavy battery into waters where the frigates could not go, but their shallow draught made them poor performers under sail, especially to windward, and very wet.

The smaller sloops were similar, all single-decked with platforms below, but did not necessarily suffer from the same defects in their underwater lines as the larger ones just described; in fact, most of them were quite long-legged. In the Revolutionary Wars they were built in great numbers. The draught of the *Columbine* of 1803 has over sixty names of other brigs to be built to her lines. She was to be armed with sixteen 32-pounder carronades and two 6-pounders, was 100 feet on the deck and 30 feet 6 inches in the

A gun-brig of 1801. Over sixty were built to the draught of the Columbine *alone, mostly in private yards.*

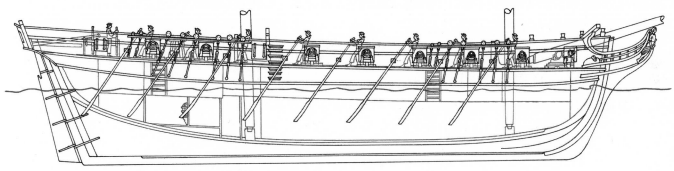

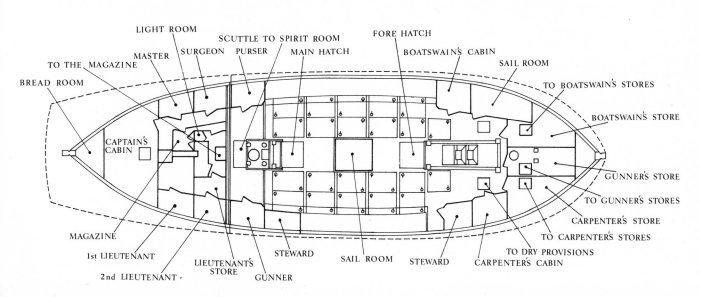

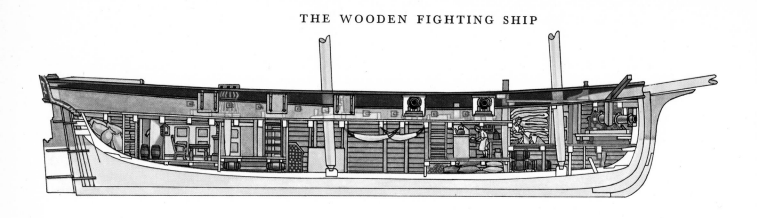

SCUTTLE TO BREAD ROOM

COMPANION

LADDER WAY

MAIN HATCH

LADDER WAY

SCUTTLE TO COALS

CHIMNEY

GRATING

SAIL ROOM

PROVISIONING STORE ROOM

SCUTTLE

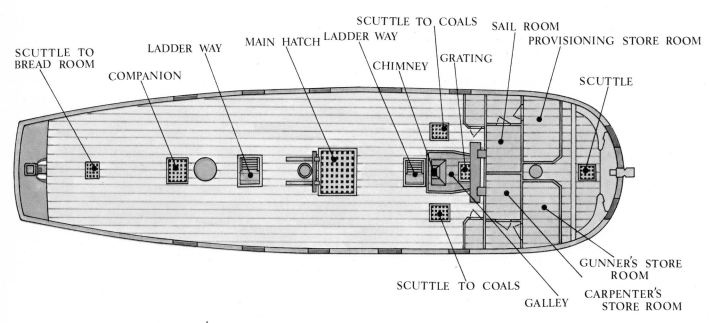

SCUTTLE TO COALS

GALLEY

GUNNER'S STORE ROOM

CARPENTER'S STORE ROOM

COMMANDER'S CABIN

SURGEON'S MATE

STEWARD'S ROOM

AFTER PLATFORM

CUPBOARD

SCUTTLE TO SPIRIT ROOM

RACKS FOR FILLED CARTRIDGES

WELL

BREAD ROOM

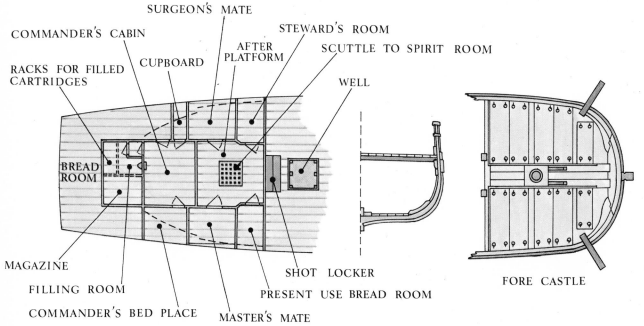

MAGAZINE

FILLING ROOM

COMMANDER'S BED PLACE

MASTER'S MATE

SHOT LOCKER

PRESENT USE BREAD ROOM

FORE CASTLE

A gun-vessel of 1800. Shallow-draught craft of this type appeared for hostilities only during the Napoleonic Wars, and in a steam-driven form during the Russian War of 1854–5.

A ketch-rigged bomb-vessel with her mortars (see page 54).
Bottom right: *The classic type single mortar bomb-ketch.*

beam, almost the same dimensions as the *Revenge* of 1575, though without her draught, and the *Columbine*'s broadside was more than half as heavy again. They were all tiller-steered and quite a few at the end of the eighteenth century had a double tiller, one above the deck and one under it. This gave an extra leverage when necessary, and in action a secondary and safer steering position.

Words have different uses at different times which makes it impossible only to indicate their meaning in one context. One word that came into English naval parlance during the Revolutionary Wars was 'corvette', which, though it had various civilian uses, in the French navy had always meant the same as we meant by sloop-of-war. Its introduction into the Royal Navy would seem unnecessary, except that by applying the word to the largest type of frigate-built sloop, it separated them for commands, the smallest sloops being lieutenants' commands, the larger sloops and the corvettes, commanders'. The sloops were armed with 6- or 4-pounders until the introduction of the carronade during the American War of Independence, after which this weapon increasingly monopolised the batteries which might increase the weight of their broad-sides as much as five times, though this would only be effective at short range.

Eighteenth-century Bomb-vessels

As in siege warfare on land, the lobbing of the large round explosive shells at sea was done by mortars, carried in the first half of the century in large ketches. This two-masted rig was preferred since there was less rigging to mask the mortars, which fired with a very high trajectory out of the centre of the bomb-vessels. These mortars, 13- or 10-inch bore, seem to have been common, were very short-barrelled chambered guns, and were mounted on revolving platforms on the centre line more or less amidships, usually two per bomb-vessel, but sometimes only one. This platform was strongly constructed to the floor of the hold and the ammunition kept in cupped shelves between the upright stanchions. The bombs also carried a broadside armament of about fourteen 4- or 6-pounders, and were about 90 feet on the deck with a 26-foot beam.

After the Seven Years' War, it was decided, presumably on sailing grounds, to build ship-rigged bombs. Possibly the first of these was the *Carcass*, which in 1773, stripped of her mortars, went with the *Racehorse* to probe for a north-east passage to the East, north of Russia, with the youthful Nelson aboard as a midshipman. This conversion of bombs in peace-time was very common, and there were never more than two or three on the

A 32-pounder, the largest gun in service at the end of the eighteenth century.

lists unless there was a war on, when there would suddenly be a dozen or more. They were, however, of a distinct design from the sloops, particularly in their deck layout. The mortars took up so much room amidships that though the deck in the ketches was flush, there was a complicated arrangement of stepped platforms below, and in the later ship-rigged bombs the decks were generally stepped aft, even to a stepped quarter-deck for a poop cabin. In the Revolutionary Wars a specialised type of bomb called a mortar-vessel was built. They were very shallow draught, just one deck and a hold, banks of oars and a fore and aft rig. Not many were built.

Eighteenth-century Rig

The basic square rig layout of the ships hardly altered from that of the seventeenth century, but the fore and aft sails grew in both number and efficiency, as the improvements in the seaworthiness of the hulls permitted far more canvas to be carried. Improvements in rig started with the smaller types of vessel and progressed to the greatest, and the first big alteration was the replacement of the sprit-sail-topmast by the jib-boom. It is difficult to understand why, since triangular sails on the fore stay had been in use in small north European boats since the sixteenth century, this change had not come sooner. In the 1719 Establishment both the sprit-sail-topmast and the jib-boom appear together, but in practice the former was usually struck. Further staysails between the fore and main, and main and mizzen-masts, came in more slowly, though they had been known since the late seventeenth century. They were not appreciably used until after the Seven Years' War, but seem to have been firmly established in the American War of Independence. The development of the mizzen-sail was one of the major changes. Since the fifteenth century it had been a triangular sail on a lateen yard. The 1740s and 1750s saw the fore part of the sail cut off and laced down the mast. It would have been a logical development to cut off the yard at the mast too, but the great yard was regarded as a possible jury-mast, so remained, in the biggest ships at any rate, until the end of the century; smaller ships did cut it down in the third quarter of the century. The next innovation was the driver. This sail was an extension of the mizzen or spanker, and in its early form required its own little yard, hoisted to the peak, and a boom from the mast. For a time the two sails remained separate, and the driver might also be used, double-sheeted to the taffrail, as a square sail from the peak in light airs. Obviously the sensible thing was to combine the two into one large sail lashed to the driver-boom, which was the case in most ships by the end of the century, though the old loose-footed spanker was still used as well.

The upward pull exerted by the new head-sails made necessary the bob-stay. Its duties got heavier through the century, but dolphin-strikers were not fitted until 1794, with the flying jib-boom, for which staying over a dolphin-striker was essential. A useful guide to dating eighteenth-century ships of the line in paintings or models was the gradual raising of the channels to which the fore and main shrouds were brought, prompted by the storm damage they and the shrouds might suffer from being set too low, and because they masked the guns, which might also set the shrouds on fire. In three-deckers this meant a rise from the middle deck to the upper deck at the beginning of the century, and from the upper deck to quarter-deck in 1794. The mizzen-channels

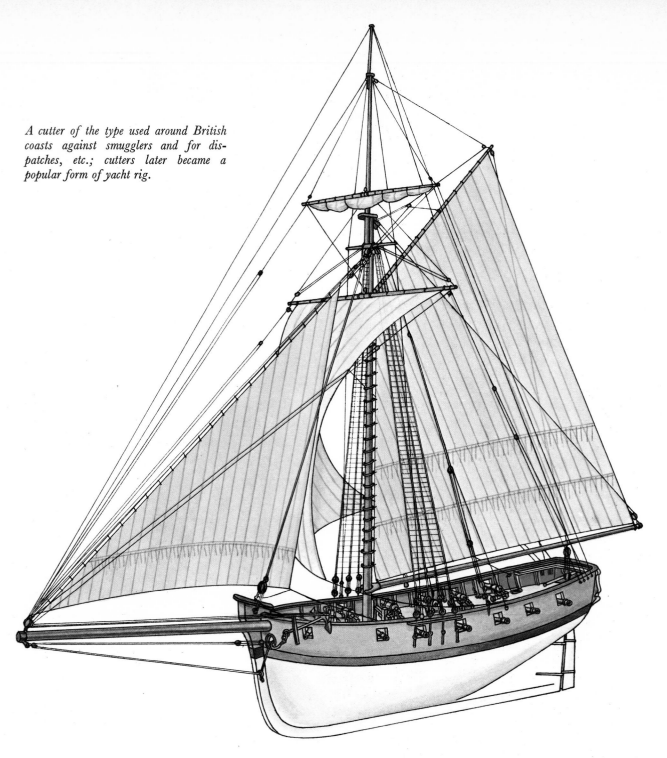

were moved up from quarter-deck to poop-deck level at the same time. In two-deckers the change was made about 1745 from the upper deck to the quarter-deck.

As the demand for more and larger lower-masts and bowsprits grew, the strain on the supply of large softwood trees made it necessary for the creation of what in the early eighteenth century was called the 'made mast' and later the 'built-up mast'. This took the form of large pieces of wood, in section like a round cake cut from the centre in eight wedges. The structure was bound together at intervals with rope woldings, or after 1800 with iron hoops, and made a stronger mast than a whole tree. The supply of timber for all purposes was a constant headache, and as regards the masts, nearly all were of white pine from America until the rebellion, when the English turned to the Baltic and the 'Riga' mast, of a stronger but heavier wood.

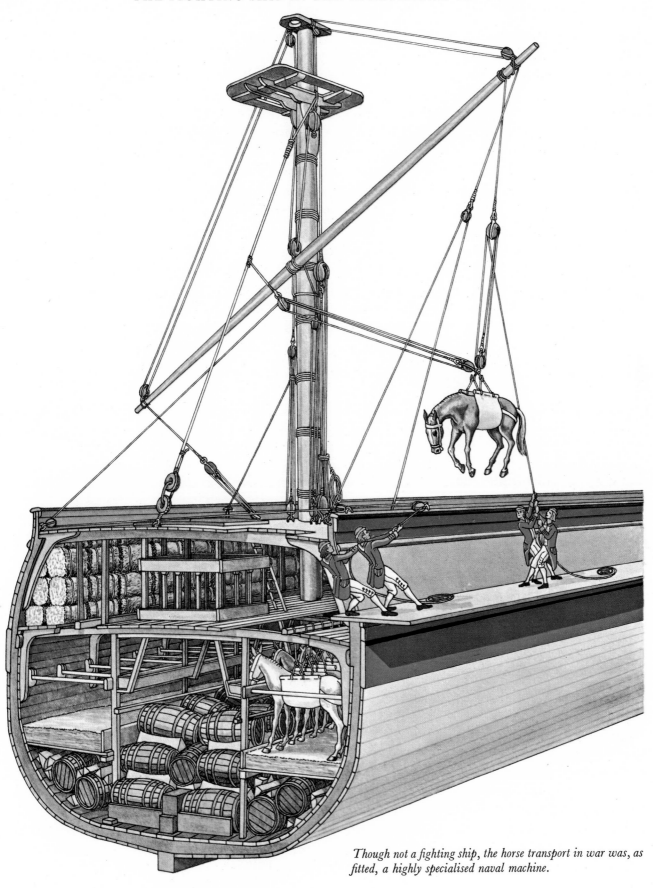

Though not a fighting ship, the horse transport in war was, as fitted, a highly specialised naval machine.

57

Eighteenth-century Hull Decoration and Appearance

As has already been noted, the scandal of the *Royal Sovereign*'s decorations caused a sharp reduction in the carved work, but decorative painting, often in the form of gold trophies on a blue background, formed bands along the sides of the ships above the upper-deck guns, a practice that continued throughout the century, though dying a rapid death in the last ten years. Until about the 1780s the hulls and spars of naval ships were, with a few exceptions in small ships, not painted, but payed. The mixture for the sides was resin, pine varnish, tar, oil and red ochre. The bottom, which needed more protection against marine animals and plant growth, had similar mixtures, reinforced with tallow, sulphur, brimstone and possibly broken glass. The wales were black-pitched, making a double black band near the water-line for about the first forty years of the century, but thereafter were joined into one broad wale. The spars were payed with resin, varnish and tallow. Mixtures varied of course, but it would be interesting to know what Captain Peter Warren precisely meant when he noted in his log in the 1740s that he had given his ship a 'pease porridge bottom'. Inside, below decks the sides were painted red, it has been said, so that the blood would not show, but more to give fierce red mouths to the gun-ports. Later deckheads tended to be white, but earlier ones were probably natural wood or painted red.

So long as they used plates of mica, called then muscovy glass, which had been universal in the seventeenth century for glazing the stern windows, these remained small and could have hardly been much more than translucent; but with the change to glass in 1703 and the simultaneous adoption of sash windows the ship's stern became designed to let in so much light and air that they resembled conservatories. Indeed we know that in the years immediately following Trafalgar, Admiral Collingwood was an enthusiastic cultivator of potted plants in his cabin. The stern walk made a reappearance at the end of the seventeenth century as an open recess to the round house and even the great cabin, but settled down to one recessed and slightly overhanging gallery in two-deckers and two in three-deckers. The figureheads on the beaks were so universally the crowned lion for ships below the second-rate that the head was referred to as the 'lyon', and it was only after individual figureheads were generally authorised in the late 1750s that the word figurehead came back.

Steering Improvements

In the seventeenth century the tiller entered the ship above the gun-deck level through a fairly wide port to allow it play, and was worked by a pole, called the whip-staff, which passed through the deck above, which itself formed the fulcrum. The men who worked the whip-staff, either on the upper deck in a two-decker, or the middle deck in a three-decker, could not see where the ship was going and received orders relayed from above. The position of the tiller flat made the gun-deck very wet in certain conditions, so a great improvement was to raise the rudder head through an opening in the underside of the counter, in a housing, to the deck above. A further great improvement harnessed the tiller to ropes from a wheel on the quarter-deck. The principle was the same as a capstan, and there is evidence that experiments were made with windlasses mounted athwartships before settling for the admirable double-wheel and drum.

Sheathing

From the fifteenth century, when ships began to venture into warmer seas, there was a pressing need to protect the underwater parts of the hulls against the dreaded teredo or ship worm, which chewed its way into the timbers and could reduce the ship to a sinking condition in a few months. The Indians had been known to use hardened leather sheathing, and at least one Japanese ship was seen to be encased in iron; but in Europe the solution in general use up to the middle of the 1770s was to pay over the bottoms with stuff containing poisonous substances such as sulphur, and sometimes pulverised glass, and then seal it with a soft wood sheathing, also payed. The teredines were expected to feed on the sheathing, but died if they tried to get through to the oak. At the end of the voyage, or from time to time, the sheathing was stripped off and renewed. A more sophisticated process introduced in the early eighteenth century was to coat the bottom with pitch and cover this with brown paper; another coat of pitch went on this and a layer of hair was stuck to it; then the wooden sheathing was fixed by a vast number of broad-headed iron nails covering the whole surface. This use of an iron facing of nails called 'filling' was also applied and more widely to wooden anchor stocks, examples of which still survive. It was effective against the teredines, but laborious and expensive, and gave the vessels that had it a very rough bottom. Of course the ordinary wooden sheathing got very foul with weed. This was a trouble particularly felt by the English, who kept their ships at sea much of the time, while the French ships, which spent most of the time in port, could usually appear with clean bottoms when they did venture abroad. Lead sheathing was tried in the third quarter of the seventeenth century, but since it could not be fastened with lead nails, and since iron ones caused electrolytic reactions, it was abandoned. It was in any case very heavy. In 1671 Charles II, inspecting the *Phoenix*, building at Deptford, asked why lead sheathing was not used. He was told that the plank sheathing was to strengthen her. The king then observed that they might as well use sarsenet to strengthen her, adding, 'Lord have mercy on the men who depend on that sheathing if the ship be not strong enough herself without it.' The final answer was copper, but again the first ship that tried it in 1758 had iron fasteners and the same electrolytic trouble occurred. However, in the case of copper, copper nails could be used, and once this was done the ships were not only teredo-proof but presented a smooth, slightly poisonous, surface to the water which did not foul so quickly, and greatly improved a ship's sailing qualities.

Signals

Although it is no part of the design of warships, the development of an articulate signals system in the late eighteenth and early nineteenth century was the most important advance in naval warfare for the period, and deserves some mention in the context of the story of the warship.

The first systematised signal code the navy had was that of Sir William Penn in the reign of James II. There had been signals by flag and gun before, but crude and few, and really the most useful one was the signal to call a council of war. This might occur at the height of the battle, as when Marten Tromp was killed at the Battle of Scheviningen in 1653 and the Dutch flag officers gathered round his body to decide

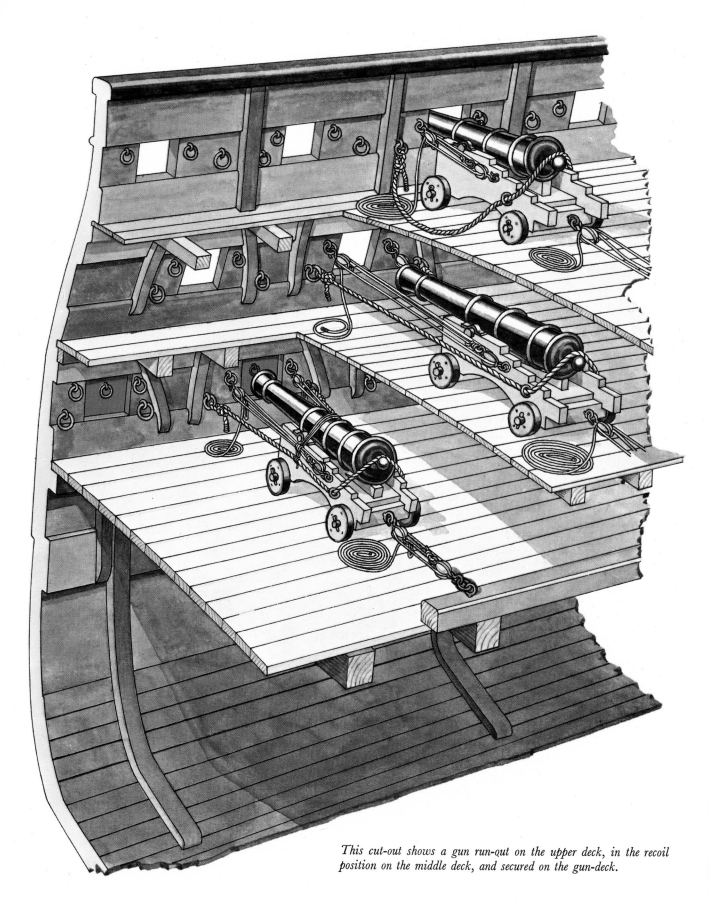

This cut-out shows a gun run-out on the upper deck, in the recoil position on the middle deck, and secured on the gun-deck.

what to do. One of the last councils of war at sea to decide the tactics of a coming sea fight must have been aboard the *Ajax* in December 1939, when Commodore Harwood summoned the captains of his other two cruisers aboard his flagship before engaging the *Admiral Graf Spee*.

The Stuart system, as of 1714, which continued up to the 1780s was for single flags, sometimes under a pendant, but only in one case two flags together, flown at various places in the rigging of the flagship to give a limited number of orders. All a private ship in the fleet could do was either to strike his main-topsail and place an ensign at the topgallant mast 'to speak with the Admiral' or put a union flag at the main-topmost backstay 'to discover danger'. Nearly all the signals were hoisted to the accompaniment of a gun.

A curiously small number of pure signal flags were used, the flags of command, the union, the ensigns and even the royal standard doubled for signal flags. One of the disadvantages of the system was that to make a code of over one hundred signals it was necessary to place flags in the yards, in the shrouds, and other places where they might not easily be seen, also the flagship had on occasion to strike her ensign, or even the flag of command to place a signal flag in their place.

In fog the admiral was down to eight gun signals, but at night there were fifteen possible signals, using set numbers of guns, and lanterns hoisted at various points. Loosing the topsails was the signal to weigh.

In the 1770s Captain Richard Kempenfelt developed the first numeral signal code,

The 24-pounder Carronade (see page 63).

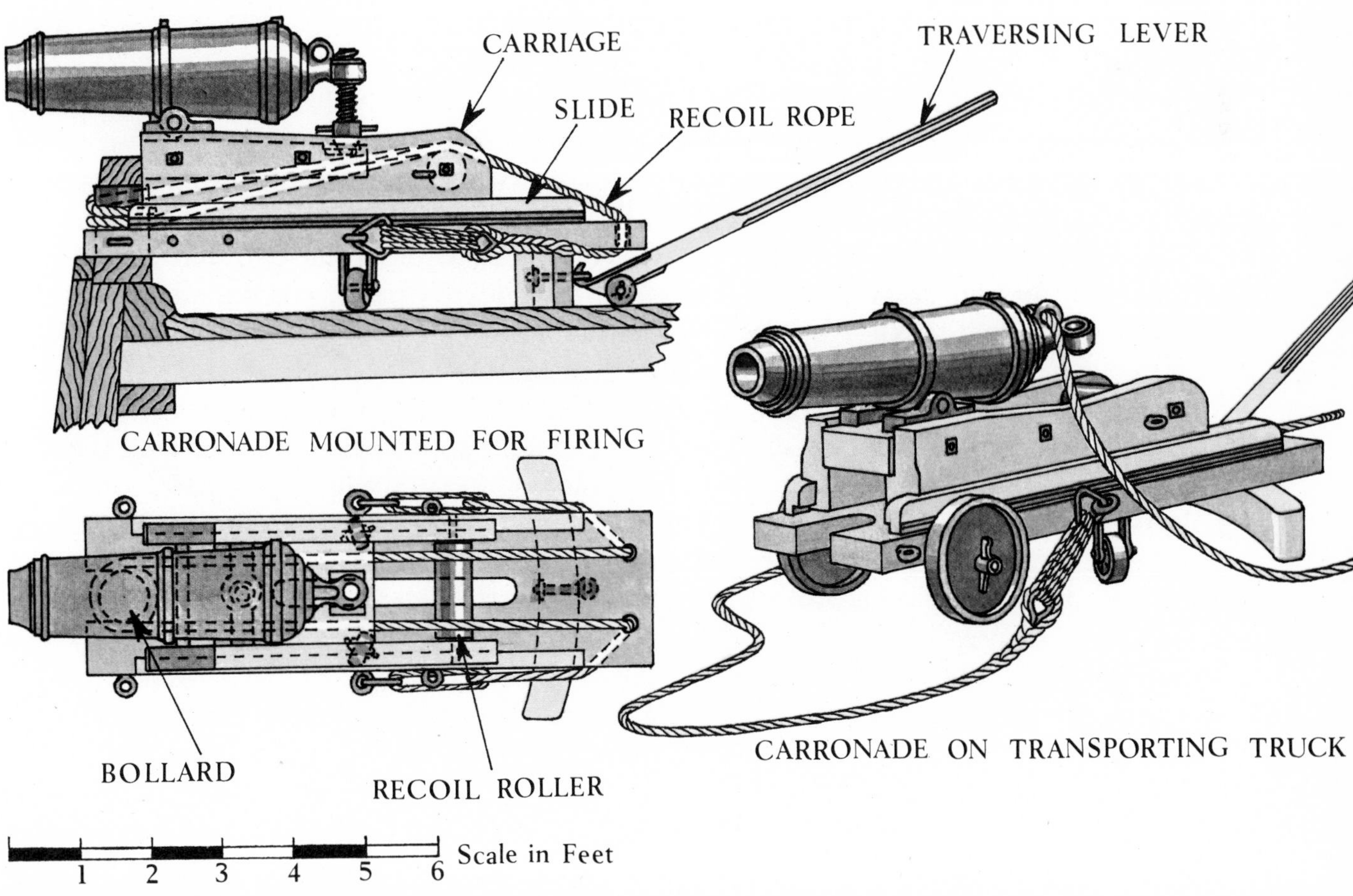

CARRIAGE   TRAVERSING LEVER

SLIDE   RECOIL ROPE

CARRONADE MOUNTED FOR FIRING

BOLLARD   RECOIL ROLLER

CARRONADE ON TRANSPORTING TRUCK

Scale in Feet
1 2 3 4 5 6

with hoists of more than one flag which read off as a number and corresponded to a given signal. As they were flown from the mast-heads they could be seen better and read off quicker. In a modified form Lord Howe used them in 1782, when they materially helped him get a convoy into Gibraltar in the face of a superior force of the enemy, which he was able to outmanœuvre.

Still, however, this system did not permit ships to speak to each other, and it was Admiral Sir Home Popham's greatly extended numeral and alphabetical code of 1801 which permitted this and which was the basis for the modern naval code. It included firstly an alphabet to spell out words if necessary; secondly a code of words; and thirdly codes of sentences and of syllables; also codes for technical terms, provisions and stores, etc. It was in this code that Nelson made his famous signal before the Battle of Trafalgar.

Eighteenth-century Naval Gunnery

The developments in this field, as in ship design, were confined on the whole to the improvements of existing types rather than the invention of new techniques. There was more system than formerly, and establishments of guns dated 1716, 1740, 1757, 1762 and 1792 defined the number and types of guns allotted to each rate. Except in the largest type of ship there was a general trend for cannon throwing increasingly heavy ball to be mounted, and this was not only due to the increase in the size of ships for the number of guns carried, but to a lesser degree to the improvement in the powder, which made a decrease in the length of the barrels justified, with a subsequent saving in weight. More important was the quality of the barrels. The English gun-founders had been acknowledged the best in Europe since the middle sixteenth century, and in the eighteenth the French were still sending people over to see how it was done. By the middle of the century Britain was embarked on her own iron age as the first industrial nation, and it was in the refinement of the iron metal that she excelled. These new iron guns were cast solid and bored out; they were now relatively safe and practically indestructible compared to the soft metalled bronze guns. They were also more accurate, though this was a relative term, and it was not until the early nineteenth century that the fitting of sights was thought worth while.

Even less change affected the carriage. The idea of perching two and a half tons of metal on an elm carriage with free-moving wooden wheels, controlled only by its breeching rope and tackle, and the whole set on a moving platform, sounds dangerous, which it sometimes was; but until well into the nineteenth century no really satisfactory form of slide to take up the recoil could be made. The great Swedish naval architect Chapman designed a wooden slide in the late eighteenth century, which was used in some French ships, but was found to be too heavy and took up too much room. The sailors in any case were used to securing most things with ropes, whether it was the ship to her anchors, or the masts, spars and sails in their places. The recoil of the gun when fired was extremely violent, and was taken up by the friction of the tackle running through the blocks. The tackles were brought to bolts on either side of the port, and great care had to be taken that neither tackle jammed or the gun would spin round and turn over. This positioning of the tackle bolts also made traverse-firing difficult and dangerous, for the different lengths of the tackles from gun to gunwale made for an uneven strain, and the gun tended to centre itself on firing. Some of the difficulties were overcome by the fitting of judiciously placed ring bolts and wedges to check the recoil. These and other ideas were successfully experimented with by Captain Sir Charles Douglas in the late 1770s and early 1780s. This enthusiast also perfected the goose-quill primer and the flintlock for cannon.

The one important eighteenth-century innovation in naval gunnery was the carronade, a type of gun invented by General Robert Melville in 1752 and made for the navy by Mr Gascoigne of the Scots firm of Carron, from 1779 the foremost among the improvers of iron gun-metal. The carronade was basically a short light-barrelled gun with a large bore. It threw its heavy ball, 32 or even 68 pounds, with a low initial velocity which at short range had a crushing effect more destructive than the swift passage of a ball at high velocity. Early carronades had trunnions and a carriage, but this was changed to lugs on to the bottom of the barrel, attached to a slide, with a worm screw at the breech to angle the barrel. There was a tackle from the slide to the gunwale and a heavy breeching to the carriage, but the use of a wooden slide was only possible with a moderate recoil. The carriage pivoted on a vertical bolt for traverse firing. Two men could work them, which was one of the main reasons why they were first adopted in bulk by the merchant service, but the navy adopted them too in the American War of Independence, when they formed a large proportion of the quarter-deck armament of the frigates, and nearly all the armament of many sloops and most gun-brigs of the French Revolutionary Wars. In an age devoted to close action, the heavy broadside that even quite small vessels armed with carronades could mount made them a popular weapon, but an entire battery of them could be disastrous; for, as several captains found to their cost, a superior sailing enemy with ordinary cannon could stand off out of range and batter them till they struck.

The French, who liked to stand off to lee and fire at the rigging, were slow to adopt the new gun; indeed their gunners, firing from an upward sloping deck, had worse recoil and running out problems with their cannon than the English, fighting to weather on a downwards sloping deck.

Conclusions on the Eighteenth Century

The names of the Petts and Anthony Deane ring down to us from the seventeenth century because they created a new type of fighting ship; but the same cannot be said for the naval architects of the eighteenth century. Men like Ward, Stacy, Hayward, Locke, Allen and Slade were merely the improvers of basic designs, and the inheritors of principles which they found no reason to alter. The extent of their improvements made the difference between summer season operations only at the beginning of the century, and blockading the north-west coast of France in winter and summer, often in dreadful conditions off a lee shore, for years during the Revolutionary Wars at the end of the century. Indeed as early as 1759 Hawke, by keeping the seas off Brest into the autumn, finally caught de Conflans and destroyed him in Quiberon Bay, in November.

It is certainly true that the French designers were more scientific in their approach to hull design, and showed the way where English designers had perforce to follow. But though it might have been fashionable for some English naval officers to say that the best ships in the service were French prizes, certainly French officers could not have had the satisfaction to claim that the worst ships in their service were English prizes. For during the long French wars, from 1688 to 1815, the loss by capture and destruction in action of English ships of the line down to the fifties was twenty-seven, while the loss to the French was one hundred and seventy-eight. Added to this armada over the same period of time were seventy-eight Spaniards, thirty-three Dutch, twenty-three Danish, one Russian and a Turk, making a grand total of three hundred and fourteen. The French have the credit of accounting for twenty-six of the twenty-seven, the odd ship, a fifty, blew up in action with a Spanish seventy-four in 1747.

The score is even more impressive during the Revolutionary Wars from 1793 to 1815 the longest and hardest-fought naval wars of all time. The English loss of ships of the line, by capture a seventy-four in 1794, another in 1795, two more in 1801, and that was all; none were destroyed. Their enemies on the other hand lost one hundred and thirty-one captured and twenty-nine destroyed. So if the success was not due to the ships, it must have been due to the men and the system.

The excellence of the French ships did not extend to their material or their construction, which was generally inferior to the English, so that promising captures soon became unserviceable and had to be scrapped. A notable example of this was the *Commerce de Marseilles* 120, the biggest ship in the world when taken in 1793 at Toulon. She was found to be so badly constructed that she was not thought fit to bear her guns, and was turned into a trooper for two voyages before being broken up.

A 32-pounder carronade.

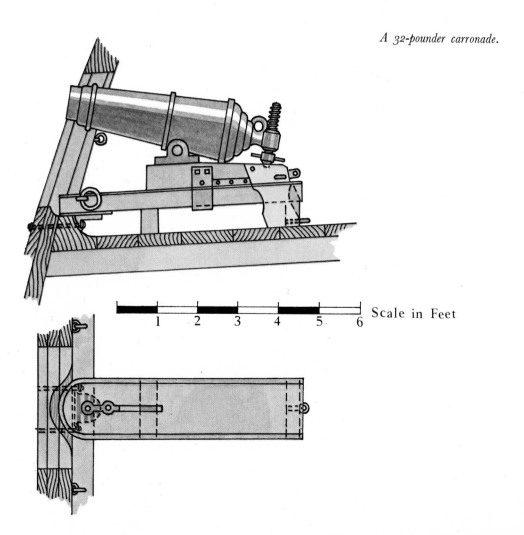

Scale in Feet

9

The Nineteenth-century
Wooden Battle Fleet

Numbers in Commission 1814–70

As the Great War drew to a close the cumulative strength of Royal Navy shows as over a thousand ship names in the Navy List. Although this list included all the hulks used for harbour duties and as prisons, there were still over nine hundred vessels of all kinds available for service, of which about six hundred and fifty were in commission at sea. Of this number between ninety and a hundred were ships of the line. Such a force of capital ships has never before or since been maintained at sea by any nation, and there were at least sixty more in reserve. The seventy-four was still the dominant type with over seventy in commission, none of the other rates reaching double figures.

After the war there was naturally a wholesale scrapping of the older ships, about half, and so long as the navy relied on sails alone the figure fluctuated between ninety and a hundred all told, with fifteen to twenty in commission and the rest in reserve or building. On the conversion to a steam assisted battle fleet in the early 1850s, the number dropped below the nineties and was little over sixty ten years later. Indeed by the second year of the Russian war, in 1855, when steam had become to be considered essential to the management of the fleets in action, only twenty-eight were completed and at sea, so that apart from the sixteen screw-liners building the other fifty liners that had not been converted were of little further use although it was thought necessary to keep some pure sailors in commission at home, and the Mediterranean fleet was mixed. The China station, where coaling stations were almost non-existent, saw the last of the purely sailing ship of the line when the *Ganges* 84 was ordered home in 1863.

With the arrival of the first ironclad in the 1860s, the disappearance of the wooden capital ship from the effective list was as rapid as the armoured ships could be built to replace them. The Mediterranean fleet had a wooden three-decker, the *Victoria* 121, until as late as 1867, and her final appearance was with the Channel Fleet in July of the same year when the queen reviewed the fleet with the Shah of Persia. The last of all to serve on an active sea-going commission was the *Rodney* 72, which was the flagship on the China station in 1868 and 1869 and paid off at Portsmouth on the morning of 27 April 1870.

The Enemy

The foregoing figures must be taken in relation to the fleets of foreign powers, notably Russia and France, whose ambitions mounted with the years. In the year of Queen

Victoria's accession (1837) the Russians sent to sea a fleet of twenty-six sail of the line, while the British Channel Fleet had but seven, the rest being in the Mediterranean or other distant stations. Britain could have commissioned a dozen others at short notice which would have been too much for the Russians, never a first-class service, even when they were under the Empress Catherine's Scottish flag officers. However, had the Russians been joined by the French, a very serious situation could have arisen. The French had been building up their fleet and were beginning to dream again of wresting the naval crown from the British. Following their old practice of building bigger ships than the British for the equivalent rates, their one-hundred-and-twenty-gun ships of 1830 were 232 feet on the gun-deck, whereas the British were still around 205 feet. In 1839 they had twelve ships of the line in commission and twelve in ordinary; made up of six first-rates, three second-rates and fifteen third-rates, none mounting less than eighty guns. In fact, this threat from France never materialised, and when it came to fighting, it was against the Russians, with Anglo-French fleets commanded by British admirals.

Nineteenth-century Developments

It was a matter of critical comment in early Victorian times that while Britain was leading engineering revolutions in many fields, particularly in land transport by

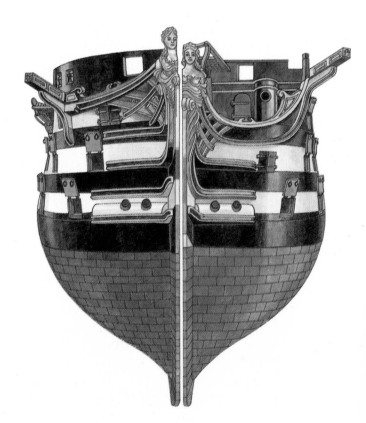

The improved method of construction with diagonal framing to stiffen the hull, and the round bow and stern introduced towards the end of the Napoleonic Wars, compared to the old method.

inventing the railway, developments in naval architecture, especially as regards the Royal Navy, appeared to be almost at a standstill. This stagnation was not only apparent but real, as will be seen by the choice of ships to go into commission. This was governed by the selection of the dozen or so ships of the line kept in the first reserve which formed a force which could quickly be put in commission for sea in an emergency, but also was the pool from which ships were commissioned to replace those coming home to pay off. These ships might be new or forty years old, like the *Hibernia* 104, launched in 1804, which went out as a flagship to the Mediterranean in 1845. A few of the liners converted to steam in the 1850s had been launched in time to fight at the end of the Napoleonic Wars.

The great stride forward was in the new method of framing perfected by Sir Robert Seppings and first tried in the *Tremendous* 74, in February 1811. In this ship additional frames were placed diagonally between the parallel frames and also between the parallel deck beams. These gave the whole structure much greater strength and rigidity. His system was generally applied to all new building when Sir Robert took over the surveyorship from Sir William Rule in 1813, and the initial benefit was that since the ships no longer worked so much in a sea, their planking did not open and they remained much drier inside. The long-term benefit was that hulls could be built much longer without hogging, and, when the time came, could bear the weight of boilers and

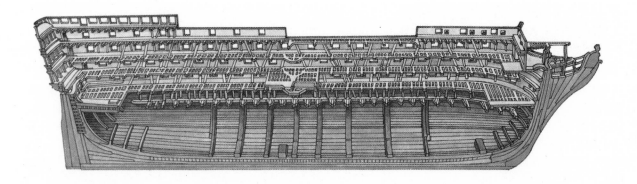

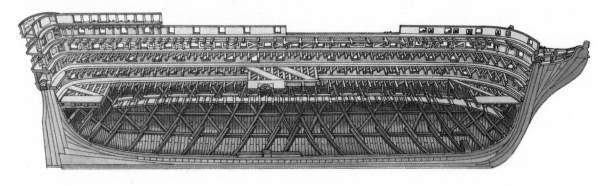

engines. The *Tremendous* was 170 feet on the gun-deck, while the biggest class of two-decker, built in the 1850's, was 250 feet. This increase in size compensated for the considerable increase in the weight of construction which made the early Seppings ships heavy sailers.

It was to improve the sailing performance that prompted Sir Robert Seppings's successor, Sir William Symonds, to change the underwater lines so that the ships had a sharper entry and a markedly steeper floor. They certainly sailed better, and a ship of the line would do about 13 knots, but they had a lively movement and would heel to the wind in a manner which made them less useful as gun platforms. The Symonds lee lurch was familiar to naval officers of the period. His two other major changes were to the designs of the bow and stern. The bows of eighteenth-century liners were framed up to the upper deck, the forward bulkhead between the upper deck and the fo'c'sle was square with round-houses and comparatively lightly built; this left the upper deck vulnerable to raking fire from ahead, and this was sorely felt by the *Victory* and *Royal Sovereign* as they slowly led their lines before a light breeze to break the Franco-Spanish line at Trafalgar. The new bow, called the round bow, was framed up to fo'c'sle level and there was a good solid bulwark above it.

Solid bulwarks for the poop-deck and fo'c'sle of liners appear in draughts dating from 1801, and for the poop alone a year or two earlier. They soon rose to be 6 feet high to give protection to those on the exposed decks. In ships without a poop-deck this led to a light bridge between the gunwales being necessary for conning the ship, a most exposed position.

To return to the dangers of raking fire a much worse vulnerability than the bow affected the stern, from ancient times the traditional living quarters of the officers. From the habitability point of view the old square stern had much to recommend it. The frames rose solid each side to poop level, but only up to the transom beams at upper-deck level in a two-decker, or middle-deck level in a three-decker. Above this rose the delightful tiers of sash windows and galleries which gave in plenty of light, and air if required, but would not stop a musket ball. Also, although of fairly light construction, their weight was mainly borne by the transom which caused straining of the main structure which could open up the seams of the planking and let in water in bad weather.

Another consideration was the extremely poor stern and chase fire of the eighteenth-century liner, which had at the most four ports opening dead astern, all at gun-deck level. This was because on the decks above even if guns were manhandled round and their barrels pushed through the stern windows, the structure could not have withstood the recoil, and if strengthened to take it, would have imposed an intolerable strain on the transom beams below it. With a built-up circular stern to poop-deck level pierced for an additional fourteen guns in two-deckers and sixteen in three-deckers, making twenty in all in the latter, a respectable stern and quarter-fire was possible. There were still the stern windows and galleries abaft the main structure, so beloved by naval officers, and these would have suffered severely from the blast of the ship's own guns. This was acceptable in the emergency of battle, but not for practice shooting. At the end of the eighteenth century an effort had been made to reduce the weight and increase the strength of the old type of stern by doing away with the open galleries and having

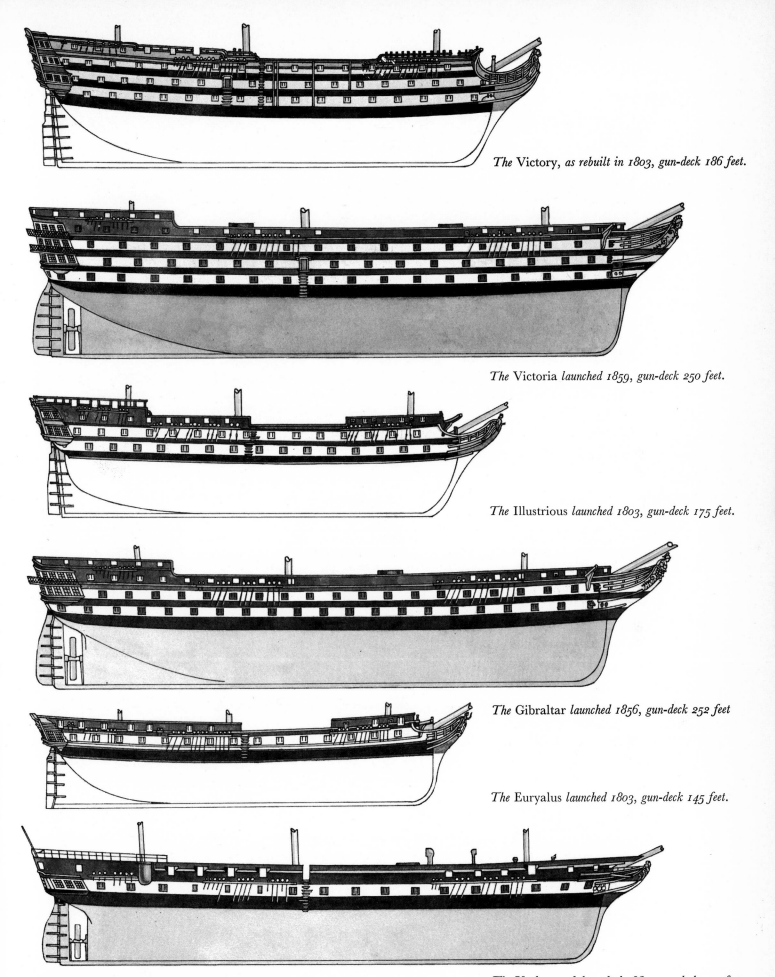

The Victory, *as rebuilt in 1803, gun-deck 186 feet.*

The Victoria *launched 1859, gun-deck 250 feet.*

The Illustrious *launched 1803, gun-deck 175 feet.*

The Gibraltar *launched 1856, gun-deck 252 feet*

The Euryalus *launched 1803, gun-deck 145 feet.*

The Undaunted *launched 1860, gun-deck 250 feet.*

0   20   40   60   80   100 Scale in Feet

The increasing lengths of wooden hulls in the first half of the nineteenth century was made possible by the added rigidity introduced with the adoption of diagonal framing.

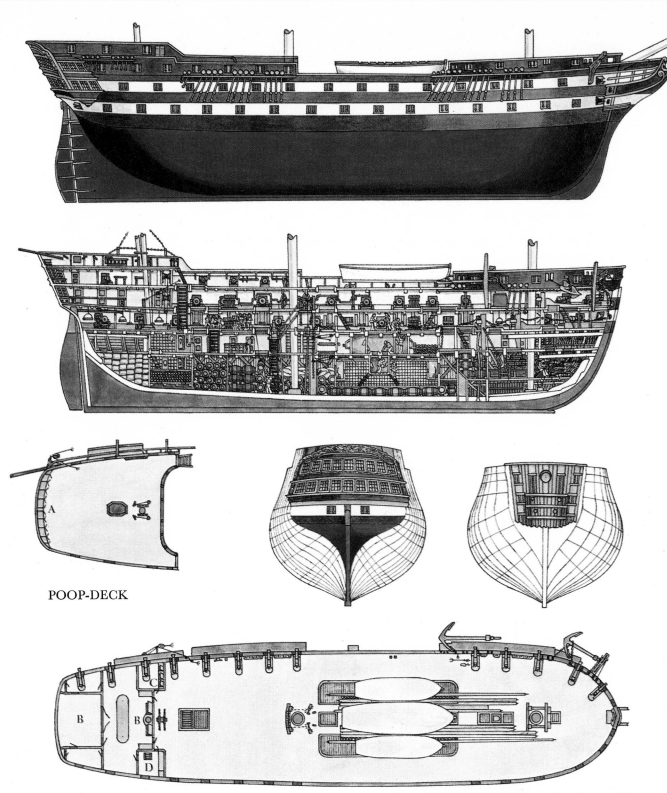

POOP-DECK

QUARTER-DECK AND FO'C'SLE

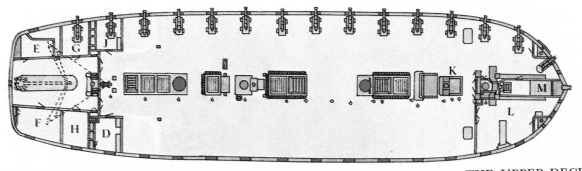

THE UPPER-DECK

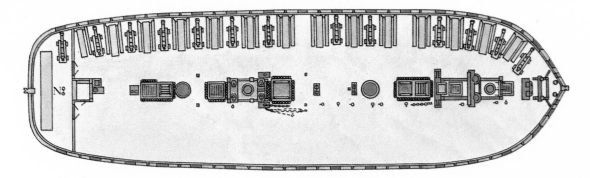

GUN-DECK

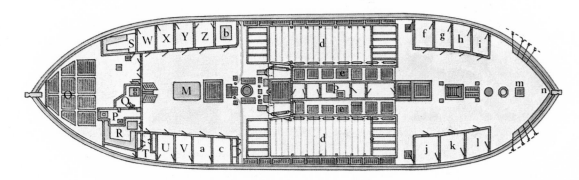

ORLOP-DECK

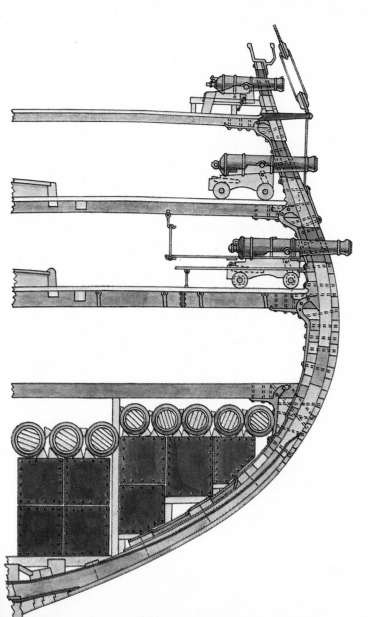

The Vanguard *of 1844, one of a class of eleven sailing two-deckers, the last to be designed without auxiliary steam propulsion, and in her case, one of several which were never converted.*

KEY TO VANGUARD

A	Colour lockers	**T**	Dispensary
B	Captain's apartments	**U**	Surgeon
C	Clerks office	**V**	Chaplain
D	Captains' steward	**W**	Purser
E	Master	**X**	2nd Lieut.
F	Commander	**Y**	3rd Lieut.
G	Captain of Marines	**Z**	4th Lieut.
H	1st Lieut.	**a**	5th Lieut.
I	Ward room	**b**	6th Lieut.
J	Ward room stewards	**c**	1st Lieut. of Marines
K	Galley	**d**	Cable Tier
L	Sick berth	**e**	Sail room
M	Amputation table	**f**	Naval Instructor
N	Gun room	**g**	2nd Lieut. of Marines
O	Gratings over Bread room	**h**	3rd Lieut. of Marines
P	Magazine passage and Scuttle to Magazine	**i**	Marine store
Q	Handing room	**j**	Gunner
R	Captain's store room	**k**	Carpenter
S	Ward store room	**l**	Boatswain
		m	Scuttle to Gunner's store
		n	Stand for Arms

complete rows of stern windows instead. This was called the closed stern, and the *Victory* was converted to one during her rebuilding of 1798 to 1803, which she still has.

By the end of the Napoleonic Wars the open gallery, by popular demand, had crept back, but Sir Robert Seppings followed up his built-up sterns with a series of extra-ordinary 'lighthouse' stern galleries, designed to facilitate the field of fire. Behind which were often iron hanging canopied stern walks, such as are associated with Regency houses, and continued in Victorian villas for decades. These stern walks continued in popularity in our capital ships and large cruisers until recent times, and only finally disappeared with the scrapping of the battleships *Queen Elizabeth* and *Warspite* after the Second World War. In 1827 a modified round stern, called the elliptical stern, in which the framing took on a much squarer form on the deck plan, was introduced by Captain Symonds. This refinement was adopted generally, and with it there was a return to the old style of quarter-gallery, though slightly bowed in the middle of the stern-line. In their final form the squared-off outer edge was modified so that the quarter-galleries curved round to the flatter line of the stern windows. The improvement in the chase fire made possible by the built-up bow was not so marked, mainly because the bowsprit, jib-booms and attendant spreaders and rigging made fire directly ahead almost impossible. There was, however, an improvement in the bow fire, particularly when a big 68-pounder was mounted on the fo'c'sles of the liners around 1850, with a slide-carriage designed to swivel on traversing-rings, and bear over wide angles on both sides of the fo'c'sle, which had enlarged ports.

Another considerable structural improvement was the closing of the waist. The gangway between the quarter-deck and fo'c'sle by the gunwales had been broadening until by the beginning of the nineteenth century it was just a large hole beamed across to carry the boats and spare yards. This hole got narrower until the surveyorship of Sir William Symonds in 1832, when he closed the waist altogether. In theory a complete tier of guns from quarter-deck to fo'c'sle was now possible, but partly for reasons of weight distribution, and more especially because a space on what was now the upper-most deck was needed for boats and spars, this was almost never done. It would have impeded the firing of truck-mounted guns so that this part of the deck was generally kept clear of guns, though some draughts show complete tiers. For this reason there are mid-nineteenth-century references to four-deckers instead of three-deckers, but if this is to be based on the number of complete decks, then they should have been called five-deckers, with their orlops. A further change introduced at the beginning of the century was the substitution of iron knees for wooden ones. This was made necessary by the acute shortage of timbers for the purpose which, if they were to have sufficient strength, had to be cut where the trunk divided and the grain of the wood curved, otherwise the knee would split. This had been one of the troubles with the *Commerce de Marseille*.

The Nineteenth-century Rates to 1856

In 1816 there was a revision of the ratings, which had been in force since 1746. First-rates remained at one hundred guns and over, but the second-rate now included ships of eighty guns and above and the third-rate began at seventy guns. Previously the third-rate had covered any ship from sixty guns to eighty and had been by far the largest and most important rate in the battle fleet, but now was reduced more or less to the seventy-fours. The fourth-rate began at fifty guns, the fifth-rate at thirty-six guns and the sixth-rate at twenty-four guns. There was a scale of men attached to the gun list, and in 1856 a new list based on the number of men employed, with different scales for steamers and pure sailors was introduced, which cut out the number of guns altogether.

Advances in gunnery and the coming of steam power might reduce the number of guns a ship carried to the point when she dropped a rate, yet was a more powerful warship than before. Also the designation of a first-rate as being a ship of one hundred guns and above became a trifle nonsensical when the number rose to one hundred and thirty-one. Indeed there were even, as early as the Napoleonic Wars, proposals for four-deckers of one hundred and sixty or one hundred and seventy guns, such as Joseph Tucker's proposed ship to be called the *Duke of Kent*. She was not built because there was no requirement for such a ship which would have been most expensive to run, but at 221 feet on the gun-deck and 62 feet 5 inches in the beam she would have been much smaller than the last three-deckers to be built. The *Howe* of 1860, which was 266 feet on the gun-deck and 61 feet 1 inch in the beam, was to have been completed with only one hundred and twenty-one guns.

The tendency was for the gradual abandonment of the smaller rates of liner and an increase in proportion of the most powerful ships, particularly in the building of the two-decker first-rates in the early 1850s. Five ships actually completed as one-hundred-and-one-gun ships, and of the twenty-five or so others that were built, all except those few that were converted into armoured ships, completed as nineties or ninety-ones.

In 1830 there were sixteen first-rates, sixteen second-rates and fifty-seven third-rates. Still an all-sailing battle fleet in 1845, the proportion was twenty-seven first-rates, twenty-eight second-rates, all two-deckers, and forty-one third-rates. The last date worthy of comparison is 1855, during the Russian war, a year before rating by guns was dropped, when the first-rates remained at seventeen; the number of second-rates had increased to thirty-six, the third-rates had dropped to thirteen and the fourth-rate was back with sixty-gun liners, all in commission.

A 32-pounder 45 cwt smooth-bore muzzle-loader of 1840, mounted on a Ferguson slide carriage.

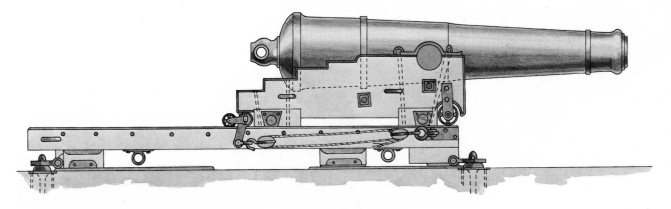

The paddle frigate Sidon of 1846. The painted ports on her paddle-boxes give an indication of how they reduced her main-deck armament. They were also vulnerable to cannon-shot.

A deck-plan of H.M.S. Sidon, showing the great awkward paddle-boxes, and the armament lay-out.

Steam Power

In the spring of 1845 there were one hundred and thirteen steam vessels in the Navy List, but not one of them belonged to the battle fleet. This may seem remarkable when one considers the commercial success of the steam-ship by this date, there being already steam services operating to America and India. The *Comet* of 1822, which served as a tug and survey vessel in home waters, was the first steam vessel built for the Royal Navy, but it was to be twenty-four years before the *Ajax* 60 was undocked in Cowes in 1846 to become the first steam-liner. She was screw-driven and powered by a four-cylinder horizontal engine of 450 horse-power by Maudsley, which was capable of driving her at 7 knots. Under sail her screw and funnel retracted, a device generally adopted.

The reason for the delay in giving steam power to the battle fleet was that it had to await the invention of the 'submarine propeller or archimedean screw', now known as the screw propeller. This was because paddle wheels would have meant doing away with at least one-quarter, perhaps a third, of the ship's broadside armament, and the machinery to drive them would have filled the entire centre section of the ship. In addition the paddles would have been extremely vulnerable to fire and would have impeded the ship's sailing performance when not in use. The screw propeller was first

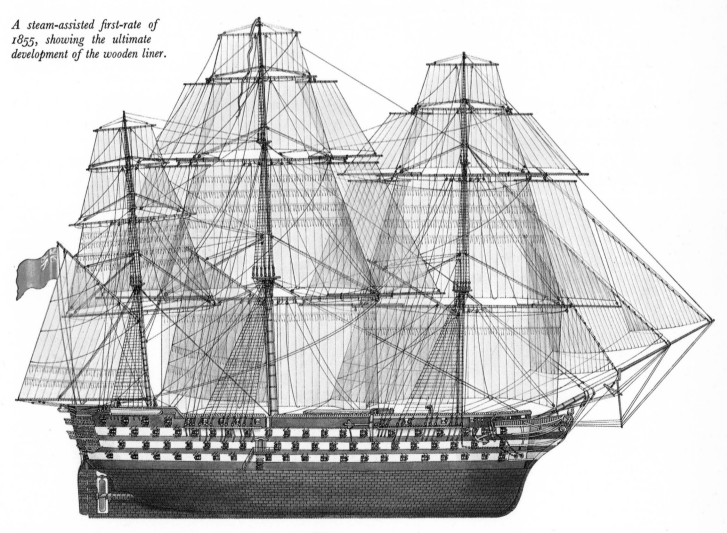

A steam-assisted first-rate of 1855, showing the ultimate development of the wooden liner.

successfully tested in a vessel called the *Archimedes* in 1840, and Brunel first tried one in a big ship when he launched his iron steamer the *Great Britain* in 1843. About this time the Admiralty became convinced of the virtues of a free-moving battle fleet based on screw propulsion, and considering that the fate of the nation might be said to have hung on their policy regarding the battle fleet, then the decision to adopt it was not too tardy.

The *Ajax*'s 7 knots gave her no more than manœuvring power, but by the sixties the engines for two-deckers were rated up to 800 horse-power which gave them a useful steaming speed of about 12 knots, the last three-deckers had engines of 1,000 horse-power. The method of altering ships on the stocks, such as the two three-deckers *Duke of Wellington* and *Marlborough*, laid down as pure sailers, was to cut off the stern and launch it; then to lengthen the hull and install the engines and boilers; finally to drag the stern ashore and reattach it to the rest of the ship. It was recognised by the time of the Crimean War that all future fleet actions would be conducted under power.

Armament of Nineteenth-century Ships of the Line

The old system, in force since the beginning of naval gunnery, of carrying a mixed armament with the greatest guns on the gun-deck and lighter ones above, had the disadvantage that several different sizes of shot and of powder charges had to be carried, and in action this might easily lead to confusion. In 1825 a Colonel Munro of the Royal Artillery submitted a proposal that a single calibre should be used for all guns, the necessary weight distribution being met by having shorter barrelled guns on the upper decks, and that this armament should be based on the 32-pounder.

This scheme was put into effect in the next few years, so that a three-decker's armament now consisted of truck-carriage mounted 32-pounders, weighing 56 cwt on the gun- and middle decks, 32-pounders of 40 cwt on the upper deck, and 32-pounders of 25 cwt, called gunnades, on the quarter-deck; the fo'c'sle had two guns of 25 cwt and two of 49 cwt. This uniformity was shortly afterwards disturbed, however, by a demand for a small number of very large chase-guns, so that 68-pounder 'millers' were added, two to each deck below the quarter-deck; later they were confined to the fo'c'sle and possibly the quarter-deck. There were some slight variations in different ships.

From the 1820s to the 1850s the French, bitterly jealous of British naval supremacy, were looking round for a weapon which would make up for their own natural short-comings and neutralise the British advantage. They pinned their hopes on M. Paixhan's shell-firing guns which he developed in the 1820s. Shell-firing from cannon as well as from mortars was not new; the French had experimented with it as far back as the beginning of the eighteenth century, and encouraging experiments were carried out by them in Napoleonic times. French ships were issued with a variety of tricky combustible projectiles before the end of the eighteenth century. The British, who had long used shell-firing mortars in their bomb-vessels for shore bombardments, regarded with distrust and distaste the idea of using shell in ship-to-ship engagements as being ungentlemanly and dangerous. Dangerous, that is to say, more to oneself from accidents in carrying them; a view that proved justified from the number of disasters to French ships from fires and explosions.

There were also limitations in the early days of shell-firing to the amount of charge that could safely be used and the ball itself being hollow was lighter for its size than a solid one, so that range and penetrating power were reduced. The effect of the explosion was also largely discounted, even though Sir Samuel Bentham, an inventive Englishman who joined Russian service, had proved, back in 1788, the effectiveness of the shell-firing gun, by destroying a Turkish squadron with them mounted in long-boats.

The attitude here, though watchful, was to leave things as they were until forced to make a change by a foreign power. So it was in 1837 when the French announced a general change to shell-firing guns that the British had also to introduce them, which was quickly done by boring out some of the 32-pounders to 8- or 10-inch calibre. So long as the shells were spherical a mixed armament of shell-firing and shot-firing guns was necessary because the shot had a better range. In the Russian war the *Duke of Wellington* 131, flagship of the Baltic fleet, had a mixed armament in the following distribution: gun-deck, ten 8-inch shell-firing and twenty-six 32-pounders (shot); middle deck, six 8-inch shell-firing and thirty 32-pounders; upper deck, thirty-eight 32-pounders; quarter-deck and fo'c'sle, twenty 32-pounders and one 68-pounder on a slide carriage and pivot mounting. A better arrangement, more generally adopted, was to have the whole of the gun-deck battery shell-firing and the batteries above shot-firing, the 32-pounders graded as before. There was a general introduction in the 1840s of the slide carriage pivoting on traversing-rings for the chase-guns, usually one in the bows and two at the stern; otherwise the truck carriage continued to be general, and was to continue to prevail in wooden-built ships until the last class of wooden corvettes paid off in the late 1880s.

There had been efforts to improve the truck carriage, the most significant of which was Captain Marshall's carriage by which the forepart of the carriage was removed and the weight taken by the barrel resting on a crutch attached to the gunwale. This crutch was hinged, the weight taken by one small truck wheel on the deck, and by moving this from side to side the gun could be laterally trained. Elevation still relied on the wooden quoin. The mounting was tested with 12-pounders aboard the *Prince Regent*, and the Marshall mounting proved itself by firing eight rounds in 7 minutes 44 seconds, manned by three men, against 9 minutes 6 seconds, for the normal truck-mounted gun manned by six men. As a result of this the system was approved for stern- and bow-chasers, but was never extended to the broadside guns, and it is doubtful whether it became general even for a short time for the chase-guns.

Although sights had been experimented with for many years, and some enthusiasts like Sir Philip Broke had fitted them at their own expense to their ships' guns, the navy did not take officially a very scientific interest in this subject until the second quarter of the century when it set up an experimental and training establishment in H.M.S. *Excellent* at Portsmouth under Captain Thomas Hastings in 1832, which he ruled for fifteen years. Initially no great strides could be taken to revolutionise naval gunnery so long as it depended on a cast, smooth-bore gun, firing spherical projectiles. It took the wrought-iron rifled gun of the 1860s firing cylindrical shells to achieve accuracy, range and penetrating power unheard of before.

Fastening

It may be said that a ship is as strong as her fastening, and unfortunately it was in its fastening that a wooden hull was apt to be most vulnerable. Fastening meant in practice the nailing of the wooden parts together. Up to the 1780s this had been done with iron nails and trenails, after that copper nails were used under the copper sheathing and in the second quarter of the nineteenth century tinned iron came into use, but copper continued to dominate the underwater fastening of wooden hulls.

Of these materials iron was the strongest and had the virtue of fusing with the wood when it started to corrode. As corrosion advanced, however, the strength of the nail ebbed and the wood around it rotted. Copper was introduced because the iron nails under the copper sheathing, when it came in, caused electrolytic action between the two metals which damaged the sheathing. It was not so strong as iron, and since it did not corrode, or hardly at all, it did not grip so hard. Still, it was strong enough, and by not corroding it kept its strength and did not rot the wood around it. Its disadvantage was the expense of the copper, and a seventy-four-gun ship required 35 tons of copper just for her undersides. The hull above the sheathing therefore continued to be fastened with iron, but the tinning process cut down corrosion and gave a much longer life to nail and wood. Finally, there was the trenail, a wooden peg which was cheap and weak, but one would have thought harmless to the wood around it; not so—it was found that a trenail of one wood set into another wood caused rotting to both, and in the nineteenth century when so many different woods were in use for shipbuilding it was often impossible to avoid mixing woods.

Accommodation

The deck layout of a typical two-decker to the early Victorian period does not differ greatly from the century before. The captain remained in the coach under the poop-deck, where he had a sitting-room, dining-room, two bedrooms, clerk's office and steward's pantry. Below him on the upper deck the wardroom remained in its traditional place, and along each side of it and, somewhat forward of it, were cabins for the commander (an innovation of the 1820s), the first, second and third lieutenants, the master, captain of marines and the captain's steward. The sick-berth was forward of the galley under the fo'c'sle. The gun-deck housed the men, who messed on folding tables between the guns, and slung their hammocks above them, while right aft was the midshipmen's gunroom. The orlop-deck, which was now quite flush with a good deckhead, housed, in addition to its traditional denizens (the surgeon, surgeon's mate, purser, carpenter, gunner and boatswain), now also the fourth, fifth and sixth lieutenants, the chaplain, naval instructor, first, second and third lieutenants of marines and the captain's clerks. Their cabins either faced each other across the surgery and amputation table two-thirds the way aft, or were well forward. Being on the fourth deck down without any forced ventilation, the air must have been pretty thick at times, though by the innovation of scuttles which were angled down through the timbers from gun-deck level, the inhabitants had some natural light and visual contact with the world outside. Another refinement was piped water through lead pipes from a cistern in the poop.

The gun-deck of a late wooden ship of the line.

10

The Nineteenth-century Frigates and Other Cruising Vessels

In 1814 the Royal Navy had a round one hundred and thirty frigates in commission, of which ninety were of the larger classes of thirty-six and thirty-eight guns, and a dozen more were of forty or forty-four guns. This was a reversal of the pattern of ten years before when the thirty-twos, now down to twenty at sea, outnumbered all other classes. It was indeed the large frigate that was to take over the peace-time duties as flagships on distant stations, formerly the province of the two-decker sixty-fours and fifties. Already by 1814 two monster frigates the *Leander* and *Newcastle* had been commissioned and sent out to America to cope with the U.S. Navy's huge frigates which had been giving Britain such shocks. The *Leander* and *Newcastle* were built of pitch pine with their waists decked over and furnished with a complete tier of guns from poop to fo'c'sle, so that they were called double-banked frigates. On the draught the *Newcastle* has a coach and a double tier of stern galleries. It is most doubtful, however, if she was finished with a coach, since when she was on the American coast Commodore Sir George Collier, who was in the *Leander*, successfully passed off his ships as an American squadron, when they fell in with an American ship. The captain of this vessel, an English prize, came aboard the *Leander* in his own boat, saying to Sir George, whom he addressed as Commodore Decatur, that he knew his ship to be the *President* the moment he saw her, and Nick himself would not deceive him. When asked what ship the *Newcastle* was, he did not know, but accepted that she was the *Constitution*, saying only that she was not painted as she used to be. Having been pumped by Sir George, and communicating the pious hope that his squadron would do 'a tarnation share of mischief to the damned English sarpents, and play the devil's game with their rag of a flag', the Yankee took his leave with great apparent satisfaction; but when about to quit, the first lieutenant told him the truth of his situation, and on seeing Sir George come up in his uniform coat, he became almost frantic. The upshot of all this is that if the *Newcastle* did have a coach it would surely have been impossible to pass her off as the *Constitution*, which we know did not.

In one respect the *Leander* and *Newcastle* were small three-deckers without gun-ports on the lower deck, and they mounted fifty-eight guns and carronades, though since carronades did not count in the total until 1817 they were classed as fifties at that time. The advantages of this type of ship over equivalent two-deckers was the same as the frigates had always enjoyed. Compared to the draught of a late two-decker fifty, to be called the *Saturn*, of the same year, the dimensions of the *Newcastle* were 177 feet on the

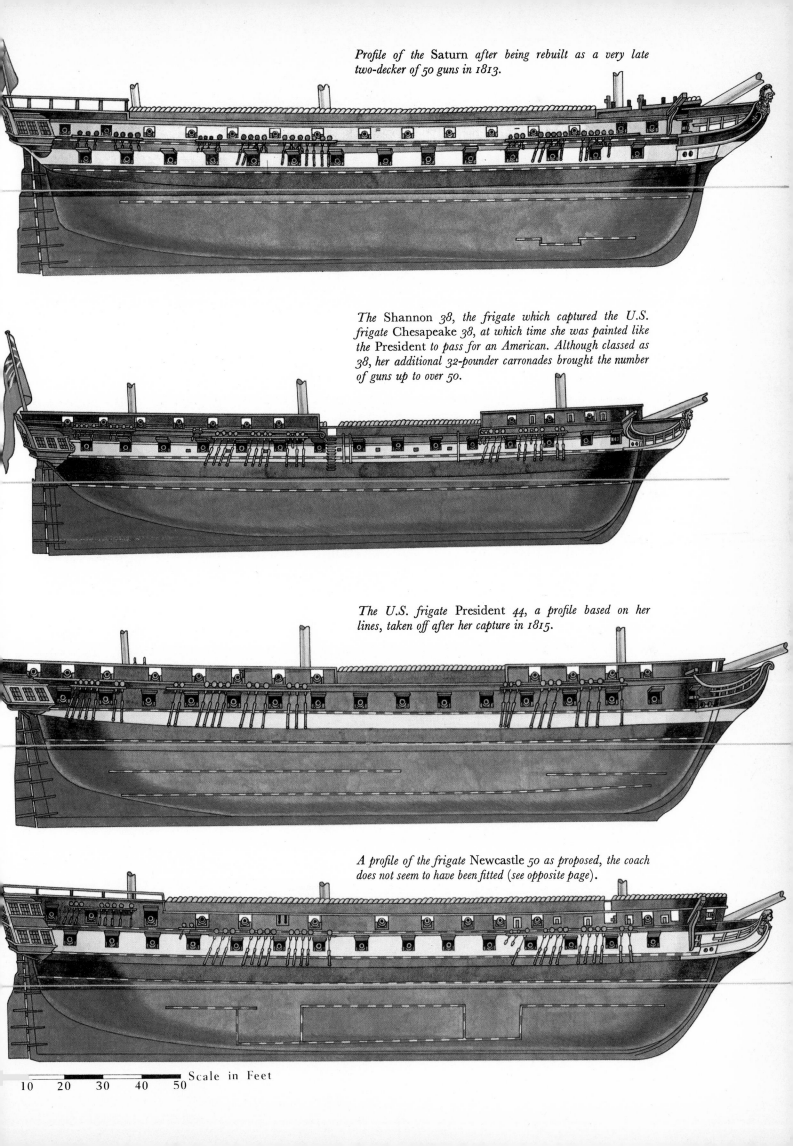

Profile of the Saturn after being rebuilt as a very late two-decker of 50 guns in 1813.

The Shannon 38, the frigate which captured the U.S. frigate Chesapeake 38, at which time she was painted like the President to pass for an American. Although classed as 38, her additional 32-pounder carronades brought the number of guns up to over 50.

The U.S. frigate President 44, a profile based on her lines, taken off after her capture in 1815.

A profile of the frigate Newcastle 50 as proposed, the coach does not seem to have been fitted (see opposite page).

Scale in Feet

10   20   30   40   50

gun-deck and 41 feet 11 inches in the beam, against 154 feet and 44 feet 4 inches, and the *Newcastle* carried her lower tier a good 9 feet above her water-line, while the *Saturn* could hardly manage 6.

Another advantage of the frigate type was that all the men lived on the lower deck where there were no guns, so that in the event of action there was much less to clear away on the deck above which carried the main battery. In two-deckers the crew lived on the gun-deck, so took longer to clear away.

The *Leander* and *Newcastle* were not built for the American war, as has been said, since the draughts are dated 1810, before Britain was much concerned with the potential of American frigates. One day when the two frigates were blockading Boston in 1814, some Americans went out in a fishing-boat to the *Leander* and asked permission to board, which was granted. During conversation with the commodore one said that 'You are a larger ship, but I do not think that your men are as stout as ours aboard the *Constitution*.' 'They may be very little, but their hearts are in the right place; and I'll thank you to inform the American captain, that if he will come out and meet the *Leander*, I will pledge my word and honour that no British ship shall be within twenty leagues; and further, if my ship mounts more guns than the *Constitution*, I will throw the additional guns overboard.' We do not know if the message was ever delivered, but the *Constitution* did not come out while the *Leander* was there and they never met.

In order to meet the sudden demand for very large frigates for the American war, three seventy-fours were razed down to flush-decked frigates. This was an emergency move, not to be repeated, but the big frigate continued to flourish into the 1860s, mostly 70 feet longer than the *Leander*.

A further feature of the nineteenth-century frigate establishment was the re-emergence of the small frigate of twenty-four or twenty-six guns. In calling them small, they were as big as a mid-eighteenth-century thirty-six, but as they carried 32-pounders instead of 12-pounders the weight of the battery had to be considered. By the 1830s the 32-pounder was in general use.

Steam-Frigates

Steam came earlier to the frigates than to the liners, as a number of paddle-driven frigates were built alongside the pure sailors until screw propulsion was adopted. The first of them was a converted forty-six-gun sailing frigate called the *Penelope* which had originally been launched in 1829, and in 1842 was cut in two and lengthened from 152 feet on the lower deck to 215 feet 2 inches to take paddle machinery. An indication of the size and weight of the paddle machinery was the reduction in the number of guns that could be carried, forty-six to sixteen. Her engine was 650 horse-power and drove her at about 10 knots. Altogether eighteen wooden and one iron paddle-frigates were built in the 1840s, the last of them completing in 1852. They served a purpose, but suffered from the inordinate amount of space the machinery took up, and the paddles were a serious hindrance to their sailing powers. It was known, indeed, for the paddle vanes to be removed in some ships on occasion; also the armament of any of them never exceeded twenty-one guns and over half of them only mounted six. Most were broken up in 1864 but one at least lasted in service until 1870.

The first steam-frigates were paddlers, but the screw-frigates followed fast. The first, the *Amphion*, was converted during construction and launched in 1846. The screw system was so obviously better than the paddles that it is remarkable that the paddlers continued to be built at the same time as the screw-vessels. The machinery to drive the shaft was situated low in the hull and did not interfere with the main-deck battery, and the drag of the screw was overcome by raising it.

The screw-frigates were very large, most of them between 230 and 250 feet on the lower deck, and with a beam of about 50 feet; and two of the later ones, the *Mersey* and *Orlando*, were 300 feet on the lower deck with a 52-foot beam, the largest unarmoured wooden hulls ever built for the navy. They were completed in 1859 and 1861 respectively, but it was found that the strains of such a length were too great for the material. Altogether forty-five screw-frigates were built, and these wore the flag on many distant stations into the middle 1870s, the last one was the *Undaunted* which came home from the Far East at the end of 1878. The last wooden frigate of all to serve was the *Newcastle*, completed as late as 1874, and when she paid off in 1880 there disappeared from view the most splendid-looking type of masted ship ever built.

Sailing Corvettes and Sloops

From the Napoleonic Wars until about 1860 a large share of the work of keeping what became known as the *Pax Britannica* was borne by the little ships of the navy, mostly the beautiful brig-rigged sloops and corvettes. These last, eighteen- or twenty-gun ships, were about 120 feet on the main-deck and 38 feet in the beam. They had two flush-decks and possibly nothing more above the battery, but they might have a quarter-deck, or even a complete deck with a well for the boats amidships, but with no guns on it; they were ship-rigged. The smaller eighteen- or sixteen-gun ship-sloops were about 113 feet on the main-deck and had a beam of about 31 feet; they were ship- or barque-rigged and sometimes had a tiny cabin aft on the main-deck, and a fo'c'sle. The lower deck would probably not be complete or flush. The brigs were laid out very much the same as those already described as serving in the late eighteenth century; the battery on an open deck, and the crew accommodated on the platforms below. They were 95 to 100 feet on the main-deck with a beam of about 32 feet. The armament of the early post-war sloops was largely based on the 32-pounder carronade, but this last was replaced in the 1830s with the 25-cwt 32-pounder gun, or gunnade, with possibly 6 feet long 18-pounders for chasers. When it came to the class below them, a large gun mounted on a slide carriage on the centre line amidships was preferred, with pivots and traversing-rings. There would be also two or four carronades, or later, from the 1840s, light guns of the same calibre.

They were usually called hermaphrodite brigs, because of their rig, which by the middle of the century was called brigantine. Sir William Symonds, the surveyor from 1832 to 1847, was particularly successful with what became known as the Symonite brigs. He had largely got his job as a result of the sailing qualities of a barque-rigged sloop which he designed, called the *Columbine*, which beat everyone else's in the sailing trials held in 1827.

In 1845 there were over sixty of these vessels in commission, but the steam-assisted

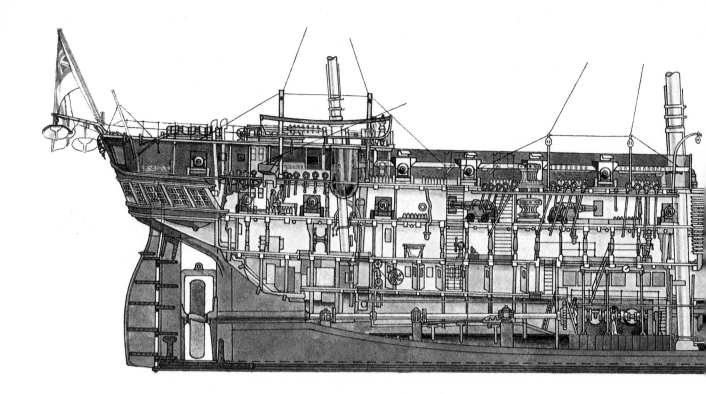

sloops were already, with over twenty in commission, gaining on the pure sailers, which disappeared from the oceans in the early 1860s.

Nineteenth-century Rigging

The sail plans of the sailing navy were perfected in the years following the Napoleonic Wars. The most obvious modifications to the appearance of the plans were the dropping of the loose-footed spanker and the general adoption of a large single driver. To compensate for this more head-sails had to be set, so that the flying jib-boom became a permanent feature. The sprit-sail yard was retained as a spreader in the ships of the line until the fifties, but in frigates and below it was replaced by two separate spreaders, fitted with jaws to the bowsprit. Another improvement to the fore and aft sails was the use of loose-footed trysails set on small masts abaft the fore and mainmasts. The square sails were, from 1811, bent to jackstays below the yards instead of being lashed to them.

In 1830, when the Royal Navy was being forced to enlarge its ships to keep up with the French, people began to worry about the practical difficulties of handling the spars and sails which would have to increase proportionately with the hulls. In fact, the crews always managed, and smartness aloft, which became a fetish in the Victorian navy, reached a remarkable standard of efficiency never equalled before.

An indication of the increase in the size of the masts and yards may be seen by

84

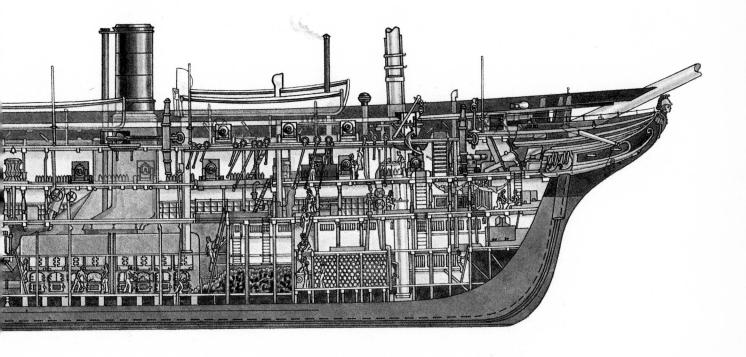

The screw steam-frigate Undaunted *of 1860, one of the last of a highly successful type of cruiser which had been evolved over a hundred years before (see pages 46–50 and 82).*

comparing some of these of the *Victory* 100 of 1765 with a one-hundred-and-twenty-gun ship of 1853:

	'Victory', 1765	*120-gun ship of 1853*
Mainmast	94 feet 10 inches	119 feet 8 inches
Main topmast	57 feet 4 inches	68 feet 1 inch
Main topgallantmast	29 feet 1 inch	34 feet 5 inches
Main yard	86 feet 5 inches	104 feet 4 inches

The general policy of standardising fittings brought in by Sir William Symonds in the 1830s also affected masts and spars which were reduced to twenty establishments, where there had formerly been eighty-eight.

The Wooden and Composite Screw-Corvettes

The difference between the screw-frigates and the screw-corvettes was not one of size, for some of the corvettes were larger than some of the frigates, but of layout. The frigates had a lower deck for accommodation, a main-deck which carried the main armament, and above that what was virtually a third deck, since the quarter-deck and fo'c'sle had been joined together, leaving only a well in the waist; this deck too carried a heavy broadside armament and chasers.

The corvettes were two-deck ships, the lower deck for accommodation and the main-deck for the battery which was out in the open. With the building of the *Eclipse* class of 1867, poops and fo'c'sles were added but these never met, or anything like, and nothing heavier than light quick-firers were ever mounted on them. The early corvettes built during or just after the Russian war of 1854–55 were about 195 feet on the main-deck and 38 feet in the beam. The next generation, the *Eclipse* class, were originally called sloops on the plans but were launched as corvettes, and were 212 feet on the main-deck and 36 feet in the beam; they had ram bows. The last wooden corvettes were the five ships of the *Amethyst* class of 1873–75. These were much easier on the eye than the ram-bowed type since they were given graceful knee-bows. They were 220 feet on the main-deck and 37 feet in the beam; their engines were around 350 horse-power, which gave a useful steaming speed of 13 knots, which was also their sailing speed. For armament they had twelve truck-mounted 64-pounder rifled-muzzle-loaders, and two more on slides as the bow- and stern-chasers. In their second commissions three of them had their truck-mounted broadside guns exchanged for ten slide-mounted guns of a lighter pattern. The early corvettes were all ship-rigged, but the last two classes, though with one exception built with ship-rigs, were all converted to barques for their second commissions.

Altogether thirty wooden and six composite corvettes were launched between 1854 and 1877, and with the launch of the *Sapphire* in September 1874 of the *Amethyst* class, wooden shipbuilding in the traditions begun in the Tudor navy came to an end.

It was fitting that the name ship of this class should close the chapter of their exploits with one last sea fight, which was with the Peruvian armoured turret ship *Huascar*. This vessel, a British-built armoured ship, was the major unit of the Peruvian navy, and in May 1877 she was seized during a revolution by the aspirant to the presidency. At first the British did not consider it their business, but when Pierolo, for that was the aspirant's name, began to stop British merchant ships, claiming government mail and seizing coal on an illegal bill drawn on the Peruvian treasury, it was time to take a hand. The Pacific flagship was the *Shah*, one of three very large iron-built unarmoured cruisers with a powerful armament. The other British warship in those waters at the time was the *Amethyst*, and the two ships intercepted the *Huascar* on 29 May. Admiral de Horsey demanded her surrender for piracy, but the 'President' haughtily refused to yield. In the resulting action the *Huascar*'s fire was naturally directed against the *Shah*, but the *Amethyst* also kept up a well-directed fire until de Horsey sent her to close the land on the Chilean side in case the *Huascar* should seek neutral sanctuary. In fact, she managed to get herself in the shallows before the town of Ilo where de Horsey could not follow and dared not fire for the houses. Although the *Huascar*'s upper works were badly damaged her armour was proof against British fire. She, on the other hand, mounted two 300-pounder Armstrong rifled-muzzle-loaders which would have destroyed the *Shah* if they had hit her in the right places. In fact, only some rigging was damaged. In the night the *Huascar* stole away and surrendered to the Peruvian squadron which was supposed to be in pursuit of her, but had not dared to take her on. Unaware of this, de Horsey had sent in a cutter with a Whitehead torpedo only to find the bird had flown. This was the last occasion when a British wooden warship with a broadside battery of muzzle-loading, truck-mounted guns was ever in action, and the only occasion when one was engaged with an armoured adversary.

Although this volume sets out to confine itself to the wooden navy, it is not reasonable to leave out the composite-built corvettes and smaller cruisers. This style of building was popular in the 1860s and 1870s until the coming in of mild steel hulls, but in the Royal Navy was not used in anything larger than the corvettes. The principle was to make the ship's frames of iron, but the keel, decks and planking were of wood. This gave a stronger and more rigid hull than a wooden-framed one, and in the hot and distant places where these ships spent their working lives the iron inside the wooden sheathing kept the temperature down below decks. One of the last composite corvette classes, the *Carolines*, were given an iron protective deck over their boilers and engines.

So far as the corvettes were concerned only one class was composite-built and this was the *Emerald* class of six, launched 1875–77. Apart from a slight difference in their underwater lines these ships were identical to the *Amethyst* class of wooden corvettes and proved magnificent sea-boats. Two examples of composite construction can be seen at and near Greenwich today: the merchant clipper *Cutty Sark* and the gunboat *Foxhound*; the latter, now called the *Arabel*, lies near by in Blackwall Reach; a third, the sloop *Gannet*, is now lying in the River Hamble as the training ship *Mercury*.

The Wooden and Composite Screw-Sloops

The old sailing sloops, because they were among the smallest of warships, might be ship-rigged, brig-rigged, or cutter-rigged; the rating was on force and the number of men carried, not on a design type. The scale for the screw-sloops was the same, but in their case their engines and boilers required them to be so big that three masts and a square rig was necessarily uniform. They were in fact scaled-down corvettes, and in 1875 any warship with more than one hundred, but less than two hundred officers and men was called a sloop.

No less than ninety-seven of these vessels went into service between the middle 1840s, when the first ones were being either built, converted from paddle sloops or from sailing sloops which had to be lengthened, until the last one was launched in May 1888. The distribution was fifty-seven wooden, thirty-nine composite and one experimental iron one, the latter built in 1846. They were generally barque-rigged, certainly all the later ones, and many classes were ram bowed. The large *Amazon* class of 1865–66 were the first to have poops and fo'c'sles. They measured 187 feet by 46 feet in the beam.

It is difficult to make any generalisation about armament when the type spans forty years, and at a time of big changes in gunnery. But it is possible to state that the early ones might have as many as seventeen smooth-bore 32-pounders, or a slightly smaller number which included a 68-pounder. In the middle 1860s the number had been reduced to four or six heavier guns such as the 7-inch rifled-muzzle-loader. This policy continued into the middle 1880s when the final armament was about ten 5-inch breech-loaders.

The sloops, being in between the corvette and gun-vessel classes, were apt to include features from either or both. Some sloops, for instance, had a complete lower deck like

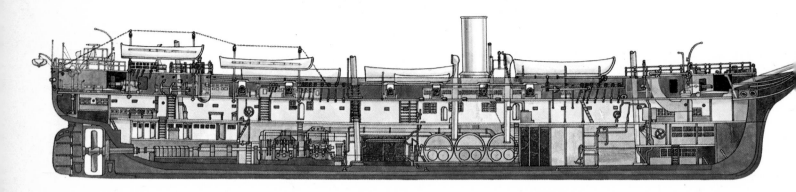

H.M.S. Amethyst, *the name ship of the last class of wooden corvettes to be built for the Navy. She was the last wooden cruiser of any kind to be built for the service; launched in 1873, she was ship-rigged.*

H.M.S. Niobe. *Launched in 1866, she was a ram-bowed wooden sloop with a fixed screw and a barque rig.*

H.M.S. Beacon, *launched 1867, the name ship of a class of composite built, twin-screw gun vessels built for service in China. They were shallow-draught, their two engines were taken from the hulls of unused and rotten Crimean gun boats. They were rigged as topsail schooners.*

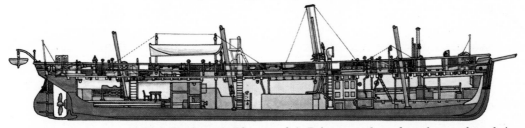

H.M.S. Tyrian *of 1861, one of the* Britomart *class of wooden gun boat designed as an improvement on the Crimean gun boats. She was rigged as a three-mast schooner, with some additional square sails on the foremast.*

*H.M.S.,*Skylark, *one of the numerous Crimean gun boats. This one was launched in 1855 and is of the* Dapper *class. They had little 60 h.p. engines and originally a light schooner rig.*

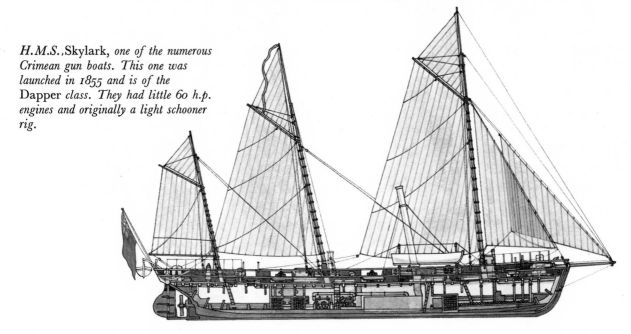

a corvette while others had it divided by the engine-room. Some had batteries mounted on the broadside and some on the centre line. In size they averaged about 170 feet between perpendiculars and 36 feet in the beam. Steaming speeds were about 10 knots.

Steam Gun-vessels and Gunboats

As with the other sailing classes, the sailing gun-brigs became due for replacement by steam-assisted vessels in the 1850s. The gunboats took the place of the brigs as the smallest British ocean-going warships, and the gun-vessels were similarly employed, but were larger.

Six little screw-steamers of the *Arrow* class were already in service at the beginning of the Russian war of 1854 and proved so effective that the Admiralty decided to order a large number, specially designed for use against Russian shore bases and fortresses in the Baltic and Crimea. The views behind this move were firstly that the shallow waters to be found in the Baltic sometimes impeded large units of the fleet getting within effective range, and secondly that it was felt that a large number of small vessels, well dispersed and mounting one or two large-calibre guns, would be less vulnerable to the fire of the Russian shore batteries than a small number of big ships.

As a result the first classes of gunboats were designed not to replace the brigs but for specialised duties in the Baltic and Black Sea, duties which had once been the province of the old bomb-vessels. These Crimean gunboats, as they were called, were given an ugly, almost square-sectioned, flat-bottomed hull, with slab sides and a stem without a knee. In an effort to keep down the weights the masts were stepped in tabernacles on the upper deck, and the original intention was to give them a miserable sail-plan of three dipping lugsails, but this was altered to gaffs of about the same sail area. By the same token small 20, 40 or 60 horse-power engines were installed, giving about 6 to 8 knots. One tall, slender funnel between the boats on davits completed the profile. There were four classes of the Crimean gunboats, varying in rig and horse-power, and altogether no less than one hundred and fifty-six were ordered, though not all by any means were completed. Many were finished too late to take part in the war for which they were designed to fight.

The armament of the first class was intended to be two 68-pounders on slides, but this was increased to three. Later classes had 32-pounders, also mounted on slides, and 24-pounder howitzers on trucks. The howitzer was a short barrelled brass gun which was designed to lob shells at a high trajectory and at low velocity. The large guns were centre-mounted ordinarily but could be moved over the iron traversing-rings to pivots at either side in action. In small ships the effect of moving so great a weight made them heel, so that the angle to which the barrel could be elevated was reduced. One advantage of the light rig and small number of guns was that the crew need only number about thirty-five, and in practice in service might have only a couple of officers aboard, if attached to a ship of the line. This was just as well, for the engines, coal bunkers, magazines and water tanks took up a good two-thirds of the internal space. The officers lived on the platforms aft and the men forward; there was no hold.

After the war some of the Crimean gunboats were refitted with a heavier rig and sent out to distant stations on general service. Their peculiar shape made them lively in heavy weather when they had to be carefully watched, and the shallow draught with no hold meant stowage problems on long passages, but they could do their work well enough. In 1857 and 1860 two further classes based on the Crimean gunboats were built, but with conventionally shaped hulls. Also at this time (1855–60) four classes of the larger gun-vessels were built; and whereas the Crimean gunboat might be 108 feet long, these vessels were between 140 feet and 185 feet. They had proper holds and better accommodation. A typical armament was one 95-cwt 68-pounder rifled-muzzle-loader and four 24-pounder howitzers; all were barque-rigged.

There was then a pause until age and decay made replacements necessary. The three new classes built around 1870 were all shallow draught, twin-screw and of composite construction. With their twin-screws and shallow draughts they were all poor sailers, and were mainly intended for river work against the Chinese. A further four classes of gun-vessel with single-screws and conventional hulls were built for ocean-going service and were about 157 feet long with a beam of 29 feet 6 inches. They were all more heavily built than the gun-vessels of the 1850s to bear the $4\frac{1}{2}$-ton 7-inch rifled-muzzle-loaders as well as the two 68-pounders; or instead of the muzzle-loaders, 64-pounder breech-loaders. The 7-inch was mounted between the funnel and the main-mast, the other two at the bow and stern. They served the Victorian navy until the end of the 1880s when they were replaced by steel third-class cruisers.

With the gunboats all the replacements of the Crimean classes were composite-built. The wooden Crimean boats had in any case lasted badly, having been built in a hurry and the later ones of green wood. The new programme began in 1867 with twenty-two vessels of shallow draught and with twin-screws, and twenty-one conventionally hulled and single-screw. These last were 125 feet between perpendiculars and 23 feet 5 inches in the beam; the twin-screw gunboats were about 30 feet longer. They were all given a barquentine rig and carried two 56-cwt 64-pounder muzzle-loaders and two 20-pounder breech-loading Armstrongs. Some of these in service in the late 1880s were given 5-inch and 4-inch breech-loaders; they could steam at 9 or 10 knots. Altogether one hundred and twenty gun-vessels and two hundred and sixty-two gun-boats were ordered for the navy between the 1850s and early 1880s.

Gunboat Diplomacy

British gunboat diplomacy often served to prevent an ugly situation becoming much uglier and reflected the greatest credit on the British officers involved. Commander Sir Lambton Loraine Bart, for instance, who from 1871 to 1874 was on the North American station in command of the *Niobe*, strictly speaking a sloop. In 1874 an American ship called the *Virginians*, which unknown to her passengers had been illegally running arms from Haiti to Cuba, was stopped by a Spanish man-of-war on the high seas and taken into Santiago. No arms were found aboard, but the blood-thirsty departmental governor, aptly named General Burriel Lynch, had all aboard declared pirates and thrown into prison, and without informing his superiors and ignoring the protests of the British and American consuls began executing the prisoners after summary trials. On hearing what was going on, the *Niobe* was dispatched by the governor of Jamaica to stop the executions. When Sir Lambton appeared before Lynch he was defied, and so was forced to threaten to sink all the Spanish warships in the harbour. This stopped the executions, and Sir Lambton received the thanks of both Houses of Parliament and the freedom of the City of New York.

Conclusion

This book, *The Wooden Fighting Ship*, has confined itself so far as possible to the development of the wooden navy; the next book will consider the metal warship from 1860 until today. So far as the battle fleet is concerned the division between wood and metal construction works well, since between August 1861 when the *Warrior* hoisted her first commissioning pendant and April 1870 when the *Rodney* paid off from the China station, less than nine years span the introduction of the iron capital ship and the elimination of the wooden one from first-line service.

With the cruisers, however, a large overlap occurs. The *Iris* and *Mercury*, launched in 1877 and 1878, although rated as dispatch vessels, were the precursors of the modern cruiser, being built of steel and relying primarily for movement on their engines. Only two years before the *Iris*, the last wooden cruiser had been launched, and similar composite-built masted cruisers continued to serve on the farthest stations of the empire until the 1890s, by which time steel cruisers with no sailing rig were serving with the fleet in large numbers.

APPENDICES

Appendix 1
A Summary of British Naval Events
from A.D. 897—1860

897 King Alfred built his new type of fighting ships (see p. 1) and defeated the Danes.

973 King Edgar was rowed in a barge on the River Dee by seven English kings as a token of their subjection to him.

991 Olaf Tryggvason took a fleet of four hundred and fifty ships to sack Sandwich and Ipswich, and going on to Maldon, defeated King Ethelred's army.

994 The same Olaf, allied to Swegen of Norway made an abortive attempt to reach London, then ravaged Kent, Sussex and Hampshire. Ethelred created a disastrous precedent by buying him off with £16,000, the first of the Danegeld.

997 A Danish fleet descended on the West Country, going up the Tamar, and carried away immense booty.

999 Another invasion ravaged Kent from Rochester, the English fleet being inferior.

1001 The Danes again descended on the West Country, bought off with £24,000.

1013 Danes under Swegen drove Ethelred into exile after a series of successful invasions following Ethelred's partially successful attempt to murder all Danes resident in England on St Brice's day, November 13th, 1002.

1052 After a confusion of pretenders and loyalties, the great Saxon Earl Godwin, with his son Harold, reasserted the English influence in the government, when he brought a fleet up to London and forced King Edward to modify his Norman leanings.

1066 William of Normandy successfully evaded a large English fleet and landed his army at Pevensey, which he led to triumph over Harold at the Battle of Hastings.

1100 The Conqueror's eldest son, Duke Robert, invaded with an army to depose his youngest brother Henry, who had seized the crown after his brother William Rufus's death. He failed to dislodge him.

1120 The loss of the *White Ship* which set out from Barfleur King Henry I's only legitimate son, Prince William, who was drowned.

1137 King Stephen invaded Normandy and restored it to the English crown, but shortly afterwards the Empress Matilda invaded England which remained in a state of virtual anarchy until 1153, when the opposing sides signed the Treaty of Wallingford.

1189 December 11th. King Richard I embarked at Dover for the Third Crusade to the Holy Land.

1213 The Battle of Damme. King John had been at war with Philip of France since 1202, except for a two-year truce. In this battle an English fleet arrived on the coast of Flanders to help the Count of Flanders against the French. They took vessels and burnt about a hundred more, most of the French being ashore.

1214 King John led an army in an unsuccessful expedition against the French.

1216 Prince Louis of France, with the sea mercenary called Eustace the Monk, who had previously fought for King John, invaded England. Defeated at Lincoln in 1217.

1217 August 24th. An English fleet defeated a French fleet under Eustace the Monk off Dover, which was bringing across another army to reinforce Prince Louis (see p. 5).

1230 April 30th. Henry III embarked on an abortive expedition to force the French to restore the English duchies in France.

1293 Norman attacks on English ships caused a fleet from the Cinque Ports to retaliate and attack the Normans in the Seine, taking six vessels.

April 14th. A battle between English and Normans was arranged to take place in mid-Channel, at a spot marked by an anchored hulk; the English won it, capturing about two hundred and forty sail.

1295 A French army landed at Dover and burnt part of the town before being driven off.

1336 August. A French success off the Isle of Wight, when a squadron of their galleys captured some of the king's ships.

1337 A French force landed at Portsmouth and

burnt and plundered most of the town; also St Peter's Port in Guernsey.

November 10th. An English squadron under the Earl of Derby landed on Gadzand in the mouth of the Scheldt, which was the home of some very damaging Flemish corsairs, and destroyed them, sacking the place.

1338 Two of King Edward III's finest ships, the *Christopher* and the *Edward*, were captured by the French fleet.

1339 A fleet under Sir Robert Morley, which included the Cinque Port's fleet, burnt five towns in Normandy and eighty ships.

1340 June 22nd. Edward III sailed to invade France to claim the crown.

June 24th. The Battle of Sluys (see p. 5).

1350 August 29th. The Battle of Winchelsea. Don Carlos de la Cerda, the Spanish freebooter, with a fleet of forty ships was attacked and defeated by the English fleet commanded by the king himself. Both the king's ship and the Black Prince's ship sank during the action, but not before the English had taken the opposing Spanish ships and transferred themselves to them. Prisoners were nearly always thrown overboard.

1372 June 22nd and 23rd. The Earl of Pembroke with a squadron sent to relieve La Rochelle, besieged by the French, was intercepted off the town by a more powerful fleet from Castille. The first day's fighting was inconclusive, but in the second Pembroke was captured with his ship and the entire English squadron taken or destroyed. The Spanish admiral was Ambrosio Bocanegra.

1377 June 29th. A force under Jean de Vienne landed near Rye and sacked the town.

1379 December 15th. Sir John Arundel's fleet with reinforcements for Brittany was scattered by a storm and twenty-six ships were wrecked on the Irish Coast including the flagship, with great loss of life.

1403 July. An English force raiding the coast of Brittany was defeated by a Breton fleet under Sire de Penhert, Admiral of Brittany, losing about forty ships.

1405 March 30th. The young Prince James of Scotland captured by the English freebooter Prendergast off Flamborough Head. The prince was kept in England by King Henry, for about 18 years.

The same year an English fleet under Prince Thomas captured three carracks in the Channel, then burnt the town of La Hogue,

Harfleur and thirty-eight others, pillaging the Normandy coast for a depth of thirty miles.

1415 August 11th. Henry sailed for France to renew the English claim on the French crown, and his success at Agincourt ended serious French resistance on the sea for many years.

1511 Andrew Barton, the Scottish pirate, brought to action by two King's ships under Lord Thomas and Lord Edward Howard, was killed and his ships taken.

War with France. Lord Edward Howard made lord admiral.

1512 August 12th. The Battle of Brest, when the French fleet under Jean de Thénouënel fought an indecisive action with the English. One of the finest English ships, the *Regent*, was burnt when the magazine of the 'Great Carrack of Brest' the *Marie la Cordelière* went up while they were grappled together.

1513 April 25th. Lord Edward Howard attacked some galleys at Le Conquêt, near Brest, and with seventeen followers entered the flagship of the French admiral, Prégent de Bidoux. Unfortunately the lord admiral's galley failed to grapple and drifted away, leaving the lord admiral and his companions to be overwhelmed and hurled over the side, where they drowned. A desultory action followed but nothing was effected.

1514 Peace with France.

1522 War with France and Scotland.

1523 Sir William Fitz-William's fleet defeated a Franco-Scottish fleet and burnt Le Tréport.

1525 Peace with France and Scotland.

1544 War with France and Scotland.

July 17th. Henry VIII landed with an army at Calais and laid siege to Boulogne, which fell.

1545 July 19th. The loss of the *Mary Rose* which foundered through keeling over her open lower ports, as she and the fleet came out of Portsmouth to meet the French fleet in the Solent. The French, under Claude D'Annebaut, were driven off.

August 15th. A fleet engagement in the Channel which was indecisive, though the French galleys under Polain did sufficiently well to persuade King Henry to increase his own galley fleet.

1546 May 18th. An engagement in the Channel between eight English and a like number of French ships. One French galley taken.

June 7th. Peace with France.

1547 War with France and Scotland; Edinburgh plundered by Lord Clinton's fleet.

1550 Peace with France.

1554 Philip of Spain on his way to England to marry Queen Mary I was met by the Lord Admiral, who took a fleet to greet him but fired a loaded cannon when the prince's ship did not dip her flag or lower her topsails to him, which she then did.

1556 War with France.

1557 January 7th. Calais lost.

1559 Peace with France.

1562/3 John Hawkins took his first cargo of slaves from Sierra Leone to the West Indies, a highly profitable venture. He therefore made a second and equally successful voyage in 1564/5, and a third in 1567, when his cousin Francis Drake joined his fleet with a little ship he had inherited, called the *Judith*.

1572 July 22nd. Drake took Nombre de Dios on the Isthmus of Panama where the Peruvian treasures were collected, and found a great heap of silver bars. In February the following year he crossed the Isthmus and intercepted a caravan of mules loaded with gold, returning to England a rich man.

1577 December 13th. Drake sailed from Plymouth on his voyage round the world, the second one to be made, returning to Plymouth Sound on September 26th, 1580.

1587 April 19th. 'The Singeing of the King of Spain's Beard.' A squadron under Sir Francis Drake entered Cadiz harbour and took or destroyed about one hundred vessels, mostly full of stores for the Armada preparing against England. The object of the expedition was to embarrass and delay this venture. Continuing to the Tagus Drake took and plundered about a hundred more.

1588 July 19th. The Spanish Armada was sighted in the mouth of the channel.
July 27th. After a week's fighting the Duke of Medina Sidonia brought his fleet to an anchor off Calais with the loss of only three ships (flagships) preparatory to embarking the Duke of Parma's army for England.
July 28th. Drake sent in fireships against the Spanish who cut their cables and were driven eostwards.
July 29th. The Battle of Gravelines. The Anglo-Dutch fleet defeated and scattered the Spaniards, who drove into the North Sea.

1589 May. A squadron under Drake and Sir John Norreys, assisted by some Dutch, took Corunna at the beginning of an attempt to put Don Antonio on to the throne of Portugal. Arriving at Lisbon, however, they found no support for the Don, and lacking the means to make a siege of it, returned to England.

1591 August 31st. The last fight of the *Revenge*.

1594 October–November. Sir Martin Frobisher retook the peninsula of Camaret near Brest from the Spanish, to help the French King. He died of a wound shortly after returning to England.

1595 August 28th. Drake and Hawkins set out on an expedition to seize the treasure of Panama. The commanders died before they could carry out their plans, Hawkins on November 13th and Drake on January 28th, 1596.

1596 June 1st. There sailed a strong squadron, including the Dutch, under Lord Howard of Effingham, the Lord Admiral, against Cadiz, which was taken on June 21st. Howard refused an offer of two million ducats to spare the shipping. The Spanish loss has been estimated at 20,000,000 ducats, or £9,300,000.

1597 The Islands Voyage under Lord Essex, aimed against Corunna and Ferrol; and then the Azores, where they intended to capture bases and await the Spanish treasure ships. The plan to attack the mainland towns was dropped in the event, but in the Azores Essex and Raleigh took Fayal. No rich prize was taken and the expedition returned home disappointed.

1602 June 3rd. Sir William Monson and Sir Richard Leveson took a great carrack at Cezimbra, worth a million ducats; two galleys were also taken.
Nine galleys that had escaped destruction at Cezimbra left to cruise on the coast of Flanders under the command of Federigo Spinola. They were intercepted by an English squadron under Sir Robert Mansell in the Straits of Dover on September 23rd. The handy English ships not only outgunned them, but rammed them and sailed over them. Only one, Spinola's own galley, managed to get safely into Dunkirk. This was the last considerable action between galleys and galleons in Northern Waters.

1603 March 24th. Death of Queen Elizabeth I.

1604 August. James I made peace with Spain.

1623 February 27th. The Dutch at Amboyna in the East Indies seized the English residents, tortured them, murdered ten and drove the rest from the Island. This act long rankled with the English at home and was one of the more conscious causes of the First Dutch War in 1652.

1625 In spite of Amboyna Anglo-Dutch squadrons of East Indiamen fought several fierce actions against the Portuguese to gain a footing in India. The principal English captain involved was John Weddell.

1625 Viscount Wimbledon's expedition against Spain. He briefly took and held Fort Puntal, near Cadiz; then abandoned it and tried to intercept the Plate fleet, but failed and returned home empty handed.

1626 War with France.

1627 June to November. The Duke of Buckingham's first expedition to assist La Rochelle against King Louis XIII, this turned out a failure.

1628 August 23rd. The Duke of Buckingham, the lord high admiral, was murdered at Portsmouth by John Felton, just before the second expedition to relieve La Rochelle sailed. The expedition went without him but their desultory efforts were soon brought to an end when La Rochelle surrendered to the French king's army. In the Mediterranean Sir Kenelm Digby, with a privateer squadron, defeated a Franco-Venetian squadron at Scanderoon, taking three French ships and sinking one.

1636 Loss of the *Anne Royal*, which bilged on her own anchor in the Medway.

1637 Building of the *Sovereign of the Seas*, the first ship to carry one hundred guns (see page 22).

1638 H.R.H. James, Duke of York, was made lord high admiral at the age of five.

1639 The Battle of the Downs, when the Dutch fleet under Marten Tromp defeated the Spanish in English waters. The English fleet, which was neutral, looked on.

1642 The Civil War, the fleet sided with Parliament under the Earl of Warwick. In August he helped to take Portsmouth from the Royalists.

1643 August. Warwick failed to take Exeter and lost three ships.

1644 May. Warwick relieved Blake who was besieged at Lyme in Dorset.

1648 Revolt of part of the fleet to the Royalists, Prince Rupert took command.

1649 Prince Rupert operated against Parliamentary shipping in home waters and later in the Mediterranean.

1650 A Parliamentary fleet under Robert Blake left England in February to seek out Prince Rupert, and appeared in the Tagus, where it blockaded the Royalist squadron until October, when Rupert escaped to the Mediterranean. Blake chased him and finally engaged and defeated him in Cartagena Bay on November 5th, though Rupert escaped.

1652/4 The First Dutch War.

1652 May 19th. The Battle off Dover, the first fleet engagement of the Dutch Wars, was fought when Britain was nominally still at peace. Marten Tromp led the Dutch fleet down on to Blake's fleet, who fired several warning shots for Tromp to dip his flag, which was finally answered with a broadside, and general action was joined and lasted all day. The Dutch lost two ships, but one the *St Maria*, 37, which was abandoned by the English as sinking, was later reboarded by the Dutch and taken to Holland. The English lost no ships.
August 27th. Van Galen defeated a squadron under Captain Richard Badiley off Elba.
September 28th. The Battle of the Kentish Knock saw the Dutch under De With beaten by the English under Blake.

1653 February 18th. Tromp had two hundred merchant ships that he was convoying home from the Mediterranean, when he was attacked by the English fleet under Blake off Portland. The action continued for a further two days, but the results were indecisive.
March 4th. Captain Badiley and his squadron had left Elba and appeared off Leghorn where Appleton's squadron of six ships lay. These were supposed to come out and join him, but were intercepted and defeated by Van Galen before Badiley could beat up to Appleton's assistance. Only one ship fought her way through, and as a result the English temporarily abandoned the Mediterranean.
June 2nd–3rd. The Battle of the Gabbard. Blake had been wounded at Portland and was ashore, so the command was shared by the two Generals at Sea, George Monck and Richard Deane. Deane was killed at the start of the action, which went well for the English and even better on the following day when the Dutch fell into confusion and

defeat. Eleven prizes were then brought in. July 31st. The Battle of Scheveningen, the final defeat of the Dutch fleet and with it the death of their great admiral, Marten Tromp. Through Blake's illness the honours were shared by Monck and William Penn.

1656 September 8th. Captain Stayner and his squadron captured a ship of the Plate fleet off Cadiz and destroyed three more.

1657 April 20th. Blake destroyed the Spanish fleet at Santa Cruz, Teneriffe.

August 7th. Blake died at sea as his squadron was entering Plymouth Sound.

1660 The Restoration of King Charles II.

1665/7 The Second Dutch War.

1665 June 3rd. The Battle of Lowestoft, when the Dutch under Obdam were heavily defeated by the English, commanded by the King's brother and lord high admiral, H.R.H. the Duke of York. The Dutch flagship, the *Eendracht*, blew up in action with the Duke, and Obdam with most of his crew were killed. The Dutch lost about thirty ships, and their fleet was unable to appear again that year.

August 3rd. Repulse at Bergen. One of the results of Lowestoft was that the returning Dutch East India fleet had to put into Bergen to avoid capture. The English bribed the Danish king into waiving his neutrality and allow them to enter Bergen harbour to take the fleet. The Danish governor, however, either because he had not received his orders, or because he chose to ignore them, supported the Dutch ships with his shore batteries, so that the English squadron was forced to withdraw and abandon this discreditable venture.

1666 June 1st–4th. The Four Days Fight. The English fleet had been foolishly split, with Monck, now the Duke of Albemarle, to the east awaiting De Ruyter, and Prince Rupert to the west watching for the French, who never came. Thus Albermarle had to fight alone for two days, greatly outnumbered, before retreating to join Rupert on the third. In spite of their better order and discipline the English suffered heavily that day, since disabled ships that fell behind were taken, and one of our finest ships, the *Royal Prince* 90, (the rebuilt *Prince Royal* of 1610, see p. 20) went aground on the Galloper Sand and had to surrender. On the fourth day Monck and Rupert fought united,

but the fleets parted exhausted, without a decision. It was the great Dutch victory in a fleet action of the wars, but not one that gave unqualified satisfaction to those of them in the know. 'If we cannot destroy the English divided,' they asked, 'how can we defeat them united?'.

July 25th and 26th. The answer came seven weeks later off the North Foreland on St James's Day and the day following, when Rupert and Albermarle decisively defeated De Ruyter. The Dutch fleet was driven off the seas for the second year running.

August 8th. Sir Robert Holmes His Bonfire. An outcome of the defeat of the Dutch fleet was that Sir Robert, with a small squadron, could sail into the Vlie and destroy about one hundred and seventy Dutch merchantmen.

1667 June 9th–28th. The English made the mistake of demanding unacceptable terms at the peace-table at Breda in May, on the strength of the previous year's victories, but at the same time did not mobilise the fleet. De Ruyter prepared swiftly and secretly and descended on the English fleet lying in ordinary in the Medway, taking Sheerness. The best English ship, the *Royal Charles* 80, was taken and three others burnt, and a few smaller ones taken or burnt; not to mention those sunk by the English to prevent the Dutch getting to Chatham. It was the greatest defeat in English naval history and enabled the Dutch to get better terms in the peace treaty that followed.

1672/3 The Third Dutch War.

1672 March 12th and 13th. Sir Robert Holmes attacked a Dutch convoy of their Smyrna fleet off the Isle of Wight, though King Charles did not declare war until the 19th; and the French followed on the 27th

May 28th. The Battle of Solebay. The Duke of York allowed himself to be caught at anchor in the bay with the result that the Allied fleet went into battle in some disorder. Partly for this reason the *Royal James* 100, the flagship of Lord Sandwich, was burnt by a fireship and the admiral drowned. The Dutch lost two ships, and the French, who were to play a feeble part in the engagements, did not get into action at all.

1673 The three actions fought this year were all aimed at neutralising the Dutch fleet so that an army could be landed on the coast of

Holland. It was De Ruyter's skill in the use of the greatly improved Dutch fleet (though smaller than the Allied one) which prevented the Allies from gaining a decisive victory, and obliged them to quit the Dutch coast for repairs. The first two battles, called the First and Second Battles of Schoonveld, May 28th and June 4th, with Prince Rupert in command of the Allies, were tactically indecisive. In the first the French lost two ships and the Dutch one, in the second neither lost any. The last action of the war, the Battle of Texel on August 11th, was very fiercely fought, and the English came near to losing the *Royal Prince* 100, which made a classic defence; but at the end only one vessel, an English yacht, was lost on either side.

1681 May 22nd. The *Kingfisher* Action. This was one of the many actions fought by ships of the 'Streights Fleet', kept in the Mediterranean to protect our merchant shipping against the Barbary corairs. On this occasion the *Kingfisher* 46, Captain Sir John Kempthorne, fought alone with seven of them from 1.0 p.m. to 1.0 a.m. and beat them off. Kempthorne was killed.

1689 May 1st. The Battle of Bantry Bay. The first fleet action of the long French Wars, the English fleet was under Admiral Arthur Herbert (afterwards the Earl of Torrington). The French were found in Bantry Bay delivering stores for King James's army. Herbert had to work to windward to meet the French, who bore down on him in good order, and in superior numbers. The French had the best of it though they took no ships. As a result of the action war was formally declared, known as the War of the English Succession 1689–97.

1690 June 30th. The Battle of Beachy Head. On this occasion the English fleet was joined by the Dutch who formed the van squadron, the whole commanded by Torrington. Even so the French could put into the contest sixty-eight ships against fifty-six, due to two squadrons of English ships being away from the main fleet. Again the battle was indecisive, only one small Dutch ship being taken, though the loss in men was heavier on the Anglo/Dutch side. The French admiral was the Comte de Tourville.

1692 May 19th–24th. The Battle of Barfleur and the subsequent destruction of the French ships at La Hogue. The Allied admiral was Edward Russell (afterwards the Earl of Orford), and this time he came in overwhelming force against Tourville, with ninety-six ships of the line to the French forty-four. In the fleet action on the 19th the French lost no ships, though they were fortunate that a fog enabled them to escape. They were chased to the French coast and a large part took shelter in the Bay of La Hogue where the allies burnt twelve of them on the 23rd and 24th. Tourville's flagship, the *Soleil Royal* 106, and two others were similarly treated near Cherbourg. James II, who was at La Hogue, thus saw his hopes of regaining the British crown literally go up in smoke.

1697 September 11th. The Treaty of Rijswijk ended the war.

1702 War with France and Spain, the War of the Spanish Succession.

1702 August 20th–24th. Benbow and Ducasse. This four-day action in the West Indies is remembered best for the gallantry of Admiral John Benbow, who died afterwards of his wounds, and the drama attending the infamous conduct of most of his captains.

October 12th. After an abortive attack on Cadiz, the Allied fleet was returning home when news came of the Spanish treasure fleet and its French escort of fifteen ships in Vigo Bay. All the French ships and the Spanish treasure ships were taken or burnt, and the spoils included £3,000,000 in specie. The Allied commander-in-chief was Sir George Rooke.

1703 November 16th. The Great Storm, in which thirteen English men of war were lost.

1704 July 24th. Rooke and the Allied fleet captured Gibralter.

August 13th. The Battle of Malaga. The Anglo-Dutch fleet evenly matched the Franco-Spanish one; the former under Rooke and the latter under a natural son of Louis XIV, the Comte de Toulouse. Neither side had a ship taken.

1703 September 23rd. Barcelona was taken, the English naval commander being Sir Clowdisley Shovell.

1707 October 22nd. Sir Clowdisley's flagship, returning home, was wrecked off The Isles of Scilly with the loss of all hands. With the *Association* 96, was lost the *Eagle* 70, *Romney* 50 and the *Firebrand*, a fireship.

1708 May 28th. Commodore Wager's action. Wager met the Spanish treasure fleet off Carthagena in the West Indies. He himself engaged the flagship which unfortunately blew up. He captured the third largest, but the second largest managed to beach herself and was burnt by her crew.

1713 The Treaty of Utrecht and peace.

1718 War with Spain.

August 11th. Sir George Byng defeated the Spanish fleet off Cape Passaro, taking or burning twenty-two of their fleet. On the whole the Spanish ships were wretchedly officered and manned throughout the century, so that there came to be a French saying, 'to chase a Spaniard is to capture one'.

1720 Peace with Spain.

1739 War with Spain, called the War of Jenkins' Ear.

November 21st. With six ships, Edward Vernon took Porto Bello, a town in what is now called Venezuela.

1740/4 Anson made his voyage round the world.

1741 March to May. Vernon's unsuccessful attempt to capture Carthagena.

1743 June 20th. Anson captured the Manila treasure ship *Nuestra Signora de Covadonga* in the Pacific. The booty from her filled thirty wagons on his return.

1744 February 11th. After watching for the French fleet to leave Toulon for two years, Mathews was rewarded at last, though England was not formally at war with France. The action proved disappointing (see p. 40) and Mathews and the French admiral, Monsieur de Court, were court-martialled and disgraced by their respective governments.

1744 October 5th. The loss of the *Victory* 100 (see p. 35).

1747 May 3rd. The first Battle of Finisterre. A French fleet destined partly for operations in North America and partly for India was intercepted by Anson's fleet, which was the stronger. In the chase both French commanders, the Marquis de la Jonquière and Monsieur Saint George, were captured, also six other warships, three indiamen and numerous other vessels. Anson was given a baronetcy.

October 14th. The Second Battle of Finisterre. A superior English fleet, this time under Sir Edward Hawke, including twelve ships of the line and two fifties, defeated a French squadron of eight ships of the line, six of which were captured, though the French commodore, Monsieur de L'Etenduere, escaped.

1748 October 1st. Knowles's action off Havana. In this not very well conducted action between six Spanish and six English ships of the line, the Spanish lost only one ship captured but a second subsequently had to be burnt by her crew. Knowles was court-martialled and sentenced to be reprimanded for not bringing his squadron into action in better order.

1749 Peace with France and Spain.

1755 February 14th. The taking of Geriah. This port with its fortress was the seat of the notorious Mahrattan pirate Tulagee Angria, whose outrages on Indian and European traders finally brought down on him a strong force of naval and Company ships and a small detachment of Mahrattan grabs, under Rear-Admiral Charles Watson, with Clive in charge of the troops. After a bombardment on the 12th the port surrendered, but refused to let in Clive the following morning, so was bombarded again, and Clive and his troops finally marched in on the 14th. They found a great quantity of cannon and stores, and £100,000 in rupees; the shipping in the harbour was destroyed.

1756/63 War with France, the Seven Years War.

1756 May-June. Byng's action off Minorca and the subsequent loss of the island with its valuable base at Port Mahon.

Although the British government knew from October 1755 that the French were preparing an expedition at Toulon to take the island, yet it was March the following year before Vice-Admiral the Hon. John Byng and a scraped together fleet were dispatched to strengthen the defences. Nothing was done to relieve the octogenarian military governor. The French military commander was the able playboy duke, De Richelieu. On May 20th the fleets of Byng and the French naval commander, Monsieur de la Galissonnière, met at Minorca, both with twelve ships in the line. In the action that followed neither side took a ship, but the British suffered the heavier damage and casualties. At a council of war aboard Byng's flagship it was decided that further attacks on the French fleet were unlikely to drive them off and it was better to return to protect Gibraltar, which was done. Port Mahon fell on June 29th, and Byng was subsequently court martialled and shot. The only benefit the English derived from this sad affair came from Richelieu's chef, who devised a new dressing which he named in honour of the occasion, mahonaise, or as we know it, mayonnaise.

1757 January 2nd. Calcutta captured from the French by Rear-Admiral Watson, and on the 23rd, Chandernagore.

October 21st. Forest's action off Cape Francois (North America). Two sixties and a sixty-four has been sent to intercept a French convoy, but when they met it, Captain Forest made out the escort to be five two-deckers and two frigates; two of them were seventy-fours. Nevertheless, after consulting Captains Suckling and Laughton he decided to accept battle, and a two-and-a-half hours action ensued. It ended with the French commodore, Monsieur de Kersaint, having his ship towed out of the line and the whole lot made off, to their discredit.

1758 February 28th. The *Monmouth* 64 took the *Foudroyant* 84 (see page 42).

April 29th. Vice-Admiral George Pocock fought an action with Comte d'Aché's squadron off Cuddalore, and had the best of it, though no ship was taken.

June 5th to 12th. The Hon. Richard Howe commanded a fleet that landed near St Malo but failed to take it.

July 26th. Admiral Boscawen took Louisbourg.

August 3rd. Pocock and D'Aché fought a second action which ended with the French in flight, though no ships were taken.

August 17th to September 10th. Howe again took the Duke of Marlborough's army to Brittany, but again it failed to take St Malo. This time, however, the adventure ended in disaster, as the French army attacked while the English was being taken to the ships in the Bay of St Cas. Over eight hundred soldiers were captured, as well as four post-captains superintending the embarkation.

December 20th. The capture of Goree. This is the island off Dakar, which was the French base in West Africa and which menaced English trade with the East. The English were obliged to take it several times during the French wars, but always gave it back.

This time Commodore the Hon. Augustus Keppel and a small squadron took it.

1759 The year of victories.

May 1st. The capture of Guadeloupe.

August 18th. The Battle of Lagos. In light winds Boscawen, with an advantage in numbers, fifteen, to twelve in the French line, brought De la Clue to action and badly beat him, taking three ships and burning two. M. de la Clue, who had ran his flagship ashore, died in Lagos of his wounds.

September 2nd. The third and fiercest action between Pocock and D'Ache which followed the same pattern as before, but this time the French casualties reached the high figure of fifteen hundred; the British figure was five hundred and sixty-nine. As a result D'Ache who had been wounded, abandoned Indian waters.

June to September. Vice-Admiral Charles Saunders was in charge of the naval side of the defeat of the French in Canada, bringing a great fleet, which included twenty ships of the line, up to Quebec for the final assault.

November 20th. The Battle of Quiberon Bay. This dramatic action was fought in a gale, when Sir Edward Hawke chased the French fleet in a running fight into Quiberon Bay where, because of the rocks, the French thought they would not be followed. The *Soleil Royal* 80, the flagship of Monsieur de Conflans, was beached and burnt by her crew before we could get to her; another flagship, the *Formidable* 80 was captured; the *Thesée* 74 was one of the rare ships to founder in action, another was taken and burnt and another wrecked. Several of those ships that sought shelter in the mouth of the River Vilaine and had got out their guns and stores to escape the British reach by going up the river, never could be got down again. It was the end of any serious French naval effort in the war.

1761 January 15th. The capture of Pondicherry. On New Year's Day that year a great storm nearly destroyed Rear-Admiral Stevens's blockading squadron; as it was, a fifty, a twenty and a fireship drove ashore and were wrecked; a sixty and a sixty-four foundered with nearly all hands, and four more were dismasted. The blockade was resumed on February 3rd, and Pondicherry was reduced by famine to surrender.

June 8th. The capture of Belle Isle. A force

was dispatched in April under Commodore Keppel and Major General Hodgson, who took the island which was held for the rest of the war.

June 8th. On the same day Commodore Sir James Douglas captured Dominica.

October 5th. The capture of Manila. On the information of Colonel Draper that the Spanish defences were weak in the Philippines, he was sent in charge of the troops and took Manila, Luzon and all the Spanish islands in the group. Rear-Admiral Cornish was in charge of the naval side.

1762 February 16th. The capture of Martinique. Rear-Admiral Rodney landed the troops in Port Royal Bay on January 16th, but Major-General Monckton found the going hard, and it took a month to reduce the island.

August 13th. The capture of Havana. This was the last and most ambitious of the amphibious operations of the Seven Years War. Admiral Sir George Pocock commanded a fleet of over fifty warships, besides storeships and hospital ships etc., and the troops were commanded by the Earl of Albemarle. The rewards from this success were considerable; stores and species to the value of £3,000,000, and twelve Spanish ships of the line that were in the harbour.

1763 February 10th. The peace treaty signed which ended the Seven Years War.

1764 June 21st. Captain the Hon. John Byron set out on his voyage round the world, with two ships, returning on May 9th, 1766.

1766 August 22nd. A further expedition under Captain Samuel Wallis set sail for the Straits of Magellan and the Pacific, where he discovered Tahiti. He returned home on May 20th, 1768. The other ship under Captain Carteret, which discovered Pitcairn Island, did not get home until March 1769.

1768 July 26th. James Cook sailed on his first voyage to the Pacific in the *Endeavour*. This was a Royal Society expedition to observe the transit of Venus, the navy providing the transport for Mr Joseph Banks and his scientists. The observation was successfully made from Tahiti on June 4th, 1769. The expedition also explored on the coasts of New Zealand and Australia, and returned home on June 12th, 1771.

1772 July 13th. Cook's second voyage, this time to find out whether there really was a great

sub-continent populated by millions of people, as was widely held. The expedition went in two ships, the *Resolution* and *Adventure*, and Cook returned with his findings on July 30th, 1775, having penetrated deep into the Antarctic icefields.

1775 Rebellion in the American colonies.

1776 July 14th. Cook's third voyage. The *Resolution* went again, this time with the *Discovery*, and the purpose was to see if there was a navigable passage from the Pacific to the Atlantic over Canada. Cook tried to find it in the summers of 1777 and 1778, but was killed in January 1779. With great persistence, his people tried again that year, without success. They finally reached the Nore on October 4th, 1780.

1778 War with France.

July 27th. The Battle of Ushant. The British fleet in the Channel under Admiral Keppel met the French fleet under the Comte d'Orvilliers off Ushant; the result was inconclusive and on the British side failure to beat the enemy was generally blamed on the poor manner in which Keppel was supported by his second-in-command, Sir Hugh Palliser. The result was two very ugly courts martial, and feelings ran so high that, at a time of great national peril, several of the best officers would not serve.

August 21st. Sir Edward Vernon captured Pondicherry.

December 30th. The capture of St Lucia. A well-conducted operation by Rear-Admiral the Hon. Samuel Barrington and Major-General James Grant, in the face of a superior French fleet under Comte d'Estaing, which failed to shift Barrington, who fought him at anchor. The French relief forces landed ashore were bloodily repulsed and D'Estaing had to leave the island to its fate.

1779 Spain declared war against England.

July 6th. Byron's action off Grenada. Vice-Admiral the Hon. John Byron was in command of a fleet of twenty-one ships of the line, which he took into action against D'Estaing's fleet, precipitantly and in bad order, and was lucky not to lose at least one.

1780 January 16th. The Moonlight Battle of St Vincent. Rodney was taking a convoy of reinforcements to Gibraltar on his way to assume command of the Leeward Islands station, when he came upon a Spanish squadron of eleven ships of the line and two frigates, commanded by Admiral Langara. The Spaniards, outnumbered two to one, fled and in a night action six were taken and one blew up.

April 17th, May 15th and May 19th. The dates of the three actions fought by Rodney in the West Indies with the new French commander there, the Comte de Guichen. All were inconclusive, but the strain of the stalking and manœuvring broke the health of the Frenchman, who asked to be recalled.

1781 February 3rd. Rodney at Saint Eustatius where, when he had taken it, he found merchandise to the value of £3,000,000.

April 16th. The action at Porto Praya. Commodore Johnstone had been sent with a squadron and troops in an attempt to take Capetown from the Dutch, who had shortly before entered the war against us. The French, hearing of it, sent a squadron of their own after Johnstone to frustrate him. This was commanded by the famous De Suffren, who found Johnstone's ships anchored in a negligent manner at Porto Praya. Had he been properly supported by all his squadron, he might have given us a serious reverse, as it was the British beat off the attack at anchor. Johnstone, who was a most unpleasant fellow and an M.P., managed to waste sufficient time to let De Suffren reach Capetown before him, and could do nothing on his arrival there but turn round and come home.

March 16th. Arbuthnot and De Touches. An action off Chesapeake Bay in which neither side lost a ship.

March 29th. Hood and De Grasse. De Grasse, the new French commander in the West Indies, was bringing a convoy from France when he met Hood, who was the British commander during Rodney's absence in England, with a fleet inferior to the French. Hood was to lee and could not close, so a long-range action took place without effect.

August 5th. The Battle of the Dogger Bank. Vice-Admiral Hyde Parker was convoying home a merchant fleet from the Baltic when he encountered Admiral Zoutmann, with a Dutch squadron, also convoying merchantmen. Both sides had seven ships in the line, though the British were the heavier gunned, and the engagement naturally enough, proved one of the most fiercely fought of the war. No ship was lost in the action, but one Dutchman sank the following day.

September 5th. The Battle of Chesapeake. Rear-Admiral Thomas Graves with nineteen sail of the line was in action with De Grasse who had twenty-four. The two fleets never really got to grips, but the fact that the British were unable to establish naval ascendancy in North American waters at that time was the chief cause of the success of the American colonial rebellion.

December 12th. De Guichen, convoying a supply fleet on its way to De Grasse through the Bay of Biscay, unfortunately found himself ahead and to lee of his charges when Rear-Admiral Richard Kempenfelt was sighted with a squadron of the Channel fleet, and took fifteen of them.

1782 January 25th. De Grasse had invested St Kitts when Hood appeared. The French came out and Hood by smart manœuvring took over the French anchorage. The next day De Grasse tried to shift Hood in a close action, but failed St. Kitts was saved.

February 17th. The first of the five fleet actions between Sir Edward Hughes and De Suffren of the east coast of India. The others were on April 12th, July 5th, September 3rd, 1782, and June 20th, 1783. Neither side lost a ship in these hard-fought actions, but on the whole the French had the strategic advantage, their high point being the taking of Trincomalee. De Suffren was the abler officer, but Hughes, 'Old Hot and Hot', had the advantage of the better discipline and organisation of his service.

April 12th. The Battle of the Saints. De Grasse's fleet was finally brought to book with a shattering defeat that included the capture of the French flagship the *Ville de Paris* 104.

October. Lord Howe relieved Gibraltar for the last time. Since the Spanish entered the war their most protracted and determined attempt to regain the Rock for Spain had resulted in a classic siege. In spite of strong opposition the British had twice before managed to relieve the place with a convoy of stores. Lord Howe's success in the face of a powerful Franco-Spanish fleet finally made the Spanish despair of success, their only reason for fighting the war, and they sued for peace.

August 29th. The loss of the *Royal George* 100.

1783 Peace with France, Holland, Spain and the United States of America.

1791 Commander George Vancouver's expedition to Nootka Sound to re-establish the British flag there, and survey the north-west coast of America. He returned October 1794.

1793 War with France, the Revolutionary Wars. August 27th. Lord Hood occupied Toulon with the connivance of the French royalists, and stayed until the middle of December, when the advance of the Republican army forced him to leave. He took with him nineteen French warships, including the *Commerce de Marseilles* 120 (see p. 64), and fourteen more had been burnt. This still left twenty-five in Republican hands. The Anglo-Spanish fleet carried away as many of the royalist population as it could, nearly 15,000, but many thousands left behind, were brutally butchered by the Republicans.

1794 March 22nd. Martinique was captured by Vice-Admiral Sir John Jervis and Lieutenant-General Sir Charles Grey. This success was followed by the capture of St Lucia on April 4th.

June 1st. The battle called the Glorious First of June. This was the first fleet action of the long Revolutionary Wars. A French fleet of twenty-six of the line commanded by Rear-Admiral Villaret-Joyeuse, left Brest to convoy an expected merchant fleet from America. Lord Howe with twenty-five of the line brought him to action, captured six of the French ships and sank one. There was no ship lost on the British side.

1795 March 14th. The Hotham's Action off Genoa. Vice-Admiral William Hotham had succeeded Lord Hood who had gone home. He managed to bring the French Mediterranean fleet to a partial action during which the French lost an eighty and a seventy-four out of a fleet of fifteen of the line. Hotham had fourteen.

June 17th. Cornwallis's retreat. A British squadron of four seventy-fours, the *Royal Sovereign* 100 and two frigates encountered the French fleet off Belle Isle and was obliged to retire as the French had twelve of the line two fifties and nine frigates. At one time it looked as if one of the British seventy-fours, the *Mars*, would be captured, having fallen to lee with damage aloft, but Cornwallis himself bore up to her aid in the *Royal Sovereign* and saved her. It was a bold and gallant gesture, and the French shortly after gave up the pursuit. The French had been purposely misled by Captain Robert Stopford of the *Phaeton* 38, who was making signals to what he pretended was Bridport's fleet; when a fleet of merchantmen were sighted the French thought it was the British fleet.

June 23rd. Bridport's Action off the Isle de Groix. Lord Bridport was in command of the channel fleet in the absence of Lord Howe. The action was a general chase, and the first French ship to strike was the *Alexandre* 74, which, as the *Alexander*, had been captured from the British the year before. Two other French ships of the line also captured, but a disappointing action.

July 12th. Hotham's Action off Hyeres. The Mediterranean fleets engaged a second time, the French doing their best to get away. The British engaged in general chase as they came up. One seventy-four struck and then burnt and blew up, but the opportunities of the situation were not exploited by Hotham to advantage.

July 26th. Rear-Admiral Peter Rainier captured Trincomalee. All the Dutch possessions in Ceylon fell by February 1796, as did all the Dutch settlements in India.

August 16th. Cape Colony was taken from the Dutch by Vice-Admiral Sir George Keith Elphinstone.

1796 April–June. Operations commanded by Rear-Admiral Sir Hugh Cloberry Christian and Lieutenant-General Sir Ralph Abercromby from Barbados led to the capture of St Lucia, St Vincent and Grenada in the West Indies.

August 3rd. A Dutch squadron of nine men-of-war commanded by Rear-Admiral Lucas arrived at the Cape and anchored in Saldanha Bay, about 60 miles from Simon's Bay where Elphinstone was moored. The British moved in on Lucas, anchored by him and invited him to surrender, which, as he was much the weaker, he did.

October 8th. War with Spain.

1797 January 14th. The destruction of the *Droits de l'Homme*. This French seventy-four had been on the abortive expedition to Ireland and was returning home with General Humbert and troops, when she was attacked by the British frigates *Indefatigible* 44 and *Amazon* 36. In snowstorms the two frigates hung on to her and so damaged her aloft that when they reached the French coast she drove ashore, as also did the *Amazon*. But whereas the *Amazon*'s crew got ashore with the loss of only six men, the *Droits de l'Homme* was wrecked on a sandbank off shore in a gale in the Bay of Audierne, and is supposed to have lost about a thousand of her people by drowning and exposure.

February 14th. The Battle of St Vincent. The poor quality of the Spanish fleet was highlighted by this action in which their Grand Fleet of twenty-seven ships of the line, which included the great *Santissima Trinidad* 136, the biggest ship in the world, and six three-deckers of 112 guns, was engaged by Sir John Jervis with fifteen of the line, and was lucky to lose only two of their hundred and twelves, an eighty and a seventy-four. Sir John's flagship was the *Victory* 100, and the day was especially memorable for the part played by Commodore Nelson in the *Captain* 74, when he took the *San Nicholas* 80 and the *San Joseph* 112.

February 18th. Trinidad captured from Spain by Rear-Admiral Henry Harvey and Lieutenant-General Sir Ralph Abercromby. July 3rd and 5th. The bombardments of Cadiz which were directed by Rear-Admiral Nelson.

July 22nd and 24th. Nelson's abortive attack on Santa Cruz, Teneriffe, where he lost his right arm.

October 11th. The Battle of Camperdown. The last fleet action between the British and Dutch. Both sides had sixteen of the line, the British commanded by Admiral Adam Duncan, the Dutch by Vice-Admiral De Winter. In a bloody action eleven Dutchmen were taken including the two flagships, but none of the prizes was afterwards fit for sea.

1798 August 1st. The Battle of the Nile. Since May, Rear-Admiral Sir Horatio Nelson had been looking for Napoleon's fleet, which however, eluded him and transported Napoleon and his army safely to Egypt. Nelson finally found it at anchor in Aboukir Bay. Of the French fleet of thirteen of the line and four frigates only two frigates and two ships of the line escaped. All the rest were captured except a frigate which was sunk, and the principal flagship the great *L'Orient* 120, which caught fire and blew up

about 10 p.m., three-and-a-half hours after the beginning of the action. The French commander-in-chief, Vice-Admiral Brueys, had been killed by a round shot about 8 p.m. This action doomed the French army in Egypt.

October 12th. Warren's action with Bompart. A French expedition to land troops in Ireland had sailed on September 16th from Brest, and consisted of nine frigates and a seventy-four, commanded by Commodore Bompart. It was intercepted by Commodore Sir John Borlase-Warren off Tory Island before it could reach Lough Swilly. Warren had three ships of the line and five frigates. The main action, when Bompart's flagship and three of the frigates struck, took place on the 12th, but three more of the frigates were taken on the 13th, 18th and 20th.

November 15th, Commodore Sir John Duckworth and General the Hon. Charles Stuart captured Minorca.

1799 August 27th. The British landed at Den Helder and captured thirteen Dutch men-of-war there. They were in ordinary and mostly old, but on the 30th Vice-Admiral Andrew Mitchell's squadron stood into the Vlieter where the Dutch fleet in commission surrendered, twelve ships altogether of which eight were of the line.

1800 February 18th. One of the two French ships of the line which had escaped from Aboukir Bay, the *Genereux* 74, was captured while trying to get a relief convoy into Malta. This island has been captured from the Knights of Malta in 1798 by Napoleon and was now blockaded by the British, augmented for a time by a Russian squadron.

March 31st. The capture of the *Guillaume Tell* 80, the other French liner to escape from the Battle of the Nile, when trying to escape from Malta.

September 4th. Malta surrendered to the British.

1801 April 2nd. The Battle of Copenhagen. Britain's answer to the hostile 'armed neutrality' of Russia, Sweden and Denmark was to send a fleet under Admiral Sir Hyde Parker to the Baltic. A detachment of ten ships of the line, two fifties and seven frigates, with bombs and sloops, went into Copenhagen harbour under the second-in-command, Lord Nelson. After a furious engagement the Danes surrendered, and with their fleet gone the Swedes and Russians settled their differences with us amicably.

July 6th. The action off Algeciras. Rear-Admiral Sir James de Saumarez with six of the line attacked a squadron of three French ships of the line and a frigate anchored in Algeciras Bay. Admiral Linois ran his ships ashore, but unfortunately during the action the *Hannibal* 74 went aground near the Spanish batteries and was forced to surrender. De Saumarez retired to Gibraltar and by tremendous efforts repaired his five ships by the 12th, on which day the French admiral, now afloat again, had been joined by five Spanish ships of the line under Vice-Admiral Moreno, two of them of 112 guns, and also a French seventy-four. Although De Saumarez had only four seventy-fours and an eighty, he immediately attacked the combined squadron, took one French seventy-four and burnt and sank both the huge Spanish one-hundred-and-twelves; a small Spanish warship was sunk.

1802 The peace of Amiens.

1803 War with France.

1804 March 8th. Goree had been taken by the French in January, but was recaptured by Captain Edward Dickson.

May 5th. The capture of Surinam by Commodore Samuel Hood.

December 12th. War with Spain.

1805 July 22nd. Calder's Action. In this, a curtain-raiser to the Battle of Trafalgar, Vice-Admiral Robert Calder with fifteen sail of the line met Villeneuve and the Franco-Spanish fleet off Finisterre with twenty. Because of the misty weather a confused and partial action ensued during which a Spanish eighty and a seventy-four were captured. At home Calder's performance was considered inadequate, and he was recalled and severely reprimanded at a court martial, somewhat unfairly.

October 21st. The Battle of Trafalgar. After much weary searching, which had taken Nelson's fleet to the West Indies and back, he had his reward when he brought the Franco-Spanish fleet under Vice-Admiral Villeneuve to action and utter defeat off Cape Trafalgar. Of the thirty-three Franco-Spanish ships of the line engaged fifteen were lost, and two more taken on the 24th. The British who went into action with twenty-seven of the line lost

none. Lord Nelson was mortally wounded early in the action but lived to hear that he had won the greatest victory in the history of naval warfare. It was the end of any serious naval challenge from Napoleon's Empire for the rest of the war.

November 4th. Captain Sir John Strachan with four of the line and two frigates engaged a squadron of four French ships of the line off Cape Ortegal and captured them.

1806 January 12th. Commodore Sir Home-Popham took Cape Colony again. It had been restored to the Dutch by the Peace of Amiens.

February 6th. Duckworth's action off San Domingo. In a highly successful action, Vice-Admiral Sir John Duckworth, with six of the line and two frigates engaged a force of five French ships of the line, one of them the great *Imperial* 120, two frigates and another vessel. The *Imperial* was driven ashore and wrecked as was another. The other three liners were captured.

1807 February 19th. Sir John Duckworth unfortunately proved less effective against the Turks; for having taken his squadron past the batteries on the Dardanelles on the 19th, he then dithered off Constantinople until retiring back to the Mediterranean.

September 2nd to 5th. The bombardment of Copenhagen by Lord Gambier's fleet.

September 7th. The surrender of the Danish fleet. This consisted of seventy vessels, eighteen of them being ships of the line. Only four of these, however, were thought worth refitting for service in the Royal Navy.

1808 April 11th. Lord Cochrane's fireships attack Basque and Aix Roads, when the French shipping there was run aground. This attack was followed up by further action by Lord Gambier's fleet, which he did not direct to the best advantage, though he was acquitted of misconduct at the court martial.

1809 January 14th. Captain James Yeo captured Cayenne from the French.

February 24th. Martinique was captured by Rear-Admiral Sir Alexander Cochrane and Lieutenant-General Beckwith.

July 28th to September. The British Expedition to Walcheren. The fleet which transported Lord Chatham's army to the Schelde was commanded by Rear-Admiral Sir John Strachan.

1810 February 16th. Rear-Admiral William Drury captured Amboyna from the Dutch.

August 9th. The capture of Banda Neira by Captain Christopher Cole with one hundred and eighty seamen and marines. The surrendered Dutch garrison numbered fifteen hundred.

1811 March 13th. Hoste's action off Lissa. In this remarkable action, Captain William Hoste with a small squadron of four frigates, consisting of two thirty-twos, a thirty-eight and a twenty-two, engaged and utterly defeated a Franco-Venetian squadron of six frigates, four of them forty-fours, two sloops and two gunboats, commanded by Commodore Dubourdieu. The action ended with two of the frigates taken and one destroyed. A fourth which had struck could not be taken possession of because Hoste had not a boat to send to her.

August 27th. The surrender of Java by the Dutch. The plans for this enterprise had been made by Rear-Admiral William Drury who, however, died before he could fulfil them. Commodore Robert Broughton and Lieutenant-General Samuel Auchmuty carried the plans through.

1812 War with the United States of America.

1813 September 10th. Commander Robert Barclay and his squadron on Lake Erie was defeated by an American squadron commanded by Commodore Oliver Perry, U.S.N. This gave the Americans control of the Upper Lakes.

1814 August 24th. The capture of Washington by Rear-Admiral George Cockburn and Major-General Ross.

September 11th. The Battle of Lake Champlain. In this bloody encounter an American squadron commanded by Captain Thomas Macdonough defeated a British squadron under Commander George Downie, who was killed.

December 14th. The Americans were defeated in a gunboat action on Lake Borgne. The British were led by Commander Nicholas Lockyer.

1815 The end of the French revolutionary and Napoleonic Wars. Peace with the United States of America.

1816 August 27th. The Bombardment of Algiers. Admiral Sir Edward Pellew with five ships of the line and some Dutch frigates, which had joined him at Gibraltar, destroyed the Dey's fleet and much of the town and fortifications of Algiers in order to obtain the release of three thousand Christian slaves. He was created Viscount Exmouth.

1824 May 11th. The capture of Rangoon; the naval forces were commanded by Commodore Grant.

1827 October 20th. The Battle of Navarino. The last fleet action we fought under sail, in which the Turko-Egyptian fleet was destroyed by an Anglo-Franco-Russian fleet commanded by Vice-Admiral Sir Edward Codrington, as part of the measures to implement the terms of the Treaty of London and end the Greco-Turkish war.

1839 January 19th. The capture of Aden by Captain Henry Smith.

1839–42 The first Chinese war.

August 23rd. The capture of Hong Kong. After the abandonment of the factory at Canton, Captain Charles Elliot took over Hong Kong. It was formally ceded to Britain in 1841.

1840 November 3rd. The Bombardment of St Jean d'Acre on the coast of Syria and the subsequent occupation of the town. This was the chief action of the operations of the British fleet, augmented by Turkish and Austrian squadrons and commanded by Admiral Sir Robert Stopford, which brought the Turkish port's rebellious vassal, Mahamet Ali, to submission.

1842 June 18th. The capture of Shanghai.

1854 War with Russia. An Anglo-French fleet commanded by Admiral Sir Charles Napier was sent to the Baltic. Another Anglo-French fleet, commanded by Vice-Admiral James Dundas, was sent to the Black Sea to support the Anglo-French army in its operations in the Crimea. Odessa was bombarded on April 22nd. The army landed on September 14th, and Sebastopol was bombarded from October 17th to the 24th. In the Baltic the Russian fleet was not brought to action, so that the blockade of the Russian ports and the bombardment of their shore defences were all that could be achieved. The principal success was the destruction of the fortress of Bomarsund.

1855 The Allied fleet returned to the Baltic, this time commanded by Vice-Admiral the Hon. Richard Dundas. The pattern of operations was similar to the year before, the highlight being the bombardment of Sweaborg from

August 9th to the 11th, where tremendous damage was done. In the Crimea further bombardments of Sebastopol were undertaken on April 9th to 28th, June 6th to 10th, 16th and 17th, July 16th to 19th, August 6th to 9th and September 5th to 7th. The southern part of the fortress and the docks were evacuated by the Russians on September 9th and 10th. Before they left they destroyed their fleet, one hundred and seventeen vessels, including five 120-gun, eight 84-gun and one 80-gun sailing ships of the line and four 60-gun frigates.

1856 Peace with Russia.

1856–60 The second China war.
October 25th. Canton was captured by the British commander-in-chief on the China station Rear-Admiral Sir Michael Seymour.

1857 June 1st. The Battle of Fatshan Creek. The Chinese had assembled between seventy and eighty armed junks near a fort in the creek, which was close to Canton. Sir Michael Seymour with two paddle tenders, seven gunboats, and oared boats from the fleet, attacked, captured and burnt all but a very few that escaped to Fatshan.

1858 May 20th. The bombardment by an Anglo-French force of the Taku forts.
June 27th. The Treaty of Tientsin. This should normally have ended the war, but the state of near-anarchy in parts of China prevented the terms of peace being properly implemented. War was formally renewed on April 8th, 1859.

1859 June 25th. A force of ten gunboats and a sloop, under the new British commander-in-chief, Rear-Admiral James Hope, was repulsed in its attempt against the Peiho forts. The admiral was severely wounded.

1860 August 21st. Rear-Admiral James Hope captured the Taku forts, and then proceeded up to Tientsin which he occupied. It required the capture of Peking by an Anglo-French army and the destruction of the Summer Palace to persuade the Chinese to ratify the peace of Tientsin permanently.
December 30th. The launching of the *Warrior*, the Royal Navy's first ironclad capital ship.

Appendix 2
British and Enemy Losses (ships of over 50 guns) 1688—1855

	Taken	Destroyed during operations	Lost by wreck	Burnt by accident
1688–1714 Wars of the English and Spanish successions	British 16 (3 retaken)	British 1	British 23	British 4
	French 11	French 19	French not known	French not known
	Spanish 6	Spanish 2	Spanish not known	Spanish not known
1718–48 Spanish War of 1718, War of Jenkins' Ear, 1739–48*	British 3 (2 retaken)	British 1	British 10 and 1 in 1716	British 1
	French 17	French none	1 in 1749 1 in 1755 French not known	French 3
	Spanish 16	Spanish 7	Spanish 3	Spanish none

* French did not join in until 1744,

	Taken	Destroyed during operations	Lost by wreck	Burnt by accident
1756–63 The Seven Years War — British	2	none	6	1
1755–63 — French	23	9	7	3
1762 — Spanish	9	3	3	none
1775–83 War of American Independence — British	3 (1 retaken)	none	14	1
1778–83 — French	14	1	1	none
1778–83 — Spanish	11	2	5	none
1780–82 — Dutch	3	1	not known	not known
1793–1801 Revolutionary Wars, Part I — British	6	none	13	6
1793–1801 — French	35	12	9	none
1795–1801 — Spanish	5	5	not known	not known
1795–1800 — Dutch	25	none	not known	not known
1801 — Danish	5	none	not known	not known
1802–15 Revolutionary Wars, Part II — British	none	none	15	1
1802–15 — French	30	7	1	none
1803–08 — Spanish	12	none	not known	not known
1803–10 — Dutch	none	4	1	not known
1807–13 — Danish	17	1	not known	not known
1808–09 — Russian	1	none	not known	not known
Navarino 1807–08 — Turkish	1	not known	not known	not known
1827 — Turko-Egyptian	none	4	not known	not known
Crimean War 1855–56 — Russian	none	18	not known	not known

1688–1855	British	French	Spanish	Dutch	Danish	Russian	Turkish
Taken	30 (6 retaken)	130	59	28	22	1	1
Destroyed during operations	2	48	19	5	1	18	4
	26	178	78	33	23	19	5

Grand Total	British	Foreign
	26	336

Of the British ships on this list lost in action, all were lost to the French, except for one of the two destroyed, the *Dartmouth* 50, which blew up in action with the Spanish *Glorioso* in 1747.

The figures above are based on the lists of William Laird Clowes.

Memoirs

OF THE

RISE AND PROGRESS

OF THE

ROYAL NAVY.

By CHARLES DERRICK, Esq.

OF THE NAVY-OFFICE.

Island of bliss! amid the subject seas
That thunder round thy rocky coasts, set up
At once the wonder, terror and delight
Of distant nations; whose remotest shores
Can soon be shaken by thy naval arm:
Not to be shook thyself; but all assaults
Baffling, as thy hoar cliff the loud sea-wave.

THOMSON.

For oh it much imports you, 'tis your all,
To keep your trade entire, entire the force
And honour of your fleets; o'er that to watch
E'en with a hand severe, and jealous eye.

IBID.

London:

PRINTED BY H. TEAPE, TOWER-HILL;

SOLD BY BLACKS AND PARRY, LEADENHALL-STREET; CADELL AND DAVIES, STRAND;
AND G. AND W. NICOL, PALL-MALL.

1806.

Appendix 3

Some Establishments of the Ships, Guns and Men 1517–1805

In 1806 the then Secretary to the Committee of Stores in the Navy Office published a book called *Memoirs of the Rise and Progress of the Royal Navy*. His name was Charles Derrick and his interest in the development of the fleet probably stemmed from the twenty years he had spent in the Surveyor's office, ten as Chief Clerk, prior to transferring to Stores and Slops. He died in 1831.

In this work are collected the earliest lists of royal ships, and for later periods, abstracts showing the number of ships in the service per rate, and also guns and men for given dates. Interspersed with these are historical observations and notes to explain points in the lists.

Since this admirable work must by now be unavailable except in a very few libraries, it has been thought useful to re-publish it here in an abridged form, which includes most of the lists and those notes relating to them. A certain amount of rearrangement has been done to make them more strictly chronological, but otherwise editing has been kept to a minimum.

Further lists to bring the record forward from Derrick's publication in 1806, to the end of the period covered by this volume in 1860, have been prepared by the author and follow in appendix 4.

Henry VIII 1509–1547

The following List of all the King's Ships in the 9th year of his reign, is taken from Mr. Pepys's Miscellanies.*

1517

	Men in Harbour.
The Henry Grace de Dieu	12
Katherine Fortune	4
Gabriel Royal	4
Great Barbara	4
John Baptist	4
Mary Rose	4
Great Bark	4
Peter Pomegranate	3
Mary George	4
Mary John	3
Less Bark	3
Mary James	1
Henry Hampton	3
Lizard	2
Two Row Barges—(one man each)	2
The Rose Galley	1
Katherine Galley	1
Sovereign	1
Great Nicholas	1
Great Galley	10
In all 21 Ships and Vessels.	

From the same source from which the foregoing List was obtained, the following is also taken, being an Account of the Names and tonnage of all the King's Ships, according to a general survey, dated 1st June, in the 13th Year of his reign:

* Vol. 8.

1521

	Tons.
The Henry Grace de Dieu	1500*
Sovereign	800
Gabriel Royal	650
Katherine Forteless†	550
Mary Rose	600
John Baptist	400
Barbara	400
Great Nicholas	400
Mary George	250
Mary James	240
Henry Hampton	120
Great Bark	250
Less Bark	180
Two Row Barges (60 tons each)	120
The Great Galley	800
In all 16 Ships and Vessels.	7260

1523

In the Year 1523, Sir William Fitzwilliams had under his command a fleet of Thirty-six large Ships, to cruize on the coasts of France; and Anthony Points had at the same time the command of a considerable fleet to guard the western seas.—but it is not known how many of the Ships were the King's own.‡

* She is in almost every other account said to have been 1000 tons only, which is certainly the most correct.

N.B.—The Sovereign was in dock at Woolwich, at this time, and was recommended, by the Officers who surveyed the Ships, to be rebuilt, "as she is a goodly ship."—It also appears that there was a great Storehouse of the King's at Erith, at this time.

† So spelt in the original; but Fortileza, according to Charnock.

‡ The Cinque Ports, with their Members, were bound by their tenure to supply the King with 57 Ships, containing 21 men and a boy in each ship, for 15 days once in the year at their own expence, if their service was required: and they were frequently obliged to furnish a great number. (See Archæologia, Vol. 6, page 195.) After the 15 days they were paid by the King.

1546

(*The Anthony Anthony Roll*) A List of the Royal Navy in 1546.

Quality.	Shyppes Names.	Tunnage.	Soldiers.	Mariners.	Soldiers & Mariners.	Gunners.	Total No of Men.
Shyppes ..	Harry Grace a Dieu	1000	349	301	...	50	700
	Mary Roase	700	185	200	...	30	415
	Peter	600	185	185	...	30	400
	Mathew.........	600	138	138	...	24	300
	Great Barke	500	136	138	...	26	300
	Jhesus of Lubeck ..	700	118	158	...	24	300
	Pawncy	450	136	140	...	24	300
	Murryan	500	138	142	...	20	300
	Struce	450	140	96	...	14	250
	Mary Hamborow..	400	119	111	...	16	246
	Xtopher of Bream.	400	119	111	...	16	246
	Trinity Harry.....	250	100	100	...	20	220
	Smaell Barke	400	105	122	...	23	250
	Swypstake........	300	100	109	...	21	230
	Mynnion.........	300	100	100	...	20	220
	Larticque	100	80	52	...	8	140
	Mary Thomas	90	25	47	...	8	80
	Hope Barke.......	80	28	28	...	4	60
	George...........	60	18	18	...	4	40
	Mary Jaymes	60	18	18	...	4	40
Galleasses	Graunde Masterys.	450	...	...	220	30	250
	Anne Gallante	450	...	...	220	30	250
	Harte...........	300	...	...	170	30	200
	Antelop..........	300	...	...	170	30	200
	Tegar...........	200	...	100	...	20	120
	Bulle	200	...	100	...	20	120
	Salamander	300	...	200	...	20	220
	Unicorne.........	240	...	124	...	16	140
	Swallowe.........	240	...	130	...	30	160
	Galie Subtile......	200	...	242	...	8	250
	Newe Barke	200	...	124	...	16	140
	Greyhounde	200	...	124	...	16	140
	Jennet	180	...	106	...	14	120
	Lyon	140	...	88	...	12	100
	Dragon	140	...	98	...	12	110
Pynnasses	Phawcon.........	80	...	54	...	6	60
	Sacar...........	80	...	54	...	6	60
	Hynde...........	80	...	54	...	6	60
	Roo	80	...	46	...	4	50
	Phenyx	40	...	46	...	4	50
	Marlyon	40	...	46	...	4	50
	Lesse Pinnas......	40	...	40	...	4	44
	Bryggendyn	40	...	40	...	4	44
	Hare	15	...	28	...	2	30
	Trego-Ronnyger ..	20	...	24	...	1	25
Roo-Baergys	Double Rose......	20	...	39	...	4	43
	Flowre de Luce....	20	...	39	...	4	43
	Portquillice.......	20	...	34	...	4	38
	Harpe	20	...	36	...	4	40
	Clowde in the Sonne	20	...	36	...	4	40
	Rose in the Sonne..	20	...	36	...	4	40
	Hawthorne.......	20	...	34	...	4	38
	Thre Ostrydge Feathers	20	...	33	...	4	37
	Fawcon in the Fetterlock	20	...	41	...	4	45
	Maydenhede......	20	...	33	...	4	37
	Rose Slype	20	...	33	...	4	37
	Jyllyver Flowre....	20	...	34	...	4	38
	Sonne	20	...	36	...	4	40

Abstract.	No	Tunnage.	Soldiers.	Mariners.	Soldiers & Mariners.	Gunners.	Total No of Men
Shyppes......	20	7940	2337	2314	...	386	5037
Galleasses	15	3740	....	1436	780	304	2520
Pynnaces.....	10	515	....	432	...	41	473
Roo-Baerges ..	13	260	....	464	...	52	516
Total	58	12455	2337	4646	780	783	8546

Edward VI 1547–1553

The following List of the Navy on the 5th January, 1548, is taken from the 6th vol. of the Archæologia, p. 218.*

1548

Names.	Where at.	Tons.	Soldiers, Mariners, &c.	Pieces of Ordnance. Brass.	Iron.
The Henry Grace de Dieu............	Woolwich.	1000	700	19	103
Peter...........⎫		600	400	12	78
Matthew		600	300	10	121
Jesus...........		700	300	8	66
Paucy..........		450	300	13	69
Great Bark		500	300	12	85
Less Bark........	Ports-	400	250	11	98
Murryan ....⎬	mouth.	500	300	10	53
Shruce of Dawske.		450	250	—	39
Christopher......		400	246	2	51
Trinity Henry....		250	220	1	63
Sweepstake		300	230	6	78
Mary Willoughby ⎭		140	160	—	23
Anne Gallant ....⎫		450	250	16	46
Salamander......	Galleys	300	220	9	40
Hart........... ⎬	at	300	200	4	52
Antelope	Ports-	300	200	4	40
Swallow.........⎭	mouth.	240	100	8	45

Name	Group	Tons			
Unicorn	Galleys at Portsmouth.	240	140	6	30
Jeannet		180	120	6	35
New Bark		200	140	5	48
Greyhound		200	140	8	37
Tiger		200	120	4	39
Bull		200	120	5	42
Lion		140	140	2	48
George		60	40	2	26
Dragon		140	120	3	42
Falcon	Pinnaces at Portsmouth.	83	55	4	22
Black Pinnace		80	44	2	15
Hind		80	55	2	26
Spanish Shallop		20	26	—	7
Hare		15	30	—	10
Sun		20	40	2	6
Cloud in the Sun	Row-Barges at Portsmouth.	20	40	2	7
Harp		20	40	1	6
Maidenhead		20	37	1	6
Gilly-flower		20	38	—	—
Ostridge-feather		20	37	1	6
Rose Slip		20	37	2	6
Flower de Luce		20	43	2	7
Rose in the Sun		20	40	3	7
Portcullis		20	38	1	6
Falcon in the Featherlock†		20	45	3	8
Grand Mrs	Deptford Strand	450	250	1	22
Marlyon		40	50	4	8
Galley Subtil, or Row Galley		200	250	3	28
Brigantine		40	44	3	19
Hoy Bark		80	60	—	5
Hawthorn		20	37	—	—
Mary Hamburgh	In Scotland.	400	246	5	67
Phœnix		40	50	4	33
Saker		40	50	2	18
Double Rose		20	43	3	6
Total		11268‡	7731	237	1848

In all 53 Ships and Vessels.

* Mr. Topham stated to the Antiquarian Society that soon after the death of Henry the Eighth a Commission issued for an inventory to be taken of all his effects of every kind: and that a List of the Names of the King's Ships then in being, together with an Account of the Tonnage, the Stores, and Ammunition of every particular Ship, and the Number of Men carried by each of them, is preserved in Mr. Brander's valuable MSS. from which he took this account.

† Or Falcon in the Fetterlock.

‡ In the Archæologia, and in Charnock, the tonnage is stated to have been 6255; Tons; but the tonnage inserted against the several ships will be found to amount to 11268 tons. The error in the first-mentioned amount must have originated in a mistake in casting up the aggregate, and has been copied since by others who were not aware of the necessity of revising it.

In the second year of his Majesty's reign, (on the 22d January), the following Ships were "thought meet to keep the Seas,—with their Tonnage, number of Men, Wages and Victuals for the same for every Month of twenty-eight days, as a Summer Guard*:"

1549

Names.	Tons.	Soldiers.	Mariners.	Gunners.	Total Number of Men.
The Great Bark	500	136	138	26	300
Less Bark	400	105	112	23	240
Sweepstake	300	100	109	21	230
Hart	300	—	180	20	200
Antelope	300	—	180	20	200
Swallow	240	—	142	18	160
New Bark	200	—	124	16	140
Grayhound	200	—	124	16	140
Flower de Luce	50	—	56	4	60
Double Rose	50	—	56	4	60
	2540	341	1221	168	1730

Wages £640 5 0
Victuals ...... 720 16 8 } For One Month.
1361 1 8

* Pepy's Miscellanies, vol. 8. p. 149.

"And the following as a Winter Guard."*

1552

Names.	Tons.	Soldiers.	Mariners.	Gunners.	Total Number of Men.
The Paunsey	450	136	140	24	300
Murrian	500	138	142	20	300
Mary Hamboro	400	108	120	18	246
Jennet	180	—	104	16	120
Dragon	140	—	104	16	120
Lion	140	—	104	16	120
Faulcon	80	—	62	8	70
Hinde	80	—	54	6	60
Phoenix	40	—	44	6	50
Mᵃ. Willoughby	140	36	80	14	130
	2150	418	954	144	1516

Wages £543 14 0
Victuals ...... 631 13 4 } ₩ Month.
1175 7 4

* Pepys's Miscellanies, vol. 8. p. 149.

The following Report of the State of the Royal Navy, on 26th August, 1552, is so valuable as to merit being inserted at full length.

1552

"GENERAL STATE OF THE KING's SHIPS."
"The State of the King's Majesty's Ships, 26 August, An. 6. R. R. Edward VI."*

The Edward† ....
Great Bark ....
Paunsey ....
Trinity ....
Salamander ....
Bull ....
Tiger ....
Willoughby ....
Primrose ....
Antelope ....
Hart ....
Greyhound ....
Swallow ....
Jennet ....
New Bark ....
Falcon ....
Sacre ....
Phœnix ....
Jer-Falcon ....
Swift ....
Sun ....
Moon ....
Seven Stars ....
Flower de Luce .....

} All these Ships and Pinnaces are in good case to serve, so that they may be grounded and caulked once a year, to keep them tight.

To be so ordered,
By the King's Command.

Peter ....
Matthew ....
Jesus ....
Sweepstakes ....
Mª. Hambrough ....
Ann Gallant ....
Hynde ....

} These Ships must be docked and new dubbed, to search their Treenails and Iron-work.
To be ordered likewise.

Less Bark ....
Lion ....
Dragon ....

} These Ships be already dry-docked; to be new made at your Lordship's pleasure.

To prepare things ready for the same.

Grand Mrs. .... Dry-docked—Not thought worthy of new making.

To lie still, or to take that which is profitable of her for other Ships.

Struse ....
Unicorn ....
George ....

} Thought meet to be sold.
The George kept, and the other Three to be sold.

Maidenhead ....
Gilly-flower ....
Port-cullis ....
Rose-Slip ....
Double-Rose ....
Rose in the Sun .....

} Not worth keeping.
To be preserved, as they may with little charge.

Bark of Bullen .... In Ireland, whose state we know not.

Item. The two Galleys and Brigantine must be yearly repaired, if your Lordship's pleasure be to have them kept.
To be repaired and kept."

"Forty-five to be kept."

* *Pepy's Miscellanies, vol. 8. p. 143.*

† *Supposed to have been the Henry Grace de Dieu; and that her name was changed by Edward, soon after his accession.*

Mary I 1553–1558

1557

"A List of Ships appointed 29th May, 1557, to serve under the Lord Admiral, together with the Number of Soldiers and Gunners in the same.*"

Names.	Burthen. Tons.	Hacbut-ters, or Arquebu-siers.	Soldiers.	Mariners.	Gunners
The Great Bark	500	50	80	190	30
Jesus	700	50	80	190	30
Trinity	300	20	40	140	20
Swallow	240	20	40	140	20
Salamander	300	20	40	140	20
Hart	300	20	40	140	20
Antelope	300	20	40	140	20
Ann Gallant	300	20	40	140	20
New Bark	200	10	20	84	16
Mary Willoughby†	160	10	20	84	16
Bull	180	10	20	84	16
Tiger	180	10	20	84	16
Greyhound	180	10	20	84	16
Jer Falcon	120	8	20	66	14
Falcon	80	6	16	54	10
George	100	6	16	54	10
Bark of Bullen	60	4	8	44	8
Saker	60	4	8	44	8
Sonne	50	4	—	34	6
Double Rose	40	—	—	26	4
Flower de Luce	30	—	—	26	4
	4380	302	568	1988	324

In all 21 Ships, &c.

* *Pepys's Miscellanies, vol. 7. p. 13.*

† *The two last letters omitted in the original.*

And mention is made in Mr. Pepys's Collection of the

Minion,	Trinity Henry,
Sacret,	and
Paunses,	Willoughby;

which, (if the two latter are the same as the Trinity and Mary Willoughby in the foregoing List,) make twenty-four in all.

The Queen died on 17th November, 1558, when the tonnage of the Navy is said to have been reduced to 7110 tons, and the number of Ships and Vessels to 26; which number very nearly corresponds with the foregoing accounts of the Ships in 1557; but the number in the following List comes still nearer; the date of which, however, I am sorry I cannot ascertain.

1558

"List and Charge of Queen Mary's Ships."
"The Names of Queen Mary's Ships, with their several numbers of Men if "they shall be appointed to serve in fashion of War.*"

Names.	Men.
The Great Bark	260
Matthew	240
Paronses, or Paunces	220
Jesus	240
Mary of Hambrᵒ	180
Trinity Henry	160
Sweepstake	200
Salamander	200
Hart	200
Antelope	200
Ann Gallant	200
Swallow	140
New Bark	120
Jennet	140
Greyhound	100
The Mª Willoughby	120
Faulcon	60
Saker	50
Jer-Falcon	90
Phœnix	40
George	40
Bull	120
Tiger	120
Seven Stars ⎫	35
Sun ⎬ Pinnaces	30
Swift ⎪	30
Flower de Luce ⎭	30
	3565

In all 27 Ships and Pinnaces

"Men to serve in them	3565		
"Wages and dead Shares....per Month of 28 Days	£1436	0	0
"Victuals .... do.	1782	10	0
	3218	10	0
"Conduct for 3000 Mariners	£450	0	0"

* Pepys's Miscellanies, vol. 8. p. 153.

Elizabeth I 1548–1603

The Royal Navy, on 4th Dec. 1565, consisted of the following Ships and Vessels.

1565

"Anno Regni Reginæ Elizª. Octavo."
"The Names of all her Highnesses Ships and other Vessels, with the several Numbers appointed for their safe keeping in Harbour, as hereafter appeareth.*"

Names.	Men in Harbour.	Names.	Men in Harbour.
Triumph	21	Willoughby	7
White Bear	21	Falcon	3
Elizª. Jonas	21	Phœnix	3
Victory	18	Sacre	3
Mary Rose	13	Bark of Bullen	3
Hope	13	Hare	3
Philip and Mary	13	Sun	3
Lion	13	George	3
Jesus	13	Speedwell ⎫	3
Minion	10	Tryright ⎬ Galleys	3
Primrose	10	Eleanor ⎭	3
Antelope	10	Make-shift	1
Jennet	10	Post	1
Swallow	10		
New Bark	7	In all 29 Ships and	
Aid	7	Vessels.	

* Taken from Pepys's Miscellanies, vol. 8. p. 175.

1578

A List of the Royal Navy, in 1578, with the burthen of the Ships, and their Number of Men.

Ships Names.	Burthen. Tons.	Mariners.	Gunners.	Soldiers.	Total Number of Men.
Triumph	1000	450	50	200	780
Elizabeth Jones	900	300	50	200	600
White Bear	900	300	50	200	600
Victory	803	330	40	100	500
Primrose	803	330	40	100	500
Mary Rose	600	200	50	100	350
Hope	600	200	50	100	350
Bonaventure	600	160	30	110	300
Philip and Mary	600	160	30	110	300
Lion (or Golden Lion)	600	150	30	110	290
Dreadnought	400	140	20	80	250
Swiftsure	400	140	20	80	250
Swallow	350	120	20	60	200
Antelope	350	120	20	60	200
Jennet	350	120	20	60	200
Foresight	300	120	20	60	200
Aid	240	90	20	50	160

Ships Names.	Burthen. Tons.	Mariners.	Gunners.	Soldiers.	Total No of Men.
Bull	160	70	10	40	120
Tiger	160	70	10	40	120
Falcon	—	60	10	20	80
Achates	80	30	10	10	60
Handmaid...........	80	30	10	10	60
Bark of Bullen	60	30	10	—	50
George.............. under	60	40	10	—	50
In all 24 Ships, &c.	10506*	3760	630	1900	6570

* *Estimating the Falcon at 120, and the George at 50 Tons.*

1588

Names.	Burthen. Tons.	Men.
Ark Royal........................	800	425
Elizabeth Bonadventure	600	250
Rainbow........................	500	250
Golden Lion	500	250
White Bear	1000	500
Vanguard	500	250
Revenge........................	500	250
Elizabeth-Jonas	900	500
Victory	800	400
Antelope	400	160
Triumph	1100	500
Dreadnought.....................	400	200
Mary Rose	600	250
Nonpareil	500	250
Hope	600	250
Galley Bonavolia	250	250
Swiftsure	400	200
Swallow........................	360	160
Foresight	300	160
Aid............................	250	120
Bull	200	100
Tiger	200	100
Tramontana	150	70
Scout	120	70
Achates	100	60
Charles	70	40
Moon..........................	60	40
Advice	50	40
Spy............................	50	40
Marline	50	35
Sun............................	40	30
Cygnet.........................	30	20
Brigantine	90	35
George Hoy	120	24
Total 34 Ships, &c.	12590	6279

In an Account, dated 1589, intituled "The Ordinary Number of Shipkeepers appointed for the keeping of the Queen's Majesty's Ships in Harbour, at Chatham, &c.—

Also an Account of Her Majesty's Ships at the Seas,*" the following Ships are inserted.

1589

Ships in Harbour.

Eliz. Jonas	Swallow
Triumph	Foresight
White Bear	Aid
Ark	Bull
Mary Rose	Tiger
Hope	Scout
Revenge	Achates
Nonpareil	Marline (or Martin)
Lion	Advice
Bonadventure	Spy
Dreadnought	Sun
Swiftsure	Cygnet (or Signet)
Brigandine	Rainbow
George Hoy	Spanish Ship
Bonaviolia	Popinjay
Jennet	

The great Ship at Woolwich
Two great new Ships at Deptford.
The Four lesser new Ships.
The great new Boats (6 in Number).

* *Pepys's Miscellanies, vol. 8. p. 280.*

An Account of Her Majesty's Ships at Sea.

Victory	Tremontane
Vanguard	Charles
Antelope	Moon.

Total of Ships, Pinnaces, and Boats 50.

The disposition shewn by the Queen to encourage all undertakings for discoveries, and planting new-found countries, excited a spirit in the nation for such expeditions; and many noblemen and gentlemen became adventurers in them.

1599

In the Archœologia,* there is a complete List of the Navy on the 23d May, 1599, taken from an original and beautiful manuscript in the possession of Dr. Leith,† which was exhibited to the Antiquarian Society, and read on 5th May, 1796; with the number of Brass and cast Iron Ordnance of the different species then appropriated to the respective Ships, viz.

Cannon	Falconets
Demi-Cannon	Port-pece Halls
Culverins	Port-pece Chambers
Demi-Culverins	Fowler-Halls
Sakers	Fowler Chambers
Mynions	and
Falcons	Curtalls.

Taken by the Queen's Commission, dated 3d March, in the 37th year of her reign, and directed to Lord Burleigh, Lord High Treasurer, Lord Howard, Lord High Admiral, Lord Hunsdon, &c. &c. and subsequent orders of the said Commissioners, the last whereof is dated 6th April, 1599.

* *Vol. 13. p. 27.*
† *Of Greenwich, who has favoured me with the use of it.*

As this is an authentic and curious piece of information, with respect to the Ordnance which the Ships carried, a matter about which historians seem, till of late, to have been almost totally in the dark, and which is now by no means generally known, it will be proper to insert the List in this place.*

1599

Names.	Cannon.	Demi-Cannon.	Culverins.	Demi-Culverins.	Sakers.	Mynions.	Falcons.	Falconets.	Port-piece Halls.	Port-piece Chambers.	Fowler Halls.	Fowler Chambers.	Curtalls.	Total No. of Pieces of Ordnance.
Achatis				6	2	5								13
Adventure			4	11	5						2	4		26
Advantage			6	8	4									18
Amity of Harwich†				4	2									6
St. Andrew		8	21	7	2				3	7	2			50
Antelope			4	13	8		1		2	4	2	4		38
Advice				4	2	3								9
Arke	4	4	12	12	6				4	7	2	4		55
Answer			5	8	2						2	4		21
Ayde				8	2	4	4							18
Bear					2									2
White Bear	3		11	7	10					2		7		40
Charles				8		2					2	4		16
Crane			6	7	6						2	3		24
Cygnet							1	2						3
Due Repulse	2	3	13	14	6				2	4	2	4		50
Dreadnought	2		4	11	10		2				4	8		41
Defiance			14	14	6				2	4	2	4		46
Daysey†				4										4
Elizabeth-Jonas	3	6	8	9	9	1	2		1	2	5	10		56
Eliza Bonaventure	2	2	11	14	4	2			2	4	2	4		47
Foresight			14	8	3	2					3	6		37
Guardland			16	14	4		‡		2	4	2	3		45
Hope	2	4	9	11	4				4	8	2	4		48
Lion	4	8	14	9		1					8	16		60
Mary Rose			4	11	10	4					3	7		39
Mere Honora			4	15	16	4						2		41
St. Matthew	4	4	16	14	4	4	2							48
Mercury or Galley-Mercury					1		1					4		6
Marlin							7							7
Moon				4	4	1								9
Nonpareil	2	3	7	8	12				4	8	4	8		56
Quittance			2	6	7	4					2	4		25
Rainbow			6	12	7	1								26
Scout					4		6							10
Swiftsure	2		5	12	8		2				4	8		41
Spy				4	2	3								9
Swallow					2	1					2	3		8
Sonne						1		4						5
Triumph	4	3	17	8	6				1	4	5	20		68
Tremontana				12	7	2								21
Tiger				6	14		2							22
Vauntguard			4	14	11	2								31
Victory			12	18	9						7	13		59
Wastspight	2	2	13	10	2								29

In all 42 Ships, &c.

* This List is attested by

> JOHN CONYERS,
> FRAS. GOFTON, } Auditors of the Prest.
>
> STEPHEN. RISLESDEN,
> J. LINEWRAYE,
> JOHN LEE, } Officers of the Ordnance.
> G. HEGGE,

† A Drumler.—This was an inferior sort of ship.

‡ In a Parenthesis is noted, "And one Spanish."

1599

GUNS.

Description of several of the sorts of *Ordnance* mentioned in some of the early Lists.*

Sorts of Ordnance.	Sir William Monson's account.		According to some other accounts.
	Bore.	Weight of the Shot.	Weight of the Shot.
	Inches.	lb	lb
Cannon	8	60	60 or 63
Demi-Cannon	6¾	33½	31
Cannon Petro	6	24½	24
Culverin	5½	17½	18
Demi-Culverin	4	9½	9
Falcon	2½	2	2
Falconet	2	1½	
Minion	3½	4	4
Sacar	3½	5½	5
Rabinet	1	½	

* See *Archæologia, vol. 6, p. 189; vol. 11, p. 170, and vol. 13, p. 27.*—See also *Chambers's Dictionary.*

1603

An Account of the Royal Navy which the Queen left at her death, with the Number of Men, and Tonnage of the Ships.*

Ships Names.	Burthen. Tons.	Mariners.	Gunners.	Soldiers.	Total No of Men.
Elizabeth Jonas	900	340	40	120	500
Triumph	1000	340	40	120	500
White Bear	900	340	40	120	500
Victory	800	268	32	100	400
Mer-Honeur (*or* Mary Honora)	800	268	32	100	400

* *Entick.*

Ships Names.	Burthen. Tons.	Mariners.	Gunners.	Soldiers.	Total No of Men.
Ark Royal†	800	268	32	100	400
St. Matthew	1000	340	40	120	500
St. Andrew	900	268	32	100	400
Due Repulse‡	700	230	30	90	350
Garland	700	190	30	80	300
Warspight	600	190	30	80	300
Mary Rose	600	150	30	70	250
Hope	600	150	30	70	250
Bonaventure	600	150	30	70	250
Lion	500	150	30	70	250
Nonpareil	500	150	30	70	250
Defiance	500	150	30	70	250
Rainbow	500	150	30	70	250
Dreadnought	400	130	20	50	200
Antelope	350	114	16	30	160
Swiftsure	400	130	20	50	200
Swallow	330	114	16	30	160
Foresight	300	114	16	30	160
Tide	250	88	12	20	120
Crane	200	70	10	20	100
Adventure	250	88	12	20	120
Quittance	200	70	10	20	100
Answer	200	70	10	20	100
Advantage	200	70	10	20	100
Tiger	200	70	10	20	100
Tramontane	140§	52	8	10	70
Scout	120	48	8	10	66
Catis‖	100	42	8	10	60
Charles	70	32	6	7	45
Moon	60	30	5	5	40
Advice	50	30	5	5	40
Spy	50	30	5	5	40
Merlin	45	26	5	4	35
Sun	40	24	4	2	30
Synnet	20	....	...	....	....
George, Hoy	100	....	...	....	....
Penny-Rose, Hoy	80	....	...	....	....
	17055	5534	804	2008	8346

In all 42 Ships, &c.

† *Named Ann Royal in 1608.*
‡ *Or Dieu Repulse, as spelt on several occasions, about this period.*
§ *See the Lists of 1604, and 1607.*
‖ *Or Cates.*

On comparing the preceding List with that, in 1578, it appears that in the last twenty-five years of Elizabeth, the Navy was almost doubled.

Before Elizabeth's time, the Navy, except in war, was not an expensive department. In her reign, the expence of it is stated to have amounted to £30,000 a year.

James I 1603–1625

SOME alterations and additions had taken place in the King's Ships in the first year of this reign, as will be seen by the following List.

1604

"A List of the King's Ships and Pinnaces, with their respective Tonnages and Men, Anno Dom. 1603.*"

Names.	Burthen. Tons.	Mariners.	Gunners.	Soldiers.	Total No of Men.
Elizabeth Jonas	900	340	40	120	500
Triumph	1000	340	40	120	500
Bear	900	340	40	120	500
Victory	700	230	30	90	350
Honour	800	268	32	100	400
Ark	800	268	32	100	400
Due Repulse	700	230	30	90	350
Garland	700	190	30	80	300
Warspight	600	190	30	80	300
Mary Rose	600	150	30	70	250
Bonaventure	600	150	30	70	250
Assurance	600	150	30	70	250
Lion	500	150	30	70	250
Defiance	500	150	30	70	250
Rainbow	500	150	30	70	250
Nonsuch	500	150	30	70	250
Vanguard	500	150	30	70	250
Dreadnought	400	130	20	50	200
Swiftsure	400	130	20	50	200
Antelope	350	114	16	30	160
Adventure	250	88	12	20	120
Crane	200	76	12	12	100
Quittance	200	76	12	12	100
Answer	200	76	12	12	100
Advantage	200	76	12	12	100
Tramontane	140	52	8	10	70
Charles	70	32	6	7	45
Moon	60	30	5	5	40
Advice	50	30	5	5	40
Spy	50	30	5	5	40
Merlin	50	30	5	5	40
Lion's Whelp	90	50	6	4 Rowers.	60
La Superlativa (Galleys†)	....	84	8	243 Rowers.	335
La Advantagia (Galleys†)	....	84	8	233 Rowers.	223
La Volatillia (Galleys†)	....	84	8	233 Rowers.	223
La Gallarita (Galleys†)	....	84	8	233 Rowers.	223

* *Meaning 1603–4.—This List is taken from Pepys's Miscellanies, vol. 2, p. 129. Its date must have been in 1604 (New Stile) and probably in March, for the reasons mentioned at the end of the List.*

† *The total number of men for each of the three last Galleys, does not correspond with the particulars.*

Mercury	Galleon	80	34	6	100	140
George	Carvel	100	10	...	....	10
Primrose	Hoy	80	2	...	....	2
A French Frigate		15	14	2	....	16
Disdain‡		....	3	..	....	3

In all 41 Ships, &c.

‡ *Mr. Phineas Pett mentions, that in January 1603-4, he was "ordered by the Lord High Admiral to build a vessel at Chatham with all possible speed, for the young Prince Henry to disport himself in above London-Bridge; her garnishing to be like the work of the Ark Royal, battlement-wise.—This little Ship was—In length by the-Keel .... 28 feet*
In breadth 12
I laid her keel the 19th January, and launched her the 6th March.—Set sail with her 9th March, and on 14th anchored right against the Tower, before the King's lodgings, his Majesty then lying there, before his riding through London. On 18th, anchored right against the Privy Stairs.—On 22d the Prince, with the Lord High Admiral, &c. &c. came on board, when we weighed and dropped down as low as Paul's Wharf, where we anchored; and there his Grace, with a great bowl of wine, christened the Ship, and called her by the name of the Disdain."—(MS. Life of Phins. Pett.)

The five last Vessels in the List of 1604, appear to have been disposed of previous to Dec. 1607, at which period the Navy consisted of the following Ships.

1607

"Dec'. 1607."
"A Catalogue of all the King's Ships, with their respective Tonnages, and Men at Sea."

Names.	Tonnage.	Men.
Elizabeth	900	500
Triumph	1000	500
Bear	900	500
Victory	900	500
Honour	800	400
Ark	800	400
Repulse	700	350
Garland	700	300
Warspight	600	300
Mary Rose	600	250
Assurance	600	250
Bonadventure	600	250
Lion	500	250
Nonsuch	500	250
Defiance	500	250
Vanguard	500	250
Rainbow	500	250
Dreadnought	400	200
Swiftsure	400	200
Antelope	350	160
Adventure	250	120
Crane	200	100
Quittance	200	100
Answer	200	100
Advantage	200	100
Tramontane	140	70
Lion's Whelp	90	60
Charles	70	45
Moon	60	45

Advice	50	40
Spy	50	40
Merlin	50	40
Superlativa ...		335
Advantagia ...		223
Volatilia ..... *		223
Galarita		223

In all 36 Ships and Vessels. 14710 8174
if each of the 4 latter Vessels was 100 Tons.

* *In the 11th vol. of the Archæologia, these Vessels are stated to have been of 100 tons each.*

Memo.—*This List is taken from Pepys's Miscellanies, vol. 2, p. 131, and vol. 5, p. 579, at the foot of which he says, "The foregoing are all the King's Ships, Pinnaces, and Galleys." By the List preceding this, it appears that the four last Vessels were large Galleys.*

1625

The accounts of the state of the Navy at the death of the King have varied exceedingly, and most of them have been very erroneous; making the number of Ships and Vessels to have been from 50 to 62, and their tonnage from 20 to 23,000 tons, whereas it appears by a report of the Commissioners appointed to examine into the state of the Navy, &c. in 1618,* that there were then but 39 Ships and Vessels, as follows, whose tonnage amounted only to 14700 tons, viz.

1618

	Tons.	
Prince Royal	1200	
White Bear	900	
More Honour	800	
Ann Royal	800	
Due Repulse	700	
Defiance	700	
Warspight	600	
Assurance	600	
Vantguard	600	
Red Lion	500	
Nonsuch	500	
Rainbow	500	May be made Serviceable.
Dreadnought	400	
Speedwell	400	
Antelope	350	
Adventure	250	
Crane	200	
Answer	200	
Phœnix	150	
Lion's Whelp	90	
Moon	100	
Seven Stars	100	
Desire	50	
George, Hoy	100	
Primrose, do.	80	
Eagle Lighter	200	

* *See Memoir on British Naval Architecture, by Ralph Willett, Esq. (Archæologie, vol. 11, p. 171.) And see Charnock.*

	Tons.
Elizabeth Jonas	500
	or 900†
Triumph	1000
Garland..................................	700
Mary Rose	600
Quittance	200
Tramontane	160
Primrose, Pinnace	30
Disdain	30
Ketch..................................	10
Superlative	100
Advantagia	100
Vollatilla	100
Gallerita	100

(bracket label: Galleys.)

(right brace label: Decayed and Unserviceable.)

	Total.....	14700
39 Ships, &c.	Or	15100

† *She was 900 Tons if she was the identical Ship that appears in preceding Lists; which, from her condition now, is highly probable.*

The aforesaid Commissioners recommend that the Navy should in future consist of the following Ships, and no more, viz.

1618

Classes of Ships, &c.	Number.	Tonnage of each.	Total Tonnage.
Ships Royal	1	1200	1200
	2	900	1800
	1	800	800
Great Ships..................	3	800	2400
	9	650	5850
	2	600	1200
Middling Ships...............	6	450	2700
Small Ships.................	2	350	700
Pinnaces	1	250	250
	2	140	280
	1	80	80
	30	....	17260

For which they assign these reasons among others, viz.

1st. —"This Navy will contain 3050 tons more than the Navy of Queen Elizabeth, when it was greatest and flourished most."

2d. —"As great a provision of long timber, planks and knees, will be required to supply these 30 Ships, as may conveniently be got in this time of great building and common devastations of woods in all places."

3d. —"These 30 Ships will require as many Mariners and Gunners as this kingdom can supply at all times, now traffick carrieth away so many and so far."

4th.—"The common building of great and warlike Ships by Merchants to reinforce the Navy, when need shall require, may well contain his Majesty's numbers and charge within these bounds."

It also appears by a report of the Commissioners appointed to enquire into the state of the Navy, &c. in 1624,* that the Navy then consisted of only 31 Ships and Vessels, of which the following is a List, viz.

1624

Prince	Rainbow
Bear	Red Lion
Mer Honour	Entrance
Ann	Convertine
Dieu Repulse	Bonadventure
Defiance	Garland
Assurance	Antelope
Wastspight	Mary Rose
Nonsuch	Speedwell
Triumph	Dreadnought
St. George	Adventure
St. Andrew	Desire
Swiftsure	Phœnix
Victory	Charles
Reformation	Seven Stars
Vantguard	

* *Pepys's Miscellanies, vol. 7. p. 203.*

As a further proof of the incorrectness of the generality of the statements mentioned page 49; as a corroborative proof of the accuracy of the reports respecting the Navy, in 1618 and 1624, as well as to shew what the Navy was just before His Majesty's death, I insert the following particular statement thereof, from the same authority as the aforesaid survey in 1618 is given.

A List of the Royal Navy, in 1624.

Names.	Burthen. Tons.	No of Pieces of Ordnance	Cannon Petro.	Demi-Cannon.	Culverines.	Demi-Culverines.	Sakers.	Minions.	Faulcons.	Port-pieces.	Fowlers.
Prince	1200	55	2	6	12	18	13	..	..	4	..
Bear	900	51	2	6	12	18	9	..	..	4	..
More Honour ...	800	44	2	6	12	12	8	..	..	4	..
Ann	800	44	2	5	12	13	8	..	..	4	..
Repulse*.......	700	40	2	2	14	12	4	..	..	2	..
Defiance*	700	40	2	2	14	12	4	..	2	..	..
Triumph*......	921	42	2	2	16	12	4	..	2	..	..
St. George*.....	880	42	2	2	16	12	4	..	2	..	..
St. Andrew*	880	42	2	2	16	12	4	..	2	..	..
Swiftsure*......	876	42	2	2	16	12	4	..	2	..	..
Victory*	870	42	2	2	16	12	4	..	2	..	..
Reformation*...	750	42	2	2	16	12	4	..	2	..	..
Warspight*.....	650	38	2	4	13	13	4	..	2	..	..
Vanguard*.....	651	40	2	..	14	12	4	..	2	..	..
Rainbow*......	650	40	2	..	14	12	4	..	2	..	4
Red Lion.......	650	38	2	..	14	12	4	..	2	..	4
Assurance	600	38	2	..	10	12	10	..	..	..	4
Nonsuch	600	38	2	..	12	12	6	..	2	..	4
Bonadventure ...	674	34	..	..	4	14	10	2	..	..	4

```
Garland........    680   32 .... 4 12 10 2 .... 4
Entrance .......   580   32 .... 4 12 10 2 .... 4
Convertine† ....   500   34 .. .. .. 18 10 2 .... 4
Dreadnought ...    450   32 .. .. .. 16 10 2 .... 4
Antelope .......   450   34 .. 4 14 10 2 ... 4
Adventure......    350   26 .. .. 12 6 4 :. .. 4
Mary Rose .....    388   26 .. ... 8 10 4 .... 4
Phœnix ........    250   20‡.. .. .. .. 12 4 2 .. 4
Crane..........    250   .. .. .. .. .. .. .. .. ..
Answer ........    250   .. .. .. .. .. .. .. .. ..
Moon..........     140   .. .. .. .. .. .. .. .. ..
Seven Stars .....  140   14 .. .. .. 2 6 6 .. .. ..
Charles ........   140   14§.. .. .. .. 2 6 4 .. ..
Desire..........   80    6 .. .. .. .. .. .. 2 4 ..
                  ─────
        Total.... 19400
                  ─────
```

In all 33 Ships, &c.

The Navy left by Queen Elizabeth consisted of
..... 42 Ships, &c...17055 Tons
That of King James, in 1624, of............
31 or 33 ..... about 19400

Decrease in Number
of Ships.......... 9 or 11
Increase in Tonnage .... about 19400

* *The Particulars of thr Ordnance do not correspond with the total.*
† *Spelt* Conventine *in the Archæologia.*
‡ *According to the particulars of the Ordnance, she carried 22 guns.*
§ *Only 12 specified in the particulars.*

MEMO.—*For a description of several of the sorts of the Ordnance in the foregoing List, see page 126.*

Charles 1 1625–1649

1633

"A List of the King's Ships, Anno 1633.*"

"Established by the Lords of the Council for the measuring His Majesty's Ships, Whitehall.*"	Length of the Keel.	Tons.	Highest Number of Men.	Guns.
"Great Ships.*"	Feet			
Prince Royal..........	115	1187	500	55
Mer Honour..........	112	828	400	40
An: Royal............	107	or 726 / 776	400	44
Triumph	110	792	350	44
St. George...........	110	783	300	44
St. Andrew	110	764	300	42
Dieu Repulse	108	876	300	40
Defiance	104	751	280	38
Vanguard	112	746	280	40
Swiftsure	106	731	300	44
Rainbow	112	742	270	40
Reformation	106	721	280	40
Victory	106	702	300	40
Warspight............	97	810	250	36
Charles	105	793	300	44
H. Mari..............	106	875	300	42
James...............	110	767	300	48
Unicorn.............	107	512	250	49
Leopard.............	103	698	250	36
Red Lion............	103	619	250	40
Nonsuch	88	610	250	38
Assurance	104	621	250	34
Convertine	96	567	250	34
Bonadventure	96	552	200	32
Garland.............	96	557	200	34
Dreadnought	92	539	200	30
Happy Entrance	96	528	200	30
St. Dennis	104	512	200	38
Antelope	92	321	180	38
Mary Rose	83	287	120	26
Adventure...........	88	512	120	24
Swallow..............	103	186 or 136	250	36
1st Whelp	62	186	70	14
2d Whelp	62	186	70	14
3d Ditto.............	62	186	70	14
4th Ditto	62	186	70	14
5th Ditto	62	186	70	14
6th Ditto	62	162	70	14
7th Ditto	62	186	70	14
8th Ditto	62	186	70	14
9th Ditto	62	186	70	14
10th Ditto	62	186	70	14
Providence	58	89	30	8
Expedition	58	89	30	8
Henrietta†	52	68	25	6
Madrid	52	68	25	6
Roebuck	58	80	30	8
Greyhound	58	80	30	8
Swan..Frigate	40	60	10	3
Nicodemus..Frigate ...	40	60	10	3
In all 50 Ships, &c.	23695 or 23595		9470	1430

* *The words between the inverted commas are precisely as they are inserted in vol. 5, p. 267, of Pepys's Miscellanies, from whence the whole of this List is taken, except the spelling of the names, which is here modernized.—It does not appear where the distinction of* Great Ships *was meant to stop.*

† *Was built for a Pinnace.*

MEMO.—*This being the earliest List of the Navy I have met with, wherein any part of the Ships principal dimensions are inserted, it was thought advisable to insert them here. And it may be observed, that this is the first List in which any nice regard appears to have been paid to the tonnage of the Ships. Previous to 1633, the tonnage of almost every Ship seems to have been rather estimated than calculated, being inserted in even numbers.*

1641

Abstract of the Royal Navy when the Rebellion broke out in 1641.

Rates or Classes.	Nº	Burthen.
		Tons.
1st.	5	5306
2d.	12	8771
3d.	8	4897
4th.	6	2206
5th.	2	600
6th.	9	631
Total......	42	22411

If this account is correct, and it has every appearance of being so, the Navy, owing to the circumstances of the times, must have fallen off in the latter part of the time that the King held the reins of government, as it consisted of 50 Ships and Vessels in 1633.* The only circumstance that creates any doubt in my mind on the subject is, the address of the House of Commons in the year 1641.

* *See the List of that date.*

Commonwealth 1649–1660

WE come now to a very busy period of our Naval History, when we had to encounter with the greatest maritime power in Europe, and when our force had been considerably reduced; Prince Rupert having quitted the kingdom in the year 1648, with 25 Ships under his command, none of which ever returned.
On the 1st March, 1652, the Navy consisted of the following Ships.

1652

"A List of all Ships, Frigates, and other Vessels belonging to the State's Navy, on 1st March, 1651.*"

Rates.	Names.	Length of the Keel.	Breadth.	Depth.	Tons.	Highest No of Men.	Guns.
		Feet	Ft. In.	Ft. In.			
1st.	Sovereign	127	46: 6	19: 4	1141	600	100
.	Resolution....	115	43: 0	18: 0	976	580	85
.	Triumph	110	36: 0	14: 6	586	300	60
2d.	George.......	110	36: 5	14:10	594	280	52
.	Andrew	110	36: 5	14: 8	587	280	52
.	James........	110	36:10	16: 2	654	280	52
.	Vanguard	112	36: 4	13:10	563	260	54
.	Rainbow	112	36: 3	13: 6	548	260	54
.	Victory	106	35: 0	15: 0	541	260	52
.	Paragon......	106	35: 9	15: 8	593	260	52
.	Unicorn......	107	35: 8	15: 1	575	260	50
.	Fairfax.......	116	34: 9	17: 4½	745	260	52
.	Speaker	106	34: 4	16: 4	691	260	52
.	Swiftsure	106	36: 0	14: 8	559	260	36

Rates.	Names.	Length of the Keel.	Breadth.	Depth.	Tons.	Highest No of Men.	Guns.
	New Frigate building....	...	.....	.....	...	..	
3d.	Garland......	96	32: 0	13:10	424	180	40
.	Entrance	96	32: 2	13: 1	403	180	40
.	Lion........	95	33: 0	15: 0	470	180	40
.	Leopard......	98	33: 0	12: 4	387	180	40
.	Bonadventure .	96	32: 5	13: 5	479	180	40
.	Worcester	112	32: 8	16: 4	661	180	46
.	Laurel	103	30: 1	15: 0	489	180	46
.	Antelope, Frigate†....	...	.....	.....	600	200	50
4th.	Tiger	99	29: 4	14: 8	442	150	32
.	Advice	100	31: 2	15: 7	516	150	34
.	Reserve	100	31: 1	15: 6½	513	150	34
.	Adventure	94	27: 9	13:10	385	150	32
.	Phoenix	96	28: 6	14: 3	414	150	32
.	Elizabeth.....	101½	29: 8	14:10	474	150	32
.	Centurion	104	31: 0	15: 6	531	150	34
.	Foresight	101½	30:10	15: 5	513	150	34
.	Pelican.......	100	30: 8	15: 4	500	150	34
.	Assurance	89	26:10	13: 6	342	150	32
.	Nonsuch	98	28: 4	14: 2	418	150	34
.	Portsmouth, Frigate.....	99	28: 4	14: 2	422	150	34
.	Dragon	96	28: 6	14: 3	414	150	32
.	President.....	100	29: 6	14: 9	462	150	34
.	Assistance	101½	30:10	15: 5	513	150	34
.	Providence ...	90	26: 0	13: 0	228	120	30
.	Expedition ...	90	26: 0	13: 0	228	120	30
.	Ruby	105½	31: 6	15: 9	556	150	40
.	Diamond.....	105½	31: 3	15: 7½	547	150	40
.	Sapphire	100	28:10	14: 5	442	140	..
.	Constant Warwick ...	85	26: 5	13: 2	315	140	32
.	Amity	...	.....	.....	...	140	..
.	Guinea, Frigate	...	.....	.....	...	140	..
.	John.........	...	.....	.....	...	120	..
.	Satisfaction ...	.	.....	.....	.	100	..
.	Success.......	.	.....	.....	.	150	..
.	Discovery	.	.....	.....	.	120	..
.	Gilliflower....	.	Not measured	.	120	..	
.	Marygold	.	.....	.....	.	100	..
.	Fox..........	.	.....	.....	.	80	..
.	Convertine ...	.	.....	.....	.	180	..
5th.	10th Whelp...	62	25: 0	12: 6	180	60	18
.	Mermaid.....	86	25: 1	12: 6	287	90	24
.	Pearl	86	25: 0	12: 6	285	90	24
.	Nightingale...	88	25: 4	12: 8	300	90	24
.	Primrose	86	25: 1	12: 6	287	90	24
.	Cygnet.......	...	.....	.....	...	80	..
.	Star	...	.....	.....	...	70	..
.	Little President	...	.....	.....	...	80	..

Abstract for 1652

Rates.	Names.	Length of the Keel.	Breadth.	Depth.	Tons.	Highest No of Men.	Guns.
.	Warwick, Frigate.....	...	.....	.....	...	90	..
.	May-flower, als. Fame‡..	...	.....	.....	...	60	..
.	Mary..Fly-boat.......	...	.....	.....	...	80	..
.	Paradox......	...	.....	.....	...	60	..
.	Roebuck	...	.....	.....	...	70	..
.	Hector.......	...	.....	.....	...	70	..
.	Truelove	...	.....	.....	...	30	..
.	Golden Sun...	...	.....	.....	...	60	..
.	Recovery.....	...	.....	.....	...	70	..
.	Concord	...	.....	.....	...	70	..
.	Bryer	...	.....	.....	...	60	..
.	Swan	...	.....	.....	...	80	..
6th.	Greyhound ...	60	20: 3	10: 0	120	80	18
.	Henrietta, Pinnace	52	15: 0	7: 6	51	25	7
.	Nicodemus ...	63	19: 0	9: 6	91	50	10
.	Drake.. ⎫	..	.....	.....	...	50	..
.	Merlin . ⎬ §..	..	.....	.....	...	50	..
.	Martin . ⎭	..	.....	.....	...	50	..
.	Scout	...	.....	.....	...	30	..
.	Samuel	...	.....	.....	...	30	..
.	Fly	...	.....	.....	...	30	..
.	Spy..........	...	.....	.....	...	30	..
.	Heart........	...	.....	.....	...	60	..
.	Weymouth ...	...	.....	.....	...	60	..
.	Minion	...	.....	.....	...	30	..
.	Hare, Ketch ..	...	.....	.....	...	30	..
.	Eagle	...	.....	.....	...	40	..
.	Dove	...	.....	.....	...	30	..
.	Elizabeth.....	...	.....	.....	...	50	..
.	Lilly	...	.....	.....	...	50	..
.	Peter of Waterford ..	...	.....	.....	...	...	..
.	Falcon	...	.....	.....	...	40	..
.	Mary, Frigate.	...	.....	.....	...	...	..
.	Galliot Hoy...	...	.....	.....	...	40	..
.	Lady, Ketch ..	...	.....	.....	...	24	..
Shallops to row with 20 Oars each	New building ...	...	.....	....	...	...	..
	New ditto	...	.....	....	...	...	..
Hulks.	Eagle, at Chatham ...	...	.....	.....	...	...	..
.	Fellowship, at Woolwich	...	.....	.....	...	...	..
.	New..buildg at Portsmth	...	.....	.....	...	...	..

* *1652 New Stile.—This List is taken from Pepys's Miscellanies, vol. 5, p. 595.*

† *Building at Woolwich.*

‡ *Supposed to mean* alias *Fame.*

§ *Building.*

Rates.	Guns.	Number.
1st.	100	1
	85	1
	60	1
2d.	54	2
	52	7
	50	1
	36	1
	Guns not known.	1
3d.	50	1
	46	2
	40	5
4th.	40	2
	34	9
	32	7
	30	2
	Guns not known.	11
5th.	24	4
	18	1
	Guns not known.	15
6th.	18	1
	10	1
	7	1
	Guns not known.	20
Shallops.........................		2
Hulks..........................		3
	Total....	102

Estimates for the maintenance and support of the Navy were first laid before Parliament in the time of the Commonwealth; and the Protector procured an annual grant of £400,000 for the expence of the Navy, which at his death, in 1658, consisted of almost double the number of Ships to what there were at the commencement of the Civil Wars, as will be seen by the following account.*

* *It may be proper to observe, in order to prevent mistake, that in the following Abstract, and in that of 1660, Sloops, and the small Vessels of inferior Classes, are included among the 6th rates, as the Sloops are in the Abstracts of 1688, 1697, and 1698; but that in after periods, Sloops, and the before-mentioned Vessels, are distinguished under the proper denominations.*

1658

Abstract of the Ships and Vessels belonging to the Proctector and the Commonwealth, on 20th November, 1658.

Rates or Classes.	Guns.	No of Ships.	Total Number of Guns.	Total Number of Men.
1st.	100	1		
	80	1	250	1600
	70	1		
2d.	66	1		
	64	4		
	56	1	694	3930
	54	2		
	52	4		
3d.	52	1		
	50	10	776	4010
	46	2		
	44	3		
4th.	44	1		
	40	4		
	38	3		
	36	19		
	34	6	1476	6630
	32	3		
	30	3		
	28	3		
5th.	34	1		
	30	2		
	28	1		
	26	5		
	25	1		
	24	4	873	4080
	22	13		
	20	9		
	18	1		
	16	1		
6th.	16	1		
	14	5		
	12	8		
	11	1		
	10	3	321	1660
	8	5		
	6	8		
	4	2		
	2	1		
Hulks......................		8	....	
Building, force not known		4	....	
Total......		157	4390	21910

Exclusive of the Guns and Men, for the four Ships building.

Charles II 1660–1685

1660

Navy at the Restoration.

Rates.	Number.	Burthen.
		Tons.
1st.	3	4139
2d.	12	10047
3d.	15	10086
4th.	146	21520
5th.	37	8663
6th.	41	3008
Total, exclusive of Hulks*	154	57463

to which I think we may with propriety add eight Hulks, as none are included in this Abstract,† and as there was that number both in 1658, and 1675. This would give a total of 162 Ships and Vessels;‡ and as there were 157, only two years before, including those building, it seems highly probable that the preceding statement is perfectly correct.— Wishing however, in all cases not absolutely certain, to produce every collateral proof in my power, it may be proper to state, that when War was declared against the Dutch in February, 1665§ the English Fleet at sea, and ready for sea, consisted of 114 sail, besides Fireships and Ketches, which could not have been the case had the whole Navy, only four years before, amounted to but 65 Ships and Vessels,‖ and there must have been some Ships building, or not equipped, exclusive of Hulks.—

Respecting Hulks, and the total tonnage of the Navy, see what follows the above Table.

† *Several there must of course have been.*

‡ *The tonnage of which must have amounted to 62250 tons, at least, and probably to 62594 tons, as stated in* Columna Rostrata, *p. 251; and which may therefore be considered an accurate account of the tonnage.*

§ *This was the second Dutch War.*

‖ *In October 1665, Lord Clarendon told the Parliament that the Naval and Military Stores were entirely exhausted.*

1675

On Thursday, 22d April, 1675, it was ordered by the House of Commons, "that Mr. Pepys do, on Saturday morning next, at ten of the clock, bring into the House a true state of the present condition of the Navy, and of the stores and provisions thereof.†" This was accordingly done on the day appointed: and the following is an abstract of the Navy, and the tonnage thereof, as stated by Mr. Pepys in the aforesaid account.

1675

Abstract of the Royal Navy on the 24th April, 1675.

Rates of Classes.	Guns.	Number.	Burthen.
			Tons.
1st.	102	1	1416
	100	5	6954
	98	1	1102
	96	1	1328

Rate	Guns	No.	Burthen
2d.	100	1	1004
	84	1	1038
	80	1	868
	78	1	1082
	75	1	906
	70	1	891
	68	2	1724
	56	1	866
3d.	74	1	994
	72	1	859
	70	2	2044
	68	2	1790
	66	2	1967
	64	3	2228
	60	7	5612
	58	3	2199
	42	1	734
4th.	60	1	666
	56	3	1852
	54	5	3163
	52	3	1652
	50	8	4479
	48	7	3744
	46	3	1438
	44	1	470
	42	2	651
	40	4	1652
5th.	40	2	615
	34	2	562
	32	2	599
	30	6	1740
	28	3	764
	24	1	180
6th.	20	1	141
	18	2	328
	16	1	182
	14	2	330
	8	1	90
	4	1	35
Sloops		13	554
Dogger..................		1	73
Fireships		3	584
Galley		1	260
Ketches		2	194
Smacks		5	57
Yachts‡		14	1064
Hoys		4	234
Hulks..................		8	4628
Total......		151	70587

* See Pepys's Naval Minutes, p. 268.—The names, dimensions &c. of these 9 Ships, are given in the Appendix (No. 6).

† See Pepys's Miscellanies, vol. 5, p. 185.

‡ This is the first time that Yachts appear in this Collection. Mr. Pepys mentions that "in the year 1660, the Dutch gave his Majesty a Yacht, called the Mary; until which time we had not heard of such a name in England."

When the Parliament were assembled in February 1677, the King acquainted them with the decayed condition of the Navy, and asked money for repairing it. The House of Commons, the same session, voted £586,000 for building 30 Ships,* and strictly appropriated the money to that service. Estimates were given in of the expence, but it was afterwards found that they fell short near £100,000.† The King, in October, 1675, had likewise desired supplies for building of Ships, and £300,000 was then voted for that service, under very particular restrictions.

1678

It is a little surprising that historians should have so very much mistaken Mr. Pepys, as to assert, from his authority, that the Navy, in August, 1678, consisted only of the following Ships and Vessels; viz.

Rates.	Number.
1st.	5
2d.	4
3d.	16
4th.	33
5th.	12
6th.	7
Fireships.	6
	83

and 30 capital Ships building;— whereas, the numbers of which the whole Navy consisted, differed considerably from this statement; for the 83 Ships therein described, were those that were actually in sea-service: and besides that there are always some Ships lying up, in want of repair, it is impossible the whole Navy could at that time have been in sea-service, at so short a notice as four months, the period mentioned by Mr. Pepys respecting the 83 Ships under consideration.

* See a particular account of these Ships after the Abstract of 1685.—— See also their names, dimensions, and establishments of men and guns, in Appendix (No. 6, and 28.)

† The Ships and their furniture cost £670,000.

1676

Abstract of the Royal Navy, in 1676.

Rates or Classes.	Guns.	No of Ships.	Burthen.	Total Number of Guns.	Total Number of Men.
1st.	100	4	10850	778	5925
	96	3			
	90	1			
2d.	84	1	8372	666	4320
	82	2			
	80	1			
	70	3			
	64	2			
3d.	74	1	16689	1298	7634
	72	1			
	70	5			
	66	1			
	64	2			
	62	4			
	60	6			

Rates or Classes.	Guns.	No of Ships.	Burthen.	Total Number of Guns.	Men.
4th.	54	9			
	50	1			
	48	16			
	46	4	20995	1890	9200
	44	2			
	42	6			
	32	1			
	30	1			
5th.	32	4			
	30	6	3236	364	1575
	28	2			
6th.	18	1			
	16	6	1103	118	565
	4	1			
Sloops	12	492	88	420	
Dogger..........	1	73	....		
Fireships	5	1049	38	205	
Galley	1	260	....		
Ketches	2	189	20	100	
Smacks..........	5	175	....		
Yachts	15	1163	90	316	
Hoys............	3	168	....		
Hulks...........	7	4190	....		
Total....	148	69004	5350	30260	

Exclusive of the Guns and Men for the Dogger, Smacks and Galley,

Some decayed Ships and Vessels may certainly have been broken up, or otherwise disposed of, between the date of this Abstract and August 1678, as it was a time of peace, and as money was sparingly expended on the Navy after 1674, as before observed; still, however, on comparing the Ships from the 1st to the 6th rates inclusive and Fireships, in this Abstract, with those in sea-pay in August 1678, and making allowance for the Ships lying up in want of repair at that period, and for the other classes of Vessels, and the Hulks, all which are included in the said Abstract, it may be reasonably supposed that the Navy in August 1678, consisted of nearly, if not quite, as many Ships as in 1676.

1677

ESTABLISHMENT OF GUNS AND MEN.

Proposed for the 30 *new Ships* to be built by act of Parliament, according to the opinion of the Navy Board, Officers of the Ordnance, and several Commanders, at a public meeting held at the Navy Office, humbly presented to His Majesty, in obedience to his command, the 16th May 1677.

Guns	Rates 1st.	2d.	3d.
	No		
Cannon	26	....	
Demi-Cannon.......................		26	26
Culverines...................	28	26	....

Guns	Rates 1st.	2d.	3d.
	No		
Twelve-pounders			26
Sakers, Upperdeck..............	28	26	....
Forecastle..............	4	....	4
Quarter-deck...........	12	10	10
Three-pounders	2	2	4
	100	90	70

Memo.—*It is supposed the Cannon were ....42 Pounders.*
Demi-Cannon . 32
Culverines 18

Men.	Rates 1st 100 Guns	2d 90	3d 70
	No		
8 to each Cannon	208	....	
6 ditto Demi-Cannon		156	156
5 ditto Culverin	140	130	....
4 ditto 12-pounder............................			104
3 ditto Saker..................	132	108	42
2 ditto 3-pounder..............	4	4	8
The remainder of the Complements to consist of..........	296	262	160
	780	660	470

The following is a particular account of the *Ordnance* required for the whole of the Royal Navy, on 1st January 1685, as appears by a List of the Navy, in the 11th vol. of Pepys's Miscellanies, p. 111, viz.

	Fortified. No		Drakes No
Cannon of 7	192	......	..
Demi-Cannon..............	994	......	66
24-Pounders	346	......	..
Culverines...................	993	......	211
12-Pounders	1004	......	..
Demi-Culverines...........	748	......	360
Do.......do.....Cutts......	250	......	..
8-Pounders	282	......	..
6-Pounders	382	......	..
Sakers	947	......	93
Saker Cutts.................	218	......	..
Minions....................	118	......	..
3-Pounders	324	......	..
Falcons	46	......	..
Falconets..................	4	......	..
Rabinets	3	......	..
Total....	6851	......	730

the whole of which are therein stated to have been in store, or on board the Ships except 40 twelve-pounders, and 15 Sakers, or Saker-cutts.*

* Both the List of the Navy, and the Abstract of the Ordnance inserted therein, are signed (at least the original ones were) by four persons.

At what particular period, after January 1685, several of the before-mentioned species of Ordnance were changed, or when their names in general were changed I do not know; but in the year 1716, as appears by the following general establishment of Guns for the Navy, all are described by the respective weights of their shot, and by them only; as has been the practice ever since, with perhaps the single exception of the Carronades which have been pretty much used in the Navy, of late years.

1685

Abstract of the Royal Navy at the demise of Charles II. on 6th February, 1685.

Rates or Classes.	Guns.	Number	Burthen.
			Tons.
1st.	100	5	12547
	96	4	
2d.	90	10	
	84 and 80	3	17364
	70 .. 60	2	
3d.	74 .. 70	31	38161
	66 to 60	8	
4th.	54 .. 44	32	22680
	42 .. 30	13	
5th.	34 .. 28	11	2977
6th.	18 .. 4	8	1041
Fireships		12	2288
Sloops		4	210
Yachts		19	1762
Small Vessels		10	301
Hulks		7	4227
Total		179	103558

James II 1685–1688

1688

Abstract of the Royal Navy on the 18th December 1688.

Rates or Classes.	Number.	Burthen in Tons.	Force.		Highest Value of Rigging and Sea-Stores for one Ship of each Class
			Men.	Guns.	
1st.	9	13041	6705	878	£5181
2d.	11	14905	7010	974	4296
3d.	39	37993	16545	2640	2976
4th.	41	22301	9480	1908	2195
5th.	2	562	260	60	1031
6th.	6	932	420	90	634
Bombs	3	445	120	34	634
Fireships	26	4983	905	218	1031
Ketches	3	243	115	24	391
Smacks	5	89	18	. . . .	
Yachts	14	1409	353	104	550
Hoys	6	480	22	. . . .	
Hulks	8	4509	50	. . . .	
Total	173	101892	42003	6930	. . . .

The number of Ships and Vessels at the commencement of this reign, was 179;* the decrease therefore is only six, notwithstanding the decayed state of the Navy at that time.

* See the List of 6th February 1685.

Gloria Britannica
or the
Boast of the British Seas.
A.D. 1689 The Royal Navy of England

No.		Where Built.	By Whome.	Year.	L	B	D	Dr.	Tuns.	MEN. Peace abroad and at home	War. home	abroad	GUNS. Abroad and Peace in both	home
	First Rates.													
9	Britania	Chatham	Sir P Pet	1682	146	47	19	24	1620	605	710	815	90	100
	St Andrew	Woolwich	Byland	1670	128	44.4	17.9	21.6	1338	510	620	730	86	96
	Charles	Deptford	John Shish	1667	128	42.3	18.3	21	1229	500	605	710	86	96
	Royal Charles	Portsm	Sir Ant Deane	1673	136	44.8	18.3	20.6	1531	560	670	780	90	100
	Royal James	Portsm	Sir A Deane	1675	132	45	18.4	20	1422	560	670	780	90	100
	London	Deptford	Shish	1670	129	44	19	20.6	1328	5.0	620	730	86	96
	St Michael	Portsm	J Tippets	1669	125	40.8	17.5	19.8	1101	430	520	600	80	90
	Prince	Chatham	Mr P Pet.	1670	131	44.4	19	21.6	1463	560	670	780	90	100
	Soveraign	Woolwich	Mr P Pet.	1637	131	48	19.2	23.6	1605	605	710	815	90	100
	Second Rates.								Tuns					
16	Albemarle	Harwich	Isaac Bets	1681	142	44	18.6	18	1462	500	580	660	82	90
	Coronation	Ports.	J Bets.	1685	137	45	18.6	20	1475	,,	,,	,,	,,	,,
	Dutchess	Deptf	J Shish	1679	137	45	18.3	19	1475	,,	,,	,,	,,	,,
	Duke	Woolw	Th Shish	1682	142.6	45.2	18.9	20	1546	,,	,,	,,	,,	,,
	Ossory	Ports.	Betts	1682	140	44.7	18.2	20	1300	,,	,,	,,	,,	,,
	French Ruby	Taken.		1666	112	38.2	16.6	18.6	868	350	435	570	72	80
	St George	Deptf	Burrel	1622	116	38	15	18	891	310	385	460	62	72
	Katherine	Woolw.	Pet	1664	124	41	17.3	20	1108	360	450	540	74	82
	Neptune	Deptf	J Shish	1683	124	41	17.3	20	1475	500	580	660	82	90
	Rainbow	Deptf	Bright	1617	114	38	15	17.6	868	270	335	410	54	64
	Sandwich	Harwich	Betts	1679	132	44.6	18.3	18	1395	500	580	660	82	90
	Triumph	Deptf	Burrel	1623	116	38	15.6	18	891	130	185	460	62	70
	Vanguard	Portsm.	Furzer	1678	126	45	18.2	18	1357	500	580	660	82	90
	Victory rebuilt	Chat.	Ph. Pett	1663	121	40	17	19	1029	350	440	530	72	82
	Unicorn	Woolw.	Boat	1633	120	37.6	15.1	17.4	823	270	335	410	54	64
	Windsor Castle	Woolw.	J Shish	1678	142	44	18.3	20	1462	500	580	660	82	90
	Third Rates.				L	B	D	Dr.	Tuns.	MEN.			Guns.	
38	Anne	Chatham	Ph Pett	1678	128	40	17	18	1089	300	380	460	62	70
	Berwick	Chat.	Ph Pett	1679	128	40	17	18	,,	,,	,,	,,	,,	,,
	Burford	Woolw	Th Shish	1679	137.8	40.3	17.3	18	1174	,,	,,	,,	,,	,,
	Breda	Harw.	Betts	1679	124	40	16	18	1050	,,	,,	,,	,,	,,
	Captain	Woolw.	Th Shish	1678	138	40	17.2	18	1164	,,	,,	,,	,,	,,
	Defiance	Chat	Ph. Pett	1675	117	38	16	17.6	881	270	345	420	60	70
	Dunkirk	Wool	Burrel	1651	112	34.4	14	17	662	210	270	340	52	60
	Dreadnought	Blackwall	Johnson	1653	116	34.6	14.2	16.6	732	215	280	355	54	62
	Edgar	Bristol	Baily	1668	124	39.8	16	18.4	994	370	290	445	62	72
	Eagle	Ports	Furzer	1679	120	40.9	17	18	1057	300	380	460	62	70
	Elizabeth	2 Blackw.	2 Johnson	,,	132	40.6	16.6	18.6	1151	,,	,,	,,	,,	,,
	Essex	1 Deptf.	1 Castle	,,	124	40.3	,,	18	1068	,,	,,	,,	,,	,,
	Expedition	Portsm	Furzer	1678	120	40.9	17.6	,,	1057	,,	,,	,,	:,	,,
	Exeter	Blackw.	Johnson	1679	123	40.4	16.9	,,	1070	,,	,,	,,	,,	,,
	Grafton	Wool	G Shish	,,	138	40.2	17.2	,,	1184	,,	,,	,,	,,	,,
	Hampton Court	Deptf	Shish	1678	131	40	17	18.6	1105	,,	,,	,,	,,	,,
	Harwich	Harwich	A Deane	1674	123.9	39	15.8	17.6	993	270	345	420	60	70
	Henrietta	Horslydown	Bright	1653	116	35.7	14.4	17	781	215	280	355	54	62
	Hope	Deptf	Castle	1678	124	40	16.9	18.6	1058	300	380	460	62	70
	Kent	Blackwall	Johnson	1679	,,	40.2	17	18	1064	,,	,,	,,	,,	,,
	Lenox	Deptf.	J Shish	1678	131	39.8	17	18	1096	,,	,,	,,	,,	,,
	Lyon	Chatham	Apsly	1640	108	35.4	15.6	17.6	717	210	270	340	52	60
	Mary	Woolw.	Pett.	1649	116	36.3	14.6	17	777	215	280	355	54	62
	Monk	Portsm.	J Tippets	1659	108	35	14	16	703	210	270	340	52	60
	Monmouth	Chatham	Ph Pett.	1666	118.9	37	15.6	18	856	255	320	400	58	66
	Montague rebuilt	,,	Pet	1654 1675	117	36.6	15	17.4	829	215	280	352	54	62
	Northumberland	Bristol	Pope	1679	130	40.2	17	18	1115	300	380	460	62	70
	Royal Oak	Deptf.	Shish.	1674	125	40.6	18.3	18.8	1107	310	390	470	62	70

Name	Place	Builder	Year	L	B	D	Dr						
Plymouth	Wapping	Taylor	1653	110	34.8	14.6	17	742	210	270	340	52	62
Pendenis	Chatham	Ph Pett	1679	128½	40	17	18	1093	300	380	460	62	70
Restoration	Harwich	Ts. Betts	1678	123½	39.8	17	18	1032	,,	,,	,,	,,	,,
Resolution	,,	A Deane	1667	120	37.2	15.6	17	885	270	345	420	60	70
Rupert	,,	,,	1665	119	37.2	15.6	,,	832	255	320	400	60	70
Stirling Castle	Deptf	T Shish	1679	131	36.3	17.3	18	1114	300	380	460	,,	,,
Suffolk	Blackw.	Johnson	1680	132	40	16.6	,,	1151	,,	,,	,,	,,	,,
Swiftsure	Ports.	A Deane	1673	123	40.6	15.6	17.6	978	270	345	420	60	70
					38.8								
Warspight	Blackw.	Johnson	1666	118	38.9	15.6	,,	742	,,	,,	,,	,,	,,
York	,,	,,	1680	115	35	14.2	17	734	300	380	460	62	70
Lyon rebuilt	Chatham	Taylor	1658										

Fourth Rates.

Name	Place	Builder	Year	L	B	D	Dr						
Adventure	Woolw	Pet	1646	92	27.9	12	14	392	120	160	190	38	48
Advice	,,	,,	1650	100	31	12.9	15	544	150	200	230	42	48
Antelope	,,	Cary	1653	101	,,	13	16	560	,,	,,	,,	,,	,,
Assistance	Deptf	Johnson	1650	102	32	,,	15.6	550	,,	,,	,,	,,	,,
Assurance	,,	Pet	1646	89	27	11	13.6	340	115	150	120	36	42
Bonaventure rebuilt	,,	,,	1663	102.9	30.8	124	15.6	514	150	200	250	42	40
Bristol	Ports.	T. Tippets	1653	104	31.1	18	15.8	584	,,	,,	,,	,,	,,
Centurion	Ratcliff	Pet	1650	104	31	13	16	531	150	200	230	42	48
Charles Gally	Woolw.	,,	1676	114	28.6	8.7	12	492	220	220	220	32	32
Constant Warwick	Ports.	J. Tippets	1646										
rebuilt			1666	90	28.2	12	12.8	379	115	150	180	36	42
Crown	Rotherith	Castle	1653	100	31.7	13	16	535	150	200	230	42	48
Deptford	Woolw.	Th Shish	1688										
St David	Woleston	Furzer	1666	107	34.9	14.8	16.8	685	185	240	280	46	54
Diamond	Deptf	Pet	1651	105	31.3	13	16	548	150	200	230	42	48
Dover	Shoram	Castle	1654	100	31.8	,,	,,	530	,,	,,	,,	,,	,,
Dragon	Chat.	Godard	1647	96	30	12	15	470	140	185	220	40	46
Falcon	Woolw.	Pet	1666	88	27.4	12	13	349	115	150	180	36	42
Foresight	Deptf	Shish	1650	102	31.1	12.9	14.6	522	150	200	230	42	48
Greenwich	Woolw.	Pet	1666	108	33.9	14.6	15	654	185	240	280	46	54
Hampshire	Deptf	Peter Pet	1653	101.9	29.9	13	14.5	479	140	105	220	40	46
Happy Return	Yarmouth	Edgar	1654	104	33.2	,,	17	609	185	240	280	46	54
James Gally	Blackw.	Deane	1676	,,	28.1	10.2	12	436	200	200	200	30	
Jersey	Mauldm	Sterlin	1654	102	32	13.1	15.6	556	150	200	230	42	48
Kingfisher	Woodbridge	Pet	1675	110	33.8	13	13	663	140	185	220	40	48
Leopard	Deptf	Shish	1658	109	33.9	15	17.3	645	185	240	280	46	54
Mary Rose	Woodbridge	Munday	1653	102	32	13	16	566	150	200	230	42	48
Mordant	Deptf	Castle	1681	110	31.1	15	12	663	,,	,,	,,	,,	,,
Mary Gally	Rotherhith	Deane	,,										
St Alban	Deptf	Hardy	1688										
Newcastle	Rotherh	Pet	1653	108	33.1	13.2	12	628	185	240	280	46	54
Nonsuch	Ports.	Deane	1668	88.1	27.8	11	13	368	115	150	180	36	42
Oxford	Bristol	Baily	1674	109	34	15.6	17.8	670	185	240	280	46	54
Phoenix	Portsm	Deane	1671	90	28.6	11.2	13	389	115	.150	180	36	42
Portland	Wapping	Taylor	1652	105	33	13	16	608	155	210	240	44	50
Portsmouth	Portsm	Eastward	1649	100	29.6	12.6	16	463	140	105	220	40	46
Princess	Forest Deane	Furzer	1660	104	33	14.3	16.6	602	185	240	280	46	54
Reserve	Woodbridge	Pet	1650	100	29.6	12.4	15	513	150	200	230	42	48
Ruby	Deptf	Pet. sen.	1651	105	31.6	13	16	539	,,	,,	,,	,,	,,
Swallow	Pitch House	Taylor	1653	101	32	15	15.6	549	,,	,,	,,	,,	,,
Sweepstakes	Yarmouth	Edgar	1666	97	28.8	11	13.8	376	115	150	180	36	42
Tyger	Deptf	Pet	1647										
rebuilt	,,	Shish	1681	99	29.4	12	14.8	453	120	160	190	38	44
Tyger	Prize Algier		1678	112	33	12.8	15	649	150	210	230	42	48
Woolwich	Woolw.	Pett	1675	112	35.9	15	16.4	761	185	240	280	46	54
Yarmouth	Yarm.	Edgar	1653	105	33	13.3	17	608	,,	,,	,,	,,	,,

Fifth Rates.

Name	Place	Builder	Year	L	B	D	Dr						
Dartmouth	Portsm	J Tippets	1655	80	25	10	12	266	90	115	135	28	32
Garland	Southamp	Furzer	1654	81	24.6	,,	11.6	260	85	110	130	,,	38
Guernsey	Waldwick.	Shish	,,	80	24	,,	12	245	,,	,,	,,	,,	30
Hunter	Dutch prize		1672	80	25	10.6	13.6	265	,,	,,	,,	,,	,,
Mermaid	Limehouse	Graves	1651	76	,,	10	12	286	90	115	135	,,	32
Norwich	Chatham	Pet	1655	80'6	24.6	10.6	,,	253	85	110	130	,,	30
Orange Tree	Algier.		1677	76	26.4	9	11	280	,,	,,	,,	,,	,,
Pearl	Ratcliff	Pet	1651	86	25	10	12	285	,,	,,	,,	28	,,
Richmond	Portsm	Tippets	1655	72	23.6	9.9	11.6	211	80	105	125	26	28
Rose	Yarmouth	Edgar	1674	75	24	10	12.6	229	,,	,,	,,	,,	,,

No.	Where Built.	By Whome.	Year.	L	B	D	Dr.	Tuns.	MEN. Peace abroad and at home	War. home	War. abroad	GUNS. Abroad and Peace in both	home
Saphire	Harwich	Deane	1675	86	27	11	13.2	333	90	115	139	28	32
Swan	Bought of Capt Young.		,,	74	25	10	11	246	,,	,,	,,	,,	,,
Success	Chatham	Taylor	1657	85	25.6	,,	12	294	,,	,,	,,	,,	,,
Sixth Rates.				L	B	D	Dr.						
Drake	Deptford	Peter Pett	1652	38	18	7.8	9	146	45	65	75	14	16
Fanfare	Harwich	Deane	1655	44	12	5.6	5.6	33	18	25	30	4	4
Francis	,,	,,	1666	66	20	9.2	8.8	140	45	65	75	14	16
Greyhound	,,	,,	1672	75	21.6	9	8.6	184	,,	,,	,,	,,	,,
Lark	Blackwall	,,	1675	74	22.6	9.2	9	199	50	70	85	16	18
Roebuck	Harwich	,,	1660	64	19.6	9.10	8.6	129	45	65	75	94	16
Soudadoes		T Shish.	1673	74	21.6	10	9.6	188	,,	,,	,,	,,	,,
Hulkes.				L	B	D	Dr.						
Alphin	Dutch prize		1673	120	33.6	12	19	716	4	4	4		
America	Bought		1678	111	27.6	14.5	15.8	446	28	20	20		
Arms of Horne	,,		1673	110	30.3	12	18	516	8	8	8		
Arms of Rotterdam	East India prize		,,	119	39.6	18.9	18.6	987	7	7	7		
Elias	Dutch prize		1653	90	27	10	12.8	350	2	2	2		
Slothony	,,		1665	112	36	17	18	772	7	7	7		
Stadthouse	,,		1667	90	30.4	11.6	15	440	4	4	4		
Fire Ships.				L	B	D	Dr.	Tuns.					
Anne & Christopher	bought		167½	76	25.5	10	11.6	261	40	40	45	8	
Castle	,,		167½	85	27	11	,,	329	,,	,,	,,	,,	
Eagle	Wapping	Taylor	1654	85.6	25.6	10	12	295	—	45	—	12	
Holmes	bought		1671	80	22.9	12.9	13.6	220	—	35	—	8	
John & Alexander	,,		1678	69	22	9.8	11	178	,,	,,	,,	,,	
Peace	,,		,,	64	20	10	10.8	145	24	30	24	6	8
Providence	,,		,,	66	22.4	9.9	10.6	175	,,	,,	,,	,,	,,
Sampson	,,		,,	78	24.1	10.8	12	240	40	40	45	8	12
Sarah	,,		,,	,,	,,	10.1	,,	,,	—	20	—	4	6
Spanish Merchant	,,		,,	79	26.9	10.6	11.6	250	—	36	—	6	8
Ivanhoe		R. Page	1665	52	19.1	8.6	7.6	100	20	20	25	6	
Young Sprag	bought of Sprag		1672	46	18	9	8.6	79	,,	,,	,,	6	
Yatchts.				L	B	D	Dr.	Tuns.					
Anne	Woolw.	Pett	1661	52	19	7	7	100	20	20	30	6	8
Bezan	Given by the Duchess		,,	34	14	7	3.6	35	—	4	—	4	
Charlotte	Woolw.	Pet	1677	61	21	9	8	142	20	20	30	6	8
Cleaveland	Portsm	Deane	1671	53	19	7.6	7.6	107	,,	,,	,,	,,	,,
Deale	Woolw	Pet.	1673	32	13	5.8	5.8	28	—	4	—	4	
Jimmy	Lambert.	Pett.	1662	31	12.6	3.6	3.6	25	,,	,,	,,	,,	,,
Isle of Wight	Portsm	Furzer	1673	,,	12.6	6	6	23	,,	,,	,,	,,	,,
Katherine	Chatham	Pet.	1674	56	21.4	8.6	7.9	135	20	20	30	6	8
Kitchin	Rotherhith	Castle	1670	52	19	8.6	8	103	,,	,,	,,	,,	,,
Mary	Chatham	Pett	1677	66.6	21	8.9	7.6	166	,,	,,	,,	,,	,,
Merlin	Ratcliff	T Shish	1665	53	19	6	7.4	109	,,	,,	,,	,,	,,
Monmouth	Rotherh.	Castle	,,	52	19.	8	7.3	103	,,	,,	,,	,,	,,
Navy	Portsm	Deane	1673	48	17	7.7	7.1	74	,,	,,	,,	,,	,,
Portsmouth	Woolw	Pet	1674	57	19	7.4	7	133	,,	,,	,,	,,	,,
Queenbro	,,	,,	1671	31.6	13.4	6.6	6	29	—	4	—	4	
Richmond	Bought		1672	45	16	9	7.6	64	20	20	30	6	4
Henrietta	Woolw.	T Shish	1679	64.6	21	8	4	106	,,	,,	,,	6	8
Tubbs.	Greenw	Ph Pett.	1682	62.4	21.2	10	8	142	,,	,,	,,	,,	,,
Ketches.				L	B	D	Dr.	Tuns.					
Deptford	Deptf.	T. Shish	1665	52	18	9.4	8.4	89	30	40	50	4	
Quaker	Bought.		1674	54	18.2	9	9.6	80	,,	,,	,,	10	
Hoyes.													
Harwich		Gressingham	1660	38	16	8	8	52		5			
Lighter	Portsm	Deane	1672	,,	18	7.6	7.6	65		3			
Marygold	,,	T Tippets	1653	32	14	7	7	33		3			
Smacks.													
Bridget	Deptf	Shish	1672	32	11.8	5.6	4.6	21		2			
Little London	Chatham	Pet	,,	26	11	5.8	4	46½		,,			
Royal Escape	Bought		1660	30.6	14	7.9	7	34		,,			

Sheerness	Chat.	Pet	1673	28	11	6	5.6	18	,,	
Shish	Deptf	T Shish	,,	38	11.4	4.6	4	24	,,	

Sloopes.

Boneta	Woolw	P. Pet	1673	61	13	5	4.6	57	10	4
Chatham	Chat.	Pet	,,	57	12	,,	4	50	,,	,,
Dove	Deptf	Shish	1672	40	10	4	,,	19	,,	,,
Emsworth		Smith	1667	,,	13	4.9	5	39	,,	,,
Experiment	Greenwich	Lawrence	1673	35	11.6	6.4	,,	24	,,	,,
Hound	Chat.	Pet	,,	57	13	5	4.6	50	,,	,,
Hunter	Portsm	Deane	,,	60.6	12	,,	,,	46	,,	,,
Invention	,,	,,	,,	44	11	,,	4	28	,,	,,
Prevention	,,	,,	1672	50	12	,,	4.6	40	,,	,,
Spy	Harwich	,,	1666	45	11	4.4	4	28	,,	,,
Whipster Brigantine	Deptf	Shish.	1672	58	14.6	5	4.6	64	,,	,,
Woolwich	Woolw	Pet	1673	61	13	,,	,,	57	,,	,,

Two Lyons
Golden Horse
Half Moon   } Prizes from Barbary.
Rose of Sally
Rose of Algier

Dumbarton   Argiles Prize.
Heldenbergh   Monmouths Ship.

Rates of Pay in 1689

	†no.	1. Rate.	no.	2. Rate.	no.	3. Rate.	no.	4. Rate.	no.	5. Rate.	no.	6. Rate.
Officers.												
Captain, daily		15s.		12s.		10s.		7s. 6d.		6s.		5s.
Lieutenant, daily.		3s.		3s.		2s. 6d.		2s. 6d.				
Master. Monthly.		7. 0.0		5. 6.0		4.13.8		4. 6.2		3.17.6		Cap. is Mast.
Mast Mate & Pilot.	6	3. 6.0	4	3. 0.0	3	2.16.2	2	2.7.10	2	2. 2.0	1	2. 2.0
Quarter-Master.	4	1.15.0	4	1.15.0	4	1.12.0	4	1.10.0	3	1. 8.0	2	1. 6.0
Quarter-Ma. Mate.	4	1.10.0	4	1.10.0	2	1. 8.0	2	1. 8.0	1	1. 6.0	1	1. 5.0
Boatswain.		4. 0.0		3.10.0		3. 0.0		2.10.0		2. 5.0		2. 0.0
Boatswains-Mate.	2	1.15.0	1	1.15.0	1	1.12.0	1	1.10.0	1	1. 8.0	1	1. 6.0
Yeomen of Sheets.	4	1.12.0	4	1.10.0	2	1. 8.0	2	1. 8.0				
Gunner.		4. 0.0		3.10.0		3. 0.0		2.10.0		2. 5.0		2. 0.0
Gunner's Mate.	2	1.15.0	2	1.15.0	1	1.12.0	1	1.10.0	1	1. 8.0	1	1. 6.0
Quarter Gunner.	4	1. 6.0	4	1. 6.0	4	1. 5.0	4	1. 5.0	1	1. 5.0	1	1. 5.0
Carpenter.		4. 0.0		3.10.0		3. 0.0		2.10.0		2. 5.0		2. 0.0
Carpenter's Mate.	2	2. 0.0	2	2. 0.0	1	1.16.0	1	1.14.0	1	1.12.0	1	1.10.0
Ordinary or Crew.*‡	9	1. 6.0	6	1. 6.0	4	1. 5.0	3	1. 5.0	1	1. 5.0	1	1. 5.0
Chysurgeon.		2.10.0		,,		,,		,,		,,		,,
Chysurg. Mate.		1.10.0		,,		,,		,,		,,		,,
Purser.		4. 0.0		3.10.0		3. 0.0		2.10.0		2.5.0		2 .0.0
Steward.		1. 5.0		1. 5.0		1 5.0		1. 3.4		1. 0.8		1. 0.0
Steward's Mate.		1. 0.8		,,		,,		,,				
Midshipmen.	8	2. 5.0	6	2. 0.0	4	1.17.6	3	1.13.9	2	1.10.0	1	1.10.0
Corporal.		1.15.0		1.12.0		1.10.0		1.10.0		1. 8.0		1. 5.0
Coxswain.		1.12.0		1.10.0		1. 8.0		1. 8.0		1. 6.0		
Trumpeter.		1.10.0		1. 8.0		1. 5.0		1. 5.0		1. 5.0		1. 4.0
Cook.		1. 5.0		,,		,,		,,		,,		1. 4.0
Armourer.		1. 5.0		,,		,,		,,				
Gunsmith.		1. 5.0		,,								

Yeomen of Powder
Cooks Mate
Coxswains Mate   } 1.4.0 in
Swabber.   each Rate.
Cooper
Able Seaman

Ordinary Seamen.
Shifter.   } 0.19.0
Barber.

Gromers at Sea   0.14.3
Boy   0. 9.6

* This list is taken from a small book called Gloria Britannica, *published by* Thomas *in 1689, and is not included in Derricks book.*
† *Number carried per ship.*
‡ *Carpenter's assistants.*

William and Mary II
1688–1702 (Mary died 1694)

Abstract of the Royal Navy at the close of the War of the English Succession in September 1697.

Rates or Classes.	Guns.	Number of Ships.	Number of Men to a Ship of each Class.
1st.	100	5	780
	94	1	750
2d.	96	1	
	94	1	700 to 600
	90	11	
3d.	80	15	
	70	23	
	68	1	490 .. 380
	66	3	
	64	1	
4th.	64	1	
	60	10	
	56	3	
	54	4	
	52	1	365 .. 180
	50	31	
	48	4	
	46	1	
	44	1	
5th.	44	4	
	42	1	
	40	1	
	36	2	
	34	4	220 to 105
	32	21	
	30	2	
	28	1	
	26	5	
	Guns not known	1	
6th.	24	18	
	18	3	
	16	2	
	14	1	110 and under
	12	2	
	10	3	
	Guns not known	11	
Bombs		19	65 to 18
Fireships		17	45 and 40
Ketches		2	10
Smacks		5	....
Yachts		18	40 to 2
Advice Boats*		5	50 and 40
Brigantines		9	35 .. 30
Tow Boats		2	....
Machine Vessels		14	10 and 4
Pinks		2	10

Storeships	5	....
Hoys	14	....
Hulks	11	....
Total....	**323**	

Many Ships and Vessels were disposed of, as usual, after the end of the War; and by the end of the ensuing year, the Navy was reduced to the following Ships.

Advice Boats, so called, officially, are said to have been employed, for the first time, in 1692, before the battle off Cape La Hogue, in order to gain intelligence of what was passing at Brest.

1698

Abstract of the Royal Navy on the 20th December 1698.

Rates or Classes.	Number.
First	6
Second	14
Third	45
Fourth	64
Fifth	34
Sixth	18
Bombs	13
Fireships	10
Ketches	2
Smacks	2
Yachts	13
Advice Boats	4
Brigantines	7
Tow-boats	2
Pink	1
Storeships	4
Hoys	16
Hulks	11
Total....	**266**

1702

Rates or Classes.	Number.	Burthen.
		Tons.
First	7	10955
Second	14	19447
Third	47	51988
Fourth	62	42940
Fifth	30	11469
Sixth	15	3611
Bombs	13	2105
Fireships	11	2956
Sloops	10	629
Ketches	2	132
Smacks	3	45
Brigantines	6	456
Advice Boats	4	339

Tow Boats....................	2	182
Pink........................	1	89
Storeships	3	911
Yachts	14	1371
Hoys	16	1177
Hulks......................	12	8218
Total....	272	159020

The Navy, at the King William's accession, consisted of

	Ships.	Tons.
	173	101892
At his death......272		159020
Increase.. 99		57128

which is an increase of more than half, both as to the number and the tonnage of the Ships.

Anne 1702–1714

QUEEN ANNE had no sooner mounted the throne, than she declared her opinion for carrying on the preparations for war, which her predecessor had begun: and in May following, war was accordingly declared, both against France and Spain.

1703

The Navy sustained a considerable loss by the great storm which happened in November, 1703*, in which the following Ships, &c. were totally lost, viz.—

2d Rate ..Vanguard..............In Chatham Harbour.
3d ....Resolution ....On the Coast of Sussex.
3d Rate ..Northumberland ....
　　　　　　Sterling Castle ...... On the Goodwin Sands.
　　　　　　Restoration.........
4th ....Mary..............
　　　　　　Reserve...............At Yarmouth.
　　　　　　Newcastle ....At Spithead.
　　　　　　York ....At Harwich.
Bomb.....Mortar ....On the Goodwin Sands.
Advice-boat, Eagle................On the Coast of Sussex.

and several other men-of-war were driven ashore, dismasted, and otherwise damaged.

The whole of the Ships named above, except the Vanguard, were in Commission; and the Queen immediately issued a proclamation, ordering, that all the widows and families of such officers and seamen as had perished by the storm in her Majesty's service, be entitled to her bounty in the same manner as if they had actually been killed in fight.†

This was one of the most tremendous storms ever known in the history of the world.—It began about the middle of November, and did not reach its

greatest height until the morning of the 27th.—The Edystone Light-house was blown down at this time.—See the Rev. Robert Winter's Sermon, on 27th November, 1798, in commemoration of this storm.
† *A fast was appointed in consequence of this storm.*

1706

Abstract of the Royal Navy on the 13th December 1706.

Rates or Classes.	Number.
First	7
Second...................	14
Third....................	47
Fourth	61
Fifth	35
Sixth	27
Sloops	8
Brigantines	3
Bombs	8
Fireships	8
Smacks	2
Advice Boat	1
Storeships	2
Yachts	16
Hoys	25
Hulks...................	13
Total....	277

1708 and 1711

Abstracts of the Royal Navy on the 25th November 1708, and 21st July 1711.

Rates or Classes.	Number on	
	25th Nov'. 1708.	21st July, 1711.
First	7	7
Second......................	13	13
Third.......................	47	46
Fourth	68	69
Fifth.......................	46	47
Sixth	27	44
Sloops	7	13
Brigantines	2	2
Bombs	7	7
Fireships	6	2
Smacks	2	2
Advice-boats.................	1	1
Storeships	4	3
Yachts	16	18
Hoys, Transports & Lighters	25	25
Hulks......................	13	14
Total....	291	313

1713

Abstract of the Royal Navy, on the 17th April, 1713.

Rates or Classes.	Number.
First	7
Second	13
Third	43
Fourth	70
Fifth	44
Sixth	30
Sloops	9
Bombs	6
Fireships	2
Storeships	3
Yachts	18
Hoys, Transports and Lighters . .	22
Hulks	11
Total. . . .	278

1714

Immediately after the end of the war, many of the small Ships and Vessels were disposed of; but the numbers of the larger classes remained nearly the same until her Majesty's death, which happened in August 1714, at which time the Navy stood as follows:

1714

Abstract of the Royal Navy, at the death of Queen Anne, on 1st August 1714.

Rates of Classes.	Guns.	Number.	Burthen.
			Tons.
1st.	100	7	11703
2d.	90	13	19323
3d.	80	16	47768
	70	26	
4th.	60	19	51379
	50	50	
Line.	131	130173	
5th.	40	24	19836
	30	18	
6th.	20	24	6435
	10	1	196
Sloops	7	869	
Bombs	4	597	
Fireship	1	263	
Storeship	1	546	
Yachts	15	1521	
Hoys, Transports & Lighters.	13	1009	
Hulks	8	5774	
Of 40 Guns and under. .	116	37046	
Total. . . .	247	167219	

By this it appears, that although there were 25 Ships less at her Majesty's decease, than at her accession, there was an increase of tonnage in the Navy, of 8199 Tons.

1716

ESTABLISHMENT OF GUNS.

By Order of the King in Council, 6th July 1716, as proposed for the Ships of each Class by the Flag Officers, Comptroller, and Surveyor of the Navy, in lieu of the former Establishment, which had been found inconvenient.

Classes of Ships.	Lower-deck.		Middle-deck.		Upper-deck.		Quarter-deck.		Forecastle.	
	No	Prs*	No	Prs	No	Prs	No	Prs	No	Prs
100 Guns	28	42	28	24	28	12	12	6	4	6
		or 32								
90	26	32	26	18	26	9	10	6	2	6
80	26	32	26	12	24	6	4	6	. . . .	
70	26	24	. . . .		26	12	14	6	4	6
60	24	24	. . . .		26	9	8	6	2	6
50	22	18	. . . .		22	9	4	6	2	6
40	20	12	. . . .		20	6	. . . .			
30	8	9	. . . .		20	6	2	4	. . . .	
20					20	6	. . . .			

N.B.—This Establishment continued in force until 25th April 1743, the Establishment of 1733 having been suspended until that time. The Establishment of 1743 superseded the above, so far as respected the Ships ordered to be built subsequent to 1st January 1740.—(See MEM°. *after the end of Table N° 31.)*

* weight of shot in pounds.

George I 1714–1727

1721

Abstract of the Royal Navy, on the 19th April 1721.

Rates or Classes.	Guns.	Number.
1st.	100	7
2d.	90	13
3d.	80	16
	70	24
4th.	60	18
	50	46
Line.	124	
5th.	40	24
	30	6
6th.	24	8
	20	19
Sloops		6
Bombs		3
Fireships		3
Storeship		1
Hospital Ship		1

Yachts 14
Hoys, Transports, & Lighters 13
Hulks 7

Of 40 Guns and under.... 105

Total...... 229

No money was voted for the building or repairs of Ships for the last six years of his Majesty's reign; but some Ships were of course both built and repaired in the said time.—The Navy, however, upon the whole, declined in this reign, in a small degree, and consisted, at the death of the King, of the following Ships and Vessels.

Abstract of the Royal Navy at the death of George I. on 11th June 1727.

Rates or Classes.	Guns.	Number.	Burthen.
			Tons.
1st.	100	7	12945
2d.	90	13	20125
3d.	80	16	21122
	70	24	26836
4th.	60	18	16925
	50	46	33829
Line...........		124	131782
5th.	40	24	13801
	30	3	1264
6th.	20	27	9760
Sloops		13	1390
Bombs		2	417
Fireships		3	1057
Storeship		1	546
Hospital Ship		1	532
Yachts		12	1378
Hoys, Transports & Lighters		14	1216
Hulks		9	7719
Of 40 guns and under..		109	39080
Total.........		233	170862

The decrease in point of number, therefore, in this reign, is 14 Ships and Vessels; but there was an increase, as to tonnage, of 3643 tons.

George II 1727–1760

1730

Abstract of the Royal Navy on the 1st December 1730.

Rates or Classes.	Guns.	Number.
1st.	100	7
2d.	90	13
3d.	80	16
	70	24
4th.	60	24
	50	40
Line..............		124
5th.	40	24
	30	1
6th.	22	1
	20	28
Sloops		13
Bombs		3
Fireships		3
Storeship		1
Yachts		12
Smacks		2
Hoys, Transports & Lighters		17
Hulks		9
Of 40 Guns and under....		114
Total......		238

For further Dimensions of Ships, see pages 148 and 149.

Men.	Rates 1st 100 Guns.	2d 90	3d 70
8 to each Cannon	208	...	...
6 ditto Demi-Cannon	...	156	156
5 ditto Culverin	140	130	...
4 ditto 12-pounder	...	...	104
3 ditto Saker	132	108	42
2 ditto 3-pounder	4	4	8
The remainder of the Complements to consist of }	296	262	160
	780	660	470

1742

Abstracts of the Royal Navy on the 1st January 1739, and 25th June 1742.

Rates or Classes.	Guns.	Number on 1st January, 1739.	25th June, 1742.
1st.	100	7	7
2d.	90	13	13
3d.	80	16	16
	70	24	25
4th.	60	30	30
	50	34	34
Line...........		124	125

Rates or Classes.	Guns.	Number on 1st January, 1739.	Number on 25th June, 1742.
5th.	44	....	
	40	22	24
6th.	24 & 20	28	33
	10	1	1
Sloops		15	19
Bombs		3	14
Fireships		3	11
Storeships		1	3
Hospital Ships			3
Snow			1
Pink			1
Yachts		11	11
Hoys, Lighters, and Transports		13	15
Hulks		7	10
Of 44 or 40 Guns, and under........		104	146
Total.........		228	271

In April 1743, the establishment of Ships Guns was altered, by order of the King and Council.

1743

ESTABLISHMENT OF GUNS.

By Order of the King in Council, 25th April 1743, for Ships ordered to be built subsequent to the 1st January 1740.

Classes of Ships.	Lower-deck. No	Lower-deck. Prs	Middle-deck. No	Middle-deck. Prs	Upper-deck. No	Upper-deck. Prs	Quarter-deck. No	Quarter-deck. Prs	Forecastle. No	Forecastle. Prs
100 Guns....	28	42	28	24	28	12	12	6	4	6
90	26	32	26	18	26	12	10	6	2	6
80	26	32	26	18	24	9	4	6	....	
64	26	32	....		26	18	10	9	2	9
58	24	24	....		24	12	8	6	2	6
50	22	24	....		22	12	4	6	2	6
44	20	18	....		20	9	4	6	....	
20					20	9	....			

N.B.—*This was the same Establishment as was settled by Order of the King in Council on January 1733, (but suspended until now) with an exception as to 50 Gunships, whose Establishment was then ordered as follows, viz.*

1744

Abstract of the Royal Navy, on the 31st December 1744.

Rates or Classes.	Guns.	Number.
1st.	100	6
2d.	90	13
3d.	80	17
	70 & 64	26
4th.	60 .. 58	31
	50	35
Line...............		128

5th.	44	30
6th.	24 & 20	40
	10	1
Sloops		33
Bombs		13
Fireships		3
Storeships		4
Hospital Ships		3
Yachts		11
Hoys, Lighters & Transports		17
Hulks & Receiving Ships		19
Of 44 Guns and under....		174
Total......		302

1745

In the year 1744 or 1745, a general complaint was made of the Ships in his Majesty's Navy, that their scantlings were not so large and strong as they should be; that they did not carry their guns a proper height above the water, (like those of other nations) that they were very crank, and heeled too much in blowing weather; and that they did not carry so great a weight of metal as the Ships of the enemy, whose batteries were said to be always open. In consequence of this, the Lords Commissioners of the Admiralty gave directions to the Flag Officers, the Surveyor of the Navy, and the Master Shipwrights of the dock-yards, to consult together,* and lay before them a scheme of dimensions and scantlings, and also a draught for a Ship of each class: and from these several draughts and schemes, their Lordships, in 1745, settled the dimensions for a Ship of each class.

* It appears by the report of the Flag Officers, that the establishment for building Ships, dated in 1719, had been for years discontinued.

1748

Abstracts of the Royal Navy on the 26th May and 26th Nov'. 1748.

Rates or Classes.	Guns.	Number on 26th May 1748.	Number on 26th Nov. 1748.
1st.	100	6	6
2d.	90	11	11
3d.	80	11	11
	74 & 66	7	10
	70 .. 64	30	31
4th.	60 .. 58	36	35
	50	39	34
Line.................		140	138
5th.	44 & 40	44	42
	30	....	1
6th.	30	....	2
	24 & 20	51	52
	10	1	1
Sloops		35	30
Bombs		10	10
Fireships		3	4

Storeships 2   2
Hospital Ships 5   3
Yachts 11 11
Hoys, Lighters, & Transports............. 22 26
Hulks 15 12

        Of 44 Guns and under.... 199 196

            Total...... 339 334

1749

Notwithstanding no money was voted by Parliament for building or repairing Ships, in any year of the preceding war, many Ships were built in the course of the war, and doubtless some were repaired.

Several old Ships and Vessels, and others not thought necessary to be retained in the service, were taken to pieces, sold, or otherwise disposed of, after the war; and on 1st January 1750, the Navy stood as follows.

1750

Abstract of the Royal Navy on the 1st January 1750.

Rates or Classes.	Guns.	Number.
1st.	100	4
2d.	90	10
3d.	80	5
	74	7
	66	4
	70 & 64	31
4th.	60	34
	50	31
Line...............		126
5th.	44 & 40	39
	30	1
6th.	24 & 20	39
	10	1
Sloops		32
Bombs		5
Storeship		1
Hospital Ship		1
Yachts		10
Hoys, Lighters & Transports		17
Hulks		10
Of 44 Guns and under....		156
Total....		282

A large sum was voted for building and repairing of Ships, for the year 1750; and every year, except one, throughout the peace, money was voted for the like services, greatly exceeding, on the whole, what had been granted in the last peace. A considerable number of Ships was therefore built and repaired in the course of the peace; and by the end of the year 1752, Six had been added to the number of those of the line of battle.

The following is an account of the numbers and tonnage of the Ships at the abovementioned period.

1753

Abstract of the Royal Navy on the 1st January 1753.

Rates or Classes.	Guns.	Number.	Burthen.
			Tons.
1st.	100	5	9602
2d.	90	13	21250
3d.	80	7	
	74	6	} 65277
	66	3	
	70 & 64	31	
4th.	60	34	} 69155
	50	33	
Line...............		132	165284
5th.	44 & 40	39	28813
6th.	30	1	
	24 & 20	37	19129
	10	1	
Sloops		34	8036
Bombs		4	1104
Storeship		1	678
Yachts		10	1195
Hoys, Lighters, & Transports		23	2037
Hulks		9	8648
Of 44 Guns, and under....		159	69640
Total......		291	234924

The number of Ships, of each respective class, continued nearly the same as in the foregoing account, until the year 1755, in which year hostilities commenced against France. In May 1756, a declaration of war took place, previous to which, considerable additions had been made to the Navy, as will appear by the following account.

1755, 1756

Abstracts of the Royal Navy on the 1st January 1755, and 1st January 1756.

Rates or Classes.	Guns.	Number on	
		1st Jany. 1755.	1st Jany. 1756.
1st.	100	5	5
2d.	90	13	13
3d.	80	7	7
	74	6	13
	66	3	3
	70 & 64	33	32
4th.	60 .. 58	34	36
	50	33	33
Line*...............		134	142

* See Mem⁰. at the foot of the list of October 1760, p. 139.

Rates or Classes.	Guns.	Number on	
		1st Jany. 1755.	1st Jany. 1756.
5th.	44	38	38
6th.	30	1	1
	24 & 20	38	44
	10	1	1
Sloops		36	42
Bombs		3	3
Fireships			2
Storeship		1	1
Hospital Ship			1
Yachts		11	11
Hoys, Lighters & Transports		24	25
Hulks............................		9	9
Of 44 Guns and under....		162	178
Total......		296	320

The Ships built by the establishment of 1745, were found to carry their guns well, and were stiff Ships, but they were formed too full in their after part: and in the war which took place in 1756, or a little before, some further improvements in the draughts were therefore adopted, and the dimensions of the Ships were also further increased.

1757

GUNS.

An Account of those carried on board the Ships of the several Classes, in the Year 1757 (particular Ships excepted).

Classes of Ships.	Lower-deck.		Middle-deck.		Upper-deck.		Quarter-deck.		Fore-castle.	
	No	Prs	No	Prs	No	Prs	No	Prs	No	Prs
100 Guns...............	28	42	28	24	28	12	12	6	4	6
90.................	26	32	26	18	26	12	10	6	2	6
	28	32	30	18	30	12	..	..	2	9
80.................	26	32	26	18	24	9	4	6	..	..
	26	32	26	12	24	6	4	6	..	..
74 Large Class	28	32	..	..	30	24	12	9	4	9
74 Common Class	28	32	..	..	28	18	14	9	4	9
70.................	28	32	..	..	28	18	12	9	2	9
64.................	26	24	..	..	26	12	10	6	2	6
	24	24	..	..	26	12	8	6	2	6
60.................	26	24	..	..	26	12	6	6	2	6
	24	24	..	..	26	9	8	6	2	6

Classes of Ships.	Lower-deck.		Upper-deck.		Quarter-deck.		Forecastle.	
	No	Prs	No	Prs	No	Prs	No	Prs
50 Guns.........	22	24	22	12	4	6	2	6
	22	18	22	9	4	6	2	6
	20	18	22	9	..	..	2	6
44	20	18	20	9	..	..	4	6
36	..	..	26	12	8	6	2	6
32	..	..	26	12	4	6	2	6
28	..	..	24	9	4	3	..	..
24	2	9	20	9	2	3	..	..
20	..	..	20	9	..	..	..	..
Sloops Ship-rigged 14	..	..	14	6	..	..	..	..
12	..	..	12	4	..	..	..	..
10	..	..	10	4	..	..	..	..
8	..	..	8	3	..	..	..	..

N.B.—The guns on board the Ships of foreign-built are not meant to be comprized in the above Account. The Sloops and small Classes of Ships carried Swivel-guns, (half-pounders).

1762

GUNS.

An Account of those carried on board the Ships of the several Classes, (particular Ships excepted) at the end of the War in 1762.

Classes of Ships.	Lower-deck.		Middle-deck.		Upper-deck.		Quarter-deck.		Fore-castle.	
	No	Prs	No	Prs	No	Prs	No	Prs	No	Prs
100 Guns............	28	42	28	24	28	12	12	6	4	6
	30	42	28	24	30	12	10	6	2	6
90.................	26	32	26	18	26	12	10	6	2	6
	28	32	30	18	30	12	..	..	2	9
80.................	26	32	26	18	24	9	4	6	..	..
74 Large Class	28	32	..	..	30	24	12	9	4	9
74 Common Class	28	32	..	..	28	18	14	9	4	9
70.................	28	32	..	..	28	18	12	9	2	9
64.................	26	24	..	..	26	18	10	9	2	9
60.................	24	24	..	..	26	12	8	6	2	6
	26	24	..	..	26	12	6	6	2	6

Classes of Ships.	Lower-deck.		Upper-deck.		Quarter-deck.		Forecastle.	
	No	Prs	No	Prs	No	Prs	No	Prs
50 Guns............	22	24	22	12	4	6	2	6
44.................	20	18	22	9	..	..	2	6
36.................	..	..	26	12	8	6	2	6
32.................	..	..	26	12	4	6	2	6
28.................	..	..	24	9	4	3	..	..
24.................	2	9	20	9	2	3	..	..
20.................	..	..	20	9	..	..	..	..
Sloops rigged as Ships								
14..	..	..	14	6	..	..	..	..
12..	..	..	12	4	..	..	..	..
10..	..	..	10	4	..	..	..	..
8..	..	..	8	3	..	..	..	..

N.B.—The guns on board the Ships of foreign-built are not meant to be comprized in the above Account. The Sloops and-small Classes of Ships carried Swivel-guns, (half-pounders).

1702 to 1713 and 1755 to 1757

SHIPS.

An account of the highest prices ℔ Ton paid for building *Ships* and *Sloops*, by Contract, in the following periods.

In Queen Anne's War (1702-13).		In 1755, 1756, and 1757.	
Rates or Classes.	Price ℔ Ton.	Rates or Classes.	Price ℔ Ton.
Gunships.		Gunships.	
90	£16 : 0 : 0	. . . .	. . . .
80	12 : 0 : 0	74	£17 : 2 : 6
70	10 : 15 : 0	70	16 : 5 : 0
64	9 : 10 : 0	. . . .	. . . .
60	10 : 6 : 6	60	15 : 15 : 0
50	9 : 3 : 0	. . . .	. . . .
42	7 : 15 : 0	44	12 : 12 : 0
40	8 : 7 : 6	36	12 : 12 : 0
32	8 : 0 : 0	32	10 : 10 : 0
26	6 : 5 : 0	28	10 : 10 : 0
24	7 : 10 : 0	20	8 : 14 : 6
Sloops	5 : 12 : 6	Sloops	8 : 5 : 0

George III 1760–1820

1760

Abstract of the Royal Navy at the Accession of King George III, on 25th October 1760.

Rates or Classes.	Guns.	Number.	Burthen.
			Tons.
1st.	100	5	9958
2d.	90	12	20907
	84	1	1918
3d.	80	7	11398
	74	28	45422
	70	11	15639
	68	1	1567
	66	3	4350
	64	24	31117
4th.	60	35	40553
Line		127	182829

MEMᵒ.—*Previous to this it will be observed, that 50 Gunships are included in the number of those of the Line; but from about the years 1755 to 1756, they seem not to have been considered as Line of Battle Ships.*

Rates or Classes.	Guns.	Number.	Burthen.
			Tons.
4th.	50	28	27348
5th.	44	25	18623
	38	2	1887
	36	5	3655
	32 & 30	22	15008

6th.	30 .. 28	25	14730
	24	22	10831
	22 & 20	14	6057
Frigates*	18	8	2498
	& under		
Sloops	16 to 8	47	10361
Bombs		14	4117
Fireships		8	2337
Busses		3	242
Storeships		2	1554
Hospital Ships		3	2791
Yachts		12	1518
Hoys, Lighters, & Transports		33	2761
Hulks		12	11957
Of 50 Guns and under		285	138275
Total		412	321104

* *Some Vessels of 18 guns and under, built about this period, were frequently denominated Frigates; but after a time, they were classed among the Sloops.*

1762

Abstract of the Royal Navy as it stood on the 3d November 1762.

Rates or Classes.	Guns.	Number.
1st.	100	5
2d.	90	15
	84	1
3d.	80	7
	74	37
	70	11
	68 & 66	3
	64	30
4th.	60	32
Line		141
4th.	50	24
5th.	44	21
	38	2
	36	4
	32	32
	30	1
	24	1
6th.	30	1
	28	22
	24	21
	20	13
Frigates*	18 & under	8
Sloops		49
Brig		1

* *See Note above*

Rates or Classes.	Guns.	Number.
Cutter	18 & under	1
Bombs		14
Fireships		11
Busses		3
Storeships		2
Hospital Ships		2
Yachts		12
Hoys, Lighters, & Transports		34
Hulks		12
Of 50 Guns and under....		291
Total....		432

From the year 1755 to 1762 inclusive, £200,000 was annually voted for the building and repairing of Ships; whereas in the preceding war, no money was ever voted for those services.

Twenty-six sail of the line, and Eighty-two smaller Ships and Vessels, including Hoys, Lighters, and Transports, were built in Merchants yards in the course of the war, which ended in 1762, or were building in those yards at the conclusion of the war: and Twenty-four sail of the line, and Twelve smaller Ships, were launched in the King's yards, between the declaration of war in 1756, and the proclamation peace in 1763.

On 3d November 1762, the following Ships were building, namely,

1762

Guns.	In the	
	King's Yards.	Merchnts Yards.
Of 100	1	....
90	3	....
74	7	5
70	1	....
64	2	5
Line....	14	10
50	1	....
32	1	2
28	1	2
Sloops 14	....	2
Of 50 Guns and under......	3	6
Total....	17	16

1764, 1767, and 1771

Abstracts of the Royal Navy on the 24th October 1764; 25th March 1767; and 1st January 1771.

Rates or Classes.	Guns.	24th Octr. 1764.	25th Mar. 1767.	1st Jany. 1771.
1st.	100	5	4	3
2d.	90	12	13	14
	84	1	1	1
3d.	80	5	5	3
	74	43	47	50
	70	10	10	9
	66	2	2	2
	64	29	29	32
4th.	60	29	22	20
Line..............		136	133	134
4th.	50	22	19	10
5th.	44	9	5	5
	38 & 36	4	4	4
	32	33	33	30
	24	1	1	1
6th.	30 & 28	22	19	18
	24 to 20	26	24	19
Sloops	18 to 8	43	43	37
Sloops on Survey		2	2	5
Brig		..	..	1
Cutters		38	34	30
Bombs		7	7	7
Fireships		2	2	1
Schooners		6	7	10
Storeships		2	3	1
Hospital Ships		1	1	....
Yachts		12	12	12
Hoys, Lighters, & Transports		34	33	27
Hulks		11	10	8
Of 50 Guns and under....		275	259	226
Total....		411	392	360

1775

Abstract of the Royal Navy on the 1st January 1775.

Rates or Classes.	Guns.	Number.
1st.	100	4
2d.	90	16
	84	1
3d.	80	3
	74	57
	70	7
	64	32
4th.	60	11
Line..................		131
4th.	50	12
5th.	44	4
	36	3
	32	35
6th.	28	24
	24	7
	22 & 20	13
Sloops	18 to 12	22
	10 & 8	16
Sloops on Survey		6

Cutters.................................	10
Bombs..................................	2
Fireship................................	1
Schooners	7
Storeship	1
Yachts..................................	13
Hoys, Lighters, & Transports	25
Hulks..................................	8
Of 50 Guns and under....	209
Total....	340

The circumstances of the war with America rendered it necessary that a great number of Frigates, Sloops, and other small Vessels, should be employed. The Navy was therefore augmented very fast, from about the end of the year 1775, with regard to Ships and Vessels of those descriptions. The following statement will shew its progressive increase up to the breaking out of the war with France, in June 1778.

1777 and 1778

Abstracts of the Royal Navy on the 4th June 1977, and 24th June 1778.

Rates or Classes.	Guns.	Number on	
		4th June 1777.	24th June 1778.
1st.	100	4	4
2d.	90	15	16
	84	1	1
3d.	80	3	3
	74	55	59
	70	4	3
	64	35	37
4th.	60	8	8
Line................		125	131
4th.	50	17	21
5th.	44	10	13
	36	2	2
	32	31	29
	28	......	4
6th.	28	28	35
	26	1	1
	24 to 20	30	34
Sloops	18 to 14	42	51
	12 .. 8	16	19
Sloops on survey		5	3
Armed Ships..........................		3	2
Brigs..............................			3
Cutters.............................		15	24
Bombs		4	4
Fireships		1	3
Schooners		13	10
Storeships		4	11

Hospital Ships	3	3
Tender................................		1
Yachts...............................	12	12
Hoy, Lighters & Transports..............	24	24
Hulks................................	10	10
Of 50 Guns and under..	271	319
Total....	396	450

1780 and 1782

Abstracts of the Royal Navy on the 1st January 1780, and 1st January 1782.

Rates or Classes.	Guns.	Number on	
		1st Jany. 1780.	1st Jany. 1782.
1st.	100	4	4
2d.	98 & 90	17	18
	84	1	1
3d.	80	3	4
	76	1	1
	74	64	73
	70	2	3
	68	....	2
	64	42	45
4th.	62	....	1
	60	9	9
Line................		143	161
4th.	52	1	1
	50	19	22
5th.	44	15	20
	40	....	2
	38	3	6
	36	6	16
	32	42	54
	30	1	1
	22	....	1
6th.	28	34	29
	26	1	2
	24	16	13
	22 & 20	14	15
Sloop	20	....	1
Sloops	18 to 14	51	71
	12 .. 8	20	20
Sloops	Guns not known	......	3
Sloops on Survey		3	3
Xebeck		1	....
Brigs................................		3	11
Armed Ships..........................		2	4
Transports			6
Armed Galleys		5	8
Storeships............................			9
Storeships (*not included above*)..............		6	4
Cutters...............................		20	30

Rates or Classes.	Guns.	Number, on	
		1st Jany. 1780.	1st Jany. 1782.
Bombs	Guns not known	4	4
Fireships		18	17
Schooners		11	11
Hospital Ships		3	5
Prison Ships		1	1
Tenders		1	1
Yachts		12	11
Hoys, Lighters & Transports		23	27
Hulks		11	10
Of 52 Guns and under....		347	439
Total......		490	600

1783

It is scarcely necessary to mention that before the conclusion of the war, the Navy had been advanced to a much higher pitch than it had ever before reached. At the signing of the preliminaries of peace, it consisted of the following Ships and Vessels, exclusive of those not then registered, the number and classes of which are specified hereafter.

1783

Abstract of the Royal Navy as it stood on the 20th January 1783.

Rates or Classes.	Guns.	Number.
1st.	100	5
2d.	98 & 90	19
	84	1
3d.	80	4
	76	1
	74	81
	70	4
	68	2
	64	49
	60	1
4th.	60	7
Line...............		174
4th.	56	2
	52	1
	50	20
5th	44	28
	40	2
	38	7
	36	17
	34	1
	32	59
	30	1
	22	1

	Guns.	Number.
6th.	28	33
	26	1
	24	11
	22	2
	20	12
Sloops	18 to 14	72
	12 .. 8	13
Sloops on Survey		2
Brigs....................................		8
Armed Ships & Vessels		4
Transports		7
Galleys		6
Storeships...........................		12
Storeships (not included above)		3
Cutters...............................		28
Bombs		4
Fireships		17
Schooners		6
Lugger...............................		1
Hospital Ships		5
Prison Ship		1
Tender...............................		1
Yachts		11
Hoys, Lighters, and Transports		34
Hulks.................................		10
Of 56 Guns and under....		443
Total......		617

The following Ships were building on the day the preliminaries of peace were signed.

1783

Guns.	In the	
	King's Yards.	Merchts Yards.
Of 100	3	....
98	5	....
74	5	24*
64		5
Line....	13	29
50	3	....
44		13
36		6
32	1	13
28		9
24		1
Sloops of 16.........................		6
Brigs..................................		2
Fireships		4
Of 50 Guns and under......	4	54
Total....	17	83

* One of which was launched the next day, (21st January), being the last of the three 74 Gun ships presented by the East India Company.

APPENDIX 3

1786

Abstract of the Royal Navy, on the 1st January 1786.

Rates or Classes.	Guns.	Number.
1st.	100	5
2d.	98 & 90	20
	84	1
3d.	80	5
	76	1
	74	70
	68	1
	64	43
4th.	60	3
Line................		149
4th.	52	1
	50	16
5th.	44	25
	40	1
	38	7
	36	15
	32	48
6th.	28	28
	24	7
	22 & 20	8
Sloops rigged as Ships.....................		27
Brigs......................		15
Nature of their rigging unknown...........		2
On survey.............................		3
Brigs..........................		6
Armed Transport..........................		1
Storeship..........................		1
Galleys............................		6
Cutters..........................		27
Bombs..........................		2
Fireships..........................		9
Schooners..........................		4
Yachts..........................		11
Hoys, Lighters & Transports...............		32
Receiving Ships..........................		11
Hulks..........................		9
Of 52 Guns and under....		322
Total......		471

From the beginning of the year 1786, to that of the year 1789, no material interruption to the building and repairing of Ships took place.—Great progress therefore continued to be made therein, particularly with regard to Ships of the Line, to which preference had been mostly given throughout the peace, as the welfare of the country required, in bringing Ships forward in the King's Yards. In the course of the beforementioned period, however, sundry old Ships were disposed of; which left the number and tonnage of the Ships and Vessels of the respective classes, as follows.

1789

Abstract of the Royal Navy on the 1st January 1789.

Rates or Classes.	Guns.	Number.	Burthen.
			Tons.
1st.	100	6	13325
2d.	98 & 90	21	40261
	84	1	1918
3d.	80	4	7847
	76	1	120878
	74	72	
	68	1	1934
	64	40	55414
4th.	60	2	2489
Line..................		148	244066
4th.	52	1	17783
	50	16	
5th.	44	23	20597
	38	7	6691
	36	15	13542
	32	47	33120
6th.	28	28	16697
	24	7	3681
	22 & 20	7	3068
	10	1	512
Sloops...........................		42	12870
Brigs...........................		6	1225
Bombs...........................		2	609
Fireships...........................		9	3821
Storeships...........................		2	1772
Armed Vessel...........................		1	220
Tender....................		1	175
Cutters...........................		23	3923
Slop-Ship........................		1	300
Yachts........................		11	1435
Hoys, Lighters, & Transports........		33	3158
Receiving Ships*...................		12	14131
Hulks...........................		9	10271
Of 52 Guns, and under....		304	169601
Total......		452	413667

Old Ships were selected in July 1783, and afterwards fitted, for the reception of Ships Companies and Stores during the time the Ships are in dock refitting. Previous to that period serviceable Ships, not in good condition, were made use of for the purpose, which did them considerable injury.

1787

It will be proper here to mention some circumstances, which in the order of time might have been noticed before. In December 1787, it was directed, that in future, Ships lying up in good condition should have the works of their magazines and store-rooms completed, that by means of such advanced state of preparation for service at sea, they might be made fit to be commissioned at a short notice; it being thought, that from the practice which had been some time adopted, of making use of Airing Stoves, the said works might be done to the Ships, without injuring their frames. And in the preceding month, four Ships were ordered in future to be kept completely fitted for the reception of new-raised men; and one Hospital Ship; in order that the Artificers of the yards might, at the commencement of an armament, be entirely employed in bringing Ships forward for sea-service.

The good effects of using Copper Bolts under the load draught of water, having been satisfactorily proved, in Ships of 44 Guns and under; and it having been found that there was no possibility of guarding the iron bolts against the effects of the copper-sheathing,* it was ordered in November 1783, that in future Ships of all classes should be copper-fastened under the load draught of water.

It has been mentioned, that, before the beginning of the year 1789, great progress had been made in bringing Ships forward into good condition: and as the Navy had arrived at a much higher state of perfection in that respect by 1st January 1790, than it had ever attained before; and as an extensive armament took place a few months afterwards,† I will describe the state and condition of the Navy as it stood at that time.

The Sandwich of 90 Guns was the first 3 decked ship coppered in December 1779 and very few Ships of the Line were coppered until after that.

* In the course of the War which ended in 1783, Ships of every class were coppered.
† A war with Spain was expected.

An Estimate of the *Expence* of building a Ship of each Class in the King's yards (including Coppering and Copper Bolting), and providing them with Masts, Yards, Rigging, Sails, Anchors, Cables, and all other Boatswain's and Carpenter's Stores, to an Eight Months Proportion, according to the Prices paid for Timber, Hemp, and other Naval Stores, in August 1789.

Ships of	Tons.	Rate ℔ Ton. Hull, including Coppering and Copper Bolting.	Rate ℔ Ton. Rigging and Stores.	Amount of the Hull.	Masts and Yards.	Rigging.	Sails.	Anchors.	Cables.	Boatswains.	Carpenters.	Hull, Masts, and Yards.	Rigging, Sails, Anchors, Cables, and all other Boatswains and Carpenters Stores.	General Total.
		£. s. d.	£. s. d.	£.	£.	£.	£.	£.	£.	£.	£.	£.	£.	£.
100 Guns.	2220	24 : 10 : 0	4 : 19 : 0	54390	2220	2790	1220	1180	1880	1320	2600	56610	10990	67600
98.	1920	23 : 10 : 0	5 : 5 : 0	45120	1920	2620	1140	970	1690	1270	2390	47040	10080	57120
80 new construction	2020	20 : 10 : 0	4 : 16 : 0	41410	2020	2700	1200	960	1500	1150	2180	43430	9690	53120
74.	1660	20 : 4 : 0	5 : 4 : 0	33530	1660	2550	1170	820	1300	1100	1690	35190	8630	43820
64.	1390	19 : 10 : 0	5 : 7 : 0	27100	1390	2120	980	630	1150	1030	1520	28490	7430	35920
50.	1050	18 : 0 : 0	5 : 10 : 0	18900	1050	1490	810	480	850	820	1320	19950	5770	25720
44.	890	17 : 5 : 0	5 : 16 : 0	15350	890	1310	710	410	770	650	1310	16240	5160	21400
38.	960	15 : 5 : 0	5 : 9 : 0	14640	960	1350	750	410	770	660	1290	15600	5230	20830
36 new construction	900	14 : 17 : 0	5 : 7 : 0	13360	900	1220	730	350	730	600	1180	14260	4810	19070
32.	700	14 : 13 : 0	6 : 6 : 0	10250	420	1140	680	280	660	560	1090	10670	4410	15080
28.	600	13 : 10 : 0	6 : 12 : 0	8100	360	970	630	260	590	520	990	8460	3960	12420
24.	530	13 : 0 : 0	6 : 6 : 0	6890	320	800	530	240	490	440	840	7210	3340	10550
20.	440	12 : 18 : 0	7 : 4 : 0	5670	260	740	520	200	470	440	800	5930	3170	9100
Sloop of	300	12 : 3 : 0	8 : 3 : 0	3640	180	520	380	130	350	340	720	3820	2440	6260

N.B. Expences of this nature are subject to great fluctuations. Since these Estimates were formed, the permanent price of timber has been much advanced; and the prices of many other articles are at present much higher than they were.

1790

State and Condition of the Royal Navy on 1st January 1790.

Rates or Classes.	Guns.	In good condition, in Ordinary.	At Sea, or in Commission for Sea-service.	In want of Repair.	Not surveyed.	Building or ordered to be built.	Repairing.	Total.
1st.	110	..	..	..	..	1	..	1
	100	3	..	..	..	1*	1	5
2d.	98 & 90	12	2	2	..	4†	1	21
	84	..	..	1	..	..	..	1
3d.	80	..	..	1	..	2	1	4
	76	1	..	..	..	..	..	1
	74	37	12	13	..	5‡	4	71
	68 & 64	20	3	18	..	..	..	41
4th.	60	..	..	1	..	..	..	1
Line...........		73	17	36	..	13	7	146
4th.	52	..	1	..	..	..	..	1
	50	1	5	8	..	1	1	16
5th.	44	14	6	2	1	..	..	23
	38	3	..	2	..	..	2	7
	36	5	2	7	..	..	1	15
	32	12	12	19	..	..	4	47
6th.	28	11	10	7	..	..	..	28
	24	1	5	1	..	..	..	7
	22 & 20	2	2	3	..	..	..	7
	10	..	1	..	..	..	..	1
Of 52 Guns and under to 6th Rates inclusive§ ..		49	44	49	1	1	8	152

Sloops rigged as Ships........................... 30

Brigs 13

Brigs.. 6

Surveying Vessel 1

Bombs... 2

Fireships 9

Storeships 2

Armed Vessel 1

Tender 1

Tenders 4

Vessels rigged as Sloops 2

Cutters... 22

Slop-Ship 1

Yachts 11

Hoys, Lighters, and Transports 53

Receiving Ships 13

Hulks... 9

Total of 52 Guns and under 332

General Total 478

* This Ship was finished, but not launched.

† One of these was finished, but not launched.

‡ One of these was finished, but not launched.

§ It is not thought necessary to describe the condition of the lower classes.

1791

Guns.	Lying up.	At Sea, or in Commission for Sea-service.	Total.
Of 100..........	4	1	5
98 & 90......	9	5	14
80..........	1	....	1
74..........	27	25	52
64..........	19	4	23
Total....	60	35	95

1791

By the end of February, the number of Ships of the line stated to be in good condition, including, as above, those at sea or in commission for sea-service, amounted to 98. This number was never exceeded, and most likely never will be; indeed eight of the said 98 Ships were found in May following to be in want of what is denominated in official language, a small, or very small repair, and were therefore struck off the list of Ships in good condition; and the number of Ships in that state continued to decrease from that time, as will be shewn further on, very many of those which had been built or repaired eight or ten years, being found to want repair faster than others were brought forward.* It also appeared on a thorough and complete investigation at this time, and from the experience of several years of peace, that such must ever be expected to be the case.

* This had appeared in upwards of thirty instances previous to the end of May 1791.

1792

State and Condition of the Navy on the 1st December 1792.

Rates or Classes.	Guns.	In good Condition, in Ordinary.	At Sea, or in Commission for Sea-service.	In want of Repair.	Not surveyed.	Building or ordered to be built.	Repairing.	Total.
1st.	110	..	..	..	..	2	..	2
	100	5	..	..	..	..	..	5
2d.	98 & 90	11	2	2	..	5	1	21
3d.	80	1	..	..	..	2*	..	3
	76	..	..	1	..	..	..	1
	74	30	9	21	..	3†	6	69
	64	16	1	22	..	..	..	39
4th.	60	..	..	1	..	..	..	1
Line...........		63	12	47	..	12	7	141

* One of which was finished, but not launched.

† One of which was finished, but not launched.

N.B.—Both these Ships were launched in 1793.

Rates or Classes.	Guns.	In good Condition, in Ordinary.	At Sea, or in Commission for Sea-service.	In want of Repair.	Not surveyed.	Building or ordered to be built.	Repairing.	Total.
4th.	52	..	..	I	..	..	..	I
	50	2	5	7	..	3	2	19
5th.	44	8	I	11	..	..	I	21
	40	I	..	..	..	..	..	I
	38	3	I	2	..	..	I	7
	36	7	2	3	..	..	2	14
	32	14	10	15	I	3	7	50
6th.	28	3	7	15	..	..	3	28
	24	..	3	2	..	..	I	6
	22 & 20	I	I	5	..	..	..	7
	12	..	I	..	..	..	..	I
Of 52 Guns, and under to 6th Rates inclusive...		39	31	61	I	6	17	155

Sloops rigged as Ships ... 30
              Brigs ... 11
Brigs ... 6
Surveying Vessel ... 1
Bombs ... 2
Fireships* ... 9
Storeships ... 2
Armed Vessel ... 1
              Tender ... 1
Tenders ... 4
Vessels rigged as Sloops ... 2
Cutters ... 19
Armed Schooners ... 3
Hospital Ship ... 1
Yachts ... 11
Hoys, Lighters, & Transports ... 50
Receiving Ships ... 16
Hulks ... 10

Total of 52 Guns, and under.... 334

General Total.... 475

* *Two of which were employed as Sloops.*

1792

GUNS.

An Account of those carried on board the Ships of the several Classes (particular Ships excepted) on the 1st October 1792.

Classes of Ships.	Lower-deck.		Middle-deck.		Upper-deck.		Quarter-deck.		Forecastle	
	No	Prs	No	Prs	No	Prs	No	Prs	No	Prs
110 Guns	30	32	30	24	32	18	14	12	4	..
100	28	42	28	24	28	12	12	12	4	..
	30	32	28	24	30	18	10	12	2	..
	30	42	28	24	30	12	10	12	2	..
	28	42	28	24	30	12	10	12	4	..

Classes of Ships.	Lower-deck.		Middle-deck.		Upper-deck.		Quarter-deck.		Forecastle	
	No	Prs	No	Prs	No	Prs	No	Prs	No	Prs
98	28	32	30	18	30	12	8	12	2	..
	28	32	28	18	30	12	8	12	4	..
	28	32	30	18	30	18	8	12	2	..
90	26	32	26	18	26	12	10	12	2	..
80	30	32	..	..	32	24	14	9	4	..
	30	32	..	..	32	24	14	12	4	..
74 Large Class	28	32	..	..	30	24	14	9	2	..
74 Guns..Common Class	28	32	..	..	28	18	14	9	4	9
Class	28	32	..	..	30	18	12	9	4	9
64	26	24	..	..	26	18	10	9	2	9
50 Common Class	22	24	..	..	22	12	4	6	2	6
50 Small Class*	20	12	..	..	22	12	6	6	2	6
44	20	18	..	..	22	12	..	..	2	6
40	..	..	..	..	28	18	8	9	4	9
38	..	..	..	..	28	18	8	9	2	12
36	..	..	..	..	26	18	8	9	2	12
32 Large Class	..	..	..	..	26	18	4	6	2	6
32 Common Class	..	..	..	..	26	12	4	6	2	6
28	..	..	..	..	24	9	4	6	..	..
24 Guns	..	..	..	..	22	9	2	6	..	..
20	..	..	..	..	20	9	..	..	..	..
Sloops Ship-rigged	18	..	..	..	18	6	..	..	..	..
	16	..	..	..	16	6	..	..	..	..
	14	..	..	..	14	6	..	..	..	..

* *Only two Ships have ever been built of this Class.*

N.B. It is not certain whether the 100 Gunships that appear by the foregoing account to have 42-pounders, have not had them exchanged for 32's; but they stand on the List of the Navy with their original Guns. The Guns on board the Ships of foreign-built, are not meant to be comprized in the foregoing account. The Sloops and small Classes of Ships carry Swivels (half-pounders) in addition to their Carriage-guns.

N.B. Since the year 1792, some alterations have taken place in the Guns of some of the Classes; and Carronades are now much used, but so unequally on board Ships of the same Class, that it is not possible to give a general statement of the Ordnance now in use.

1793

Abstract of the Royal Navy on the 1st September 1793.

Rates or Classes.	Guns.	Number.	Burthen.
			Tons.
1st.	110	2	4664
	100	5	11000
2d.	98 & 90	21	41125
3d.	80	3	6232
	76	1	115763
	74	69	
	64	39	54067
4th.	60	1	1285
Line		141	234136
4th.	52	1	21128
	50	19	

APPENDIX 3

Rates or Classes.	Guns.	Number.	Burthen.
			Tons.
5th.	44	21	18806
	40	1	1020
	38	14	13597
	36	14	12700
	32	53	37992
6th.	28	29	17206
	24	6	3069
	22 & 20	6	2636
	12	1	406
Floating Battery....................		1	386
Sloops rigged as Ships..............	42		14400
Brigs	11		2939
Brigs............................	6		1225
Surveying Vessel	1		64
Bombs	2		609
Fireships	9		3820
Storeships	2		1772
Armed Vessel	1		123
Tender	1		Not known.
Tenders...........................	4		606
Vessels rigged as Sloops	2		84
Cutters...........................	18		3254
Armed Schooners..................	3		270
Lugger...........................	1		111
Hospital Ship	1		1781
Yachts...........................	11		1450
Hoys, Lighters & Transports.........	50		4926
Receiving Ships	16		21092
Hulks...........................	10		11618
Of 52 Guns and under....		357	199090 Exclusive of the Tonnage of one Tender
Total......		498	433226 Exclusive of the Tonnage of one Tender

1792 and 1793

Guns.	In commission as fighting Ships.	
	1st Decr. 1792.	1st Sepr. 1793.
Of 100..............................		5
98 or 90	2	8
80...............................		1
74...................	9	42
64..................	1	16
Line....	12	72
50..................	5	6
44.................	1	13
40............................		1
38.................	1	6

Guns.	In commission as fighting Ships.	
	1st Decr. 1792.	1st Sepr. 1793.
36...................	2	10
32...................	10	40
28...................	7	20
24...................	3	5
22 & 20..............	1	3
Of 50 to 20 Guns......	30	104
Total....	42	176

1795, 1797, 1799, and 1801

Abstracts of the Royal Navy on the 1st January 1795, 1797, and 1799, and as it stood on the 1st October 1801.

Rates or Classes.	Guns.	Number on			
		1st Jany. 1795.	1st Jany. 1797.	1st Jany. 1799.	1st Octr. 1801.
1st.	120	1	2	2	2
	114	...	...	1	1
	112	...	...	1	1
	110	2	2	2	2
	100	5	5	5	5
2d.	98 & 90	21	20	21	21
3d.	84	2	2	2	3
	82	...	...	1	1
	80	5	4	7	8
	78	3	1	1	1
	76	1	1	1	1
	74	70	82	81	89
	72	...	...	2	1
	64	34	41	46	43
4th.	60	1	1	3	1
Line..............		145	161	176	180
4th.	56	...	2	2	2
	54	...	4	4	2
	52	1	1	...	1
	50	17	16	15	15
5th.	44	23	21	21	20
	40	1	4	7	7
	38	21	33	33	36
	36	20	24	33	43
	34	...	2	3	3
	32	51	58	54	52
	30	...	...	...	1
6th.	28	26	26	27	26
	26	...	2	2	2
	24	5	5	6	8
	22 & 20	8	9	13	14
	16	1	1	1	1
	Guns unknown	...	1	...	...

Rates or Classes.	Guns.	Number on			
		1st Jany. 1795.	1st Jany. 1797.	1st Jany. 1799.	1st Octr. 1801.
Floating Batteries.................		2	2	2	2
Sloops rigged as Ships.............		44	54	80	88
Brigs		16	42	38	44
Sloops, nature of their rigging unknown.....................		1	1	2	2
Brigs..........................	6	5	2	1	
Armed Brigs		...	2	3	2
Advice Boats.....................		...	...	...	2
Surveying Vessels.................		1	1	1	1
Bombs		2	2	14	13
Fireships		8	7	13	7
Fire Vessels.....................		12	9	10	8
Storeships		3	4	3	9
Armed Vessels		3	4	6	6
Vessels rigged as Sloops		2	1	1	1
Armed Tenders		...	...	1	2
Tenders........................		4	4	4	4
Cutters.........................		16	17	17	16
Armed Schooners.................		3	5	5	6
Galleots		3	1	1	1

Rates or Classes.	Guns.	Number on			
		1st Jany. 1795.	1st Jany. 1797.	1st Jany. 1799.	1st Octr. 1801.
Schooners (exclusive of the above)		5	3	2	3
Luggers		1	1	1	1
Hospital Ships		2	2	2	3
Prison Ships		1	3	4	8
Gun Vessels*		54	54	93	114
Barge Magazines		1	1	1	1
Latteen Settee		...	...	...	1
Yachts		11	11	11	11
Hoys, Lighters & Transports		55	60	63	67
Receiving Ships		16	15	16	17
Hulks..........................		10	10	10	10
Of 56 Guns and under....		454	530	627	684
Total....		599	691	803	864

* *Originally called* Gun Boats.

N.B.—There were some Ships and Vessels in the service, at least in our possession, on the 1st October 1801, and perhaps at each of the other periods in the foregoing statement, that had not been registered on the list of the Navy, at those periods.

Dimensions of Ships, 1677–1745

An Account shewing the *Dimensions* established, or proposed to be established at different times, for building of Ships.

Gunships 100	Establishment of				Proposed in		Establishment of 1745
	1677.	1691.	1706.	1719.	1733.	1741.	
	Ft. In.						
Length on the Gundeck	165 : 0	......	......	174 : 0	174 : 0	175 : 0	178 : 0
Of the Keel for tonnage	137 : 8	......	......	140 : 7	140 : 7	142 : 4	140 : 6½
Breadth extreme.....................	46 : 0	......	......	50 : 0	50 : 0	50 : 0	51 : 0
Depth in Hold	19 : 2	......	......	20 : 0	20 : 6	21 : 0	21 : 6
Burthen in Tons....................	1550	......	......	1869	1869	1892	2000

Gunships 90	Establishment of				Proposed in		Establishment of 1745
	1677.	1691.	1706.	1719.	1733.	1741.	
Length on the Gundeck	158 : 0	......	162 : 0	164 : 0	166 : 0	168 : 0	170 : 0
Of the Keel for tonnage	......	......	132 : 0	132 : 5	134 : 1	137 : 0	138 : 4
Breadth extreme.....................	44 : 0	......	47 : 0	47 : 2	47 : 9	48 : 0	48 : 6
Depth in Hold	18 : 2	......	18 : 6	18 : 10	19 : 6	20 : 2	20 : 6
Burthen in Tons....................	1307	......	1551	1566	1623	1679	1730

Gunships 80 with Three decks.	Establishment of				Proposed in		Establishment of 1745
	1677.	1691.	1706.	1719.	1733.	1741.	
	Ft. In.						
Length on the Gundeck	......	156 : 0	156 : 0	158 : 0	158 : 0	161 : 0	165 : 0
Of the Keel for tonnage	......	......	127 : 6	128 : 2	127 : 8	130 : 10	134 : 10¾
Breadth extreme	......	41 : 0	43 : 6	44 : 6	45 : 5	46 : 0	47 : 0
Depth in Hold	......	17 : 4	17 : 8	18 : 2	18 : 7	19 : 4	20 : 0
Burthen in Tons	......	1100	1283	1350	1400	1472	1585

Gunships 70	1677.	1691.	1706.	1719.	1733.	1741.	Establishment of 1745
	Ft. In.						
Length on the Gundeck	150 : 0	......	150 : 0	151 : 0	151 : 0	154 : 0	160 : 0
Of the Keel for tonnage	......	......	122 : 0	123 : 2	122 : 0	125 : 5	131 : 4
Breadth extreme	39 : 8	......	41 : 0	41 : 6	43 : 5	44 : 0	45 : 0
Depth in Hold	17 : 0	......	17 : 4	17 : 4	17 : 9	18 : 11	19 : 4
Burthen in Tons	1013	......	1069	1128	1224	1291	1414

Gunships 60	Establishment of				Proposed in		Establishment of 1745
	1677.	1691.	1706.	1719.	1733.	1741.	
	Ft. In.						
Length on the Gundeck	......	144 : 0	144 : 0	144 : 0	144 : 0	147 : 0	150 : 0
Of the Keel for tonnage	......	......	119 : 0	117 : 7	116 : 4	119 : 9	123 : 0½
Breadth extreme	......	37 : 6	38 : 0	39 : 0	41 : 5	42 : 0	42 : 8
Depth in Hold	......	15 : 8	15 : 8	16 : 5	16 : 11	18 : 1	18 : 6
Burthen in Tons	......	900	914	951	1068	1123	1191

Gunships 50	1677.	1691.	1706.	1719.	1733.	1741.	Establishment of 1745
Length on the Gundeck	......	......	130 : 0	134 : 0	134 : 0	140 : 0	144 : 0
Of the Keel for tonnage	......	......	108 : 0	109 : 8	108 : 3	113 : 9	117 : 8½
Breadth extreme	......	......	35 : 0	36 : 0	38 : 6	40 : 0	41 : 0
Depth in Hold	......	......	14 : 0	15 : 2	15 : 9	17 : 2½	17 : 0
Burthen in Tons	......	......	704	755	853	968	1052

Gunships 40	Establishment of				Proposed in		Establishment of 1745
	1677.	1691.	1706.	1719.	1733.	1741.	
	Ft. In.						
Length on the Gundeck	......	......	118 : 0	124 : 0	124 : 0	126 : 0	133 : 0
Of the Keel for tonnage	......	......	97 : 6	101 : 8	100 : 3	102 : 6	108 : 10
Breadth extreme	......	......	32 : 0	33 : 2	35 : 8	36 : 0	37 : 6
Depth in Hold	......	......	13 : 6	14 : 0	14 : 6	15 : 5½	16 : 0
Burthen in Tons	......	......	531	594	678	706	814

Gunships 20	1677.	1691.	1706.	1719.	1733.	1741.	Establishment of 1745
Length on the Gundeck	......	......	......	106 : 0	106 : 0	112 : 0	113 : 0
Of the Keel for tonnage	......	......	......	87 : 9	85 : 8	91 : 6	93 : 4
Breadth extreme	......	......	......	28 : 4	30 : 6	32 : 0	32 : 0
Depth in Hold	......	......	......	9 : 2	9 : 5	11 : 0	11 : 0
Burthen in Tons	......	......	......	374	429	498	508

MEMO.—*Several Ships were built by the establishments proposed in 1733 and 1741. The establishment of 1745 was not generally adhered to for more than ten years, if so long; and there has been no establishment of the kind since.*

1793 to 1801

SHIPS.

An Account of the *Increase* and *Decrease* of *Ships* of the Line, between the 1st January 1793 and 1st October 1801, when the Preliminaries of Peace were signed.

Rate.	Guns.	In the Service on 1st Janr. 1793.	Added to the List of the Navy.					Disposed of.				Total disposed of.	Registered on the List of the Navy, on 1st Octr. 1801.
			Built, building, or ordered to be built.	Bought from the India Company's Service.	Taken from the Enemy, or surrendered to us by them.	Converted from other Classes.	Total added.	Taken by the Enemy.	Taken to Pieces.	Lost.	Converted to other Classes.		
1st.	120 to 100	7	2	....	3	....	5	....	....	I	....	I	II
2d.	98 & 90	21	3	....	....	....	3	....	....	2	I	3	21
3d.	84 to 80	3	....	....	9	....	9	....	....	....	....	....	12
	78	....	....	....	3	....	3	....	2	....	....	2	I
	76 & 74	70	26	....	8	I	35	3	3	7	2	15	90
	72	....	....	....	2	....	2	....	....	....	I	I	I
	64	39	....	5	10	....	15	....	2	4	5	11	43
4th.	60	I	....	....	2	....	2	....	....	....	2	2	I
	Total......	141	31	5	37	I	74	3	7	14	11	35	180

N.B.—Ships taken before 1st October 1801, but not registered till afterwards, are not included herein.

MEN.

Highest *Complements* established at several periods, and generally borne at others, (particular Ships excepted.)

Classes of Ships.	As established in							Generally borne in		
	1677	1692	1706	1719	1733	1741	1745	1762	1783	1805
120 Guns	...	...	...	...	...	...	...	...	...	875
110	...	...	...	...	...	...	...	...	...	837
100	780	...	780	780	850	850	850	850	850	837
98 & 90	660	...	680	680	750	750	750	750	750	738
80	...	490	520	520	600	600	650	650	650	640
74 Large Class	...	...	...	...	...	...	...	650	650	640
74 Common Class	...	...	...	...	...	...	600	650	600	590
70	460	...	440	440	480	480	520	520	520	...
64	...	...	...	...	...	...	470	500	500	491
60	...	355	365	365	400	400	420	420	420	...
50	...	...	280	280	300	300	350	350	350	343
44	...	...	...	...	250	250	280	280	300	294
40	...	...	190	190	...	...	...	...	300	320
38	...	...	...	...	...	...	...	250	280	284
36	...	...	...	...	...	...	...	240	270	264
32 Large	...	...	...	...	...	...	...	...	...	254
32 Common	...	...	...	...	...	...	...	220	220	215
28	...	...	...	...	...	...	...	200	200	195
24	...	...	...	...	...	...	160	160	160	155
20	...	...	115	130	140	140	...	160	160	155
Large Sloops	...	...	...	100	...	...	110	125	125	121

N.B —Flag-ships are allowed an additional number of men.

The following Ships were building, or under orders to be built, on the day that the preliminaries of peace were signed,* and are included in the foregoing abstract, namely,

1801

Guns.	In the		Total.
	King's Yards.	Merchᵗˢ Yards	
Of 120..........	1	....	1
110..........	1	....	1
100..........	1	....	1
98..........	4	....	4
74..........	8	9	17
50..........	2	....	2
44..................	....	1	1
38..........	2	....	2
36..........	4	3	7
Sloops	1	1	2
Yachts	2	....	2
Total....	26	14	40

* *Peace of Amiens, concluded 1802.*

MEMᵒ.—*In the course of the war, several very large 74 Gun ships were built pretty much after French models; but the Ships laid down of late have been of smaller dimensions.*

1793 to 1801

SHIPS.

An Account of the *Increase* and *Decrease* of *Ships* under the Line, Sloops, and all other Vessels, between the 1st January 1793 and 1st October 1801.

Rates or Classes.	Guns.	Built, taken, purchased, or converted from other Classes.	Taken, lost, sold, or otherwise disposed of.
4th.	56	4	2
	54	6	4
	50	....	4
5th.	44	4	5
	40	6	....
	38	34	7
	36	41	10
	34	5	2
	32	21	18
	30	1	....
6th.	28	8	10
	26	2	....
	24	5	3
	22 & 20	14	7
6th.	12	....	1
	16	1	....
Floating Batteries.....................		2	....
Sloops rigged as Ships..................		86	24
Brigs		62	33
Nature of riggˢ not known..........		3	1

Brigs.................................	1	6
Armed Brigs..........................	5	3
Bombs...............................	12	1
Fireships.............................	7	9
Fire Vessels..........................	13	5
Storeships............................	7	2
Advice Boats.........................	2	....
Armed Vessels........................	6	....
Tenders........................	3	2
Galleot........................	1	....
Vessel rigged as a Sloop..............		1
Cutters..............................	8	11
Armed Schooners......................	5	2
Schooners............................	7	5
Lugger..............................	1	....
Hospital Ships........................	2	....
Prison Ships..........................	7	....
Gun Boats............................	131	18
Barge Magazine.......................	1	....
Latteen Settee........................	1	....
Yachts...............................	3	3
Receiving Ships.......................	6	5
Hulks................................	2	1
Total......	536	205

1803

Abstract of the Royal Navy as it stood on the 15th May 1803.

Rates or Classes.	Guns.	Number.
1st.	120	1
	114	1
	112	1
	110	2
	100	5
2d.	98 & 90	20
3d.	84	3
	82	1
	80	8
	78	1
	76	2
	74	87
	72	1
	64	43
4th.	60	1
	Line..................	177
4th.	56	3
	54	2
	52	1
	50	14
5th.	44	16
	40	7
	38	39
	36	43
	34	2
	32	50

Rates or Classes	Guns.	Number.
6th.	28	24
	26	1
	24	6
	22 & 20	11
	16	1
Sloops rigged as Ships.....................		83
Brigs		43
Nature of rigging not known		2
Armed Brig.............................		1
Advice Boats...........................		2
Surveying Vessel		1
Bombs		12
Fireships		4
Fire Vessel		1
Storeships		9
Armed Vessels		6
Vessel rigged as a Sloop		1
Armed Tenders		2
Tenders...............................		4
Cutters................................		12
Armed Schooners........................		5
Galleot		1
Schooners (exclusive of the above).............		3
Lugger.................................		1
Hospital Ships..........................		3
Prison Ships		6
Gun Vessels*...........................		70
Barge Magazine		1
Latteen Settee..........................		1
Yachts.................................		11
Hoys, Lighters & Transports		63
Receiving Ships		15
Hulks.................................		10
Of 56 Guns and under....		593
Total......		770

* Originally called Gun-Boats.

1803

In the year 1803, a 74 and a 36 Gunship were ordered to be built in the East India Company's docks at Bombay:* and it is expected that the building of Ships of War there, will be continued.† The Ships will be built with Teak Timber which is extremely durable.

Only very scanty supplies of Oak timber having been obtained for some time past for the dock-yards, and it being an article exceedingly wanted, the prices were much raised in the year 1802, and also in 1803.

* The Frigate (named the Salsette) is launched.
† Others have been since ordered to be built there.

1804

Orders were given in the course of this year to purchase six Ships in India to carry from 36 to 40 guns: and many Sloops and Gun Vessels were contracted for with private Ship-builders in this country.

The want of oak timber still continuing, a further advance was given to the Merchants, and other encouragements given them, this year, which had a good effect with regard to the supplies.

1805

Many Ships and smaller Vessels have been also contracted for in this year; and among them there are ten of 74 Guns. The Navy at the beginning of this year consisted of the following Ships and Vessels.

1805

Abstract of the Royal Navy, on the 1st January 1805.

Rates or Classes.	Guns.	Number.
1st.	120	1
	114	1
	112	1
	110	2
	100	5
2d.	98 & 90	18
3d.	84	3
	82	1
	80	8
	78	1
	76	2
	74	87
	72	1
	64	43
4th.	60	1
Line...............		175
4th.	56	5
	54	4
	52	2
	50	13
5th.	44	20
	40	7
	38	45
	36	43
	34	2
	32	59
6th.	28	27
	26	1
	24	5
	22 & 20	13
Sloops rigged as Ships.....................		104
Brigs		64
Nature of rigging not known		3
Armed Brigs		2
Surveying Vessel		1
Bombs		19
Mortar Boats		2
Fireships		5
Fire Vessels.............................		16
Storeships		8
Advice Boats...........................		2

Rates or Classes	Guns.	Number.
Armed Vessels		7
Tenders		2
Galleot		1
Tenders		4
Cutters.		25
Armed Schooners.		11
Schooners		4
Lugger.		1
Hospital Ships.		4
Prison Ships		5
Gun Vessels*		125
Barge Magazine		1

Rates or Classes	Guns.	Number.
Latteen Settee.		1
Yachts		11
Gun Schooners		12
Receiving Ships		15
Hoys, Lighters, and Transports		62
Hulks		11
Of 56 Guns and under.		774
Total. . . .		949

* *Originally called* Gun Boats.

Appendix 4

Some abstracts from the establishment of the Royal Navy between 1814–1860. Prepared by the author.

War-time January 1814

Rates or Classes	Guns	Number		
		In commission	In ordinary	Total
Three-deckers				
1st.	120	2	—	2
	112	2	—	2
	100	3	—	3
2nd.	98	5	3	8
Two-deckers				
3rd.	80	1	4	5
	74	85	12	97
	64	1	—	1
Total line		99	19	118
4th.	56	3	—	3
	50	5	2	7
5th.	44	2	—	2
Single-deckers (Frigates)	44	1	—	1
	40	6	2	8
	38	51	6	57
	36	51	3	54
	32	12	—	12
6th.	24	2	2	4
Post-ships	22	10	—	10
	20	13	2	15
Sloops	18	121	4	125
	16	54	1	55
	14	14	—	14
	10	28	—	28
Gun-brigs	14	3	—	3
	12	67	2	69
	10	1	—	1
Cutters	14	8	—	8
	12	8	—	8
	10	24	—	24
	8	2	—	2
	6	1	—	1
Bombs	4	10	—	10
	8			
& 2 mortars	8	—	8	
Total cruiser		500	24	524
Troop-ships		—	28	28
Store-ships		—	15	15
Surveying-vessels		—	3	3
Advice-boats and Tenders		—	4	4
Grand total		654	43	697

At the beginning of 1820, four-and-a-half years after the end of the Napoleonic Wars, the Navy's peace-time strength was as follows.

Peace-time, January 1820

Rates or Classes	Guns	Number		
		In commission	In ordinary	Total
Three-deckers				
1st.	120	—	5	5
	112	—	2	2
	108	1	1	2
	106	1	—	1
	104	—	6	6
Two-deckers				
2nd.	84	—	3	3
	80	1	5	6
3rd.	78	2	6	8
	76	3	5	8
	74	6	58	64
Total line		14	91	105
4th.	60	2	1	3
	58	1	5	6
Frigates				
	50	4	1	5
	48	1	5	6
	46	5	35	40

Rates or Classes	Guns	In commission	In ordinary	Total
6th.	44	1	1	2
	42	7	25	32
6th.	32	—	2	2
	26	9	2	11
	24	5	3	8
Sloops				
	22	1	—	1
	20	11	5	16
	18	23	41	64
	16	—	1	1
	14	1	3	4
	10	6	1	7
Bombs	—	—	5	5
Gun-brigs	12	6	8	14
Cutters	10 to 14	9	2	11
Total cruisers		92	146	238
Troop-ships	—	1	6	7
Store-ships	—	5	5	10
Discovery-ships	—	2	—	2
Surveying-vessels	—	6	1	7
Grand total		120	249	369

The next abstract is taken from the last year that the battle-fleet was a purely sailing one, 1845. The emphasis has shifted since 1820 to the employment of very large vessels in home and Mediterranean waters, and very small ones in distant parts.

September 1845—The sailing navy

Rates or Classes	Guns	Number		
		In commission	In ordinary	Total
Three-deckers				
1st.	120	3	10	13
	110	1	5	6
	104	2	5	7
Two-deckers				
2nd.	92	1	1	2
	90	2	1	3
	84	2	7	9
	80	4	2	6
3rd.	78	—	5	5
	76	—	4	4
	74	—	3	3
	72	1	28	29
Total line		16	71	87
4th.	50	7	12	19
5th.	46	—	3	3
	44	1	13	14
	42	4	22	26
	38	—	1	1
6th.	36	3	1	4
	30	—	1	1
	26	11	9	20
	24	1	3	4
Sloops	22	—	4	4
	20	1	5	6
	19	1	—	1
	18	12	5	17
	16	17	6	23
	12	7	—	7
	10	7	6	13
	6	10	2	12
Total sailing cruisers		82	93	175
Survey-vessels		6	—	6
Discovery-ships		2	2	4
Troop-ships		3	1	4
Total		109	167	276

September 1845—The steam navy

It will be noted in this and subsequent abstracts from lists of the steam navy, that rating by numbers of guns becomes rather meaningless, as some sloops mount as many or more guns than some frigates. One reason was that the paddles took up so much room that an armament of a small number of large guns was preferred, and in the early frigates this was restricted to the upper-deck only. The other reason was that if a cruiser was a post-ship, that is to say a captain's command, then she had to be rated as a frigate, even if she had been a sloop before, and vice-versa.

Class	Guns	Number		
		In commission	In ordinary	Total
Paddle-frigates	21	1	—	1
	16	2	—	2
	10	—	1	1
	6	1	2	3
Screw-sloop	11	1	—	1
Paddle-sloops	6	11	1	12
	5	3	1	4
	4	2	—	2
Paddle-vessels	6	1	—	1
	4	3	—	3
	3	6	1	7
Steam cruisers		31	6	37
Grand total, steam and sail		140	173	313

September 1855

Ten years later, in the second year of the Russian War, the strength of the Navy is shown to be enormously increased, especially in the proportion of steamers. Indeed, as it was by then accepted that the battle-fleet must fight under steam, the sailing liners scarcely deserving of the name, and none of them went to the Baltic, where the Russian battle-fleet might have been encountered.

Rates or Classes	Guns	In commission	In ordinary	Total
Steam-assisted Three-deckers 1st.	131	1	—	1
	130	—	1	1
	121	1	—	1
	102	1	—	1
	101	1	—	1
Two-deckers 2nd.	91	6	—	6
	90	3	—	3
	80	3	3	6
3rd.	70	1	—	1
	60	9	—	9
Steam line		26	4	30
Sailing Three-deckers 1st.	120	4	4	8
	116	1	—	1
	104	1	4	5
	102	1	—	1
	101	1	—	1
Two-deckers 2nd.	90	3	2	5
	84	4	6	10
	80	—	7	7
	78	—	6	6
	72	1	6	7
	70	1	2	3
Sailing line		17	37	54
Total line		43	41	84
Steam-assisted cruisers Screw-frigates	51	2	—	2
	33	1	—	1
	31	1	—	1
	21	1	—	1
Paddle-frigates	28	1	—	1
	24	1	—	1
	22	1	—	1
	21	1	—	1
	18	1	—	1
	16	5	—	5
	6	7	—	7
Screw-sloops	21	1	—	1
	20	3	1	4
	17	5	—	5
	14	6	—	6
	11	1	—	1
	9	4	—	4
	8	5	—	5
	6	1	—	1

Rates or classes	Guns	In commission	In ordinary	Total
Paddle-sloops	8	1	—	1
	6	25	3	28
	5	2	—	2
Screw-vessels	4	5	6	11
	3	2	—	2
Paddle-vessels	5	1	1	2
	4	7	3	10
	3	13	4	17
	2	1	2	3
Screw gun-boats	2	18	52	70
Mortars	—	—	3	3
Steam cruisers		123	75	198
Sailing cruisers Frigates 5th.	50	5	22	27
	44	1	7	8
	42	—	18	18
	40	2	3	5
	36	2	—	2
6th.	26	5	7	12
	24	2	—	2
Sloops	18–22	3	6	9
	10–16	16	18	34
	3–8	14	11	25
Mortars	—	—	18	18
Sailing cruisers		50	110	160
Grand total		216	226	442

September 1860

For the sake of continuity the following abstract is still based on the number of guns carried in each class, although since 1856 a ship's rating depended entirely on the number of men she carried.

A measure of the continuing build-up of the Navy's strength, is that the battle-fleet in time of peace is larger than it was ten years previously in time of war.

Classes	Guns	In commission	In ordinary	Total
Steam-assisted Three-decker ships of the line	131	1	3	4
	121	1	2	3
Two-decker ships of the line	101	3	3	6
	91	9	5	14
	90	8	7	15

86	1	—	1
81	—	1	1
80	4	6	10
70	1	—	1
60	8	1	9
Steam line	**36**	**28**	**64**
Sailing			
Three-decker ships of the line 120	1	—	1
104	1	—	1
101	1	—	1
Two-decker ships of the line 84	4	6	10
80	—	2	2
78	1	3	4
72	3	3	6
70	1	—	1
Sailing line	**12**	**14**	**26**
Total line	**48**	**42**	**90**
Screw-frigates 51	10	11	21
50	—	1	1
47	1	—	1
40	1	—	1
36	1	—	1
32	2	—	2
31	2	1	3
26	1	1	2
25	1	—	1
13	1	—	1
Screw-frigates	**20**	**14**	**34**
Paddle-frigates 28	1	—	1
22	1	—	1
18	1	—	1
16	4	1	5
Paddle-frigates	**7**	**1**	**8**
Sailing-frigate 50	—	18	18
44	—	8	8
42	—	15	15
41	1	4	5
36	1	—	1
28	—	1	1
26	2	10	12
24	—	2	2
Sailing-frigates	**4**	**58**	**62**
Total frigates	**31**	**73**	**104**
Screw-sloops 22	2	2	4
21	9	5	14
17	7	5	12
16	1	—	1
15	—	1	1
14	1	—	1
13	2	—	2
12	—	1	1
11	5	2	7
9	3	1	4
8	1	3	4
6	6	1	7
4	8	10	18
Screw-sloops	**45**	**31**	**76**
Paddle-sloops 21	1	—	1
12	1	—	1
8	2	—	2
6	18	12	30
5	2	—	2
4	1	—	1
3	2	—	2
Paddle-sloops	**27**	**12**	**39**
Sailing-sloops 22	—	1	1
20	—	1	1
19	—	1	1
18	1	4	5
16	1	7	8
14	—	4	4
12	2	15	17
8	—	3	3
6	1	3	4
4	—	1	1
Sailing-sloops	**5**	**40**	**45**
Total sloops	**77**	**83**	**160**
Screw gun-vessels 5	3	10	13
4	4	2	6
2	—	1	1
1	4	—	4
Screw gun-vessels	**11**	**13**	**24**
Steam vessels 6	—	2	2
(paddle-wheel) 5	2	—	2
4	2	1	3
3	6	11	17
2	3	2	5
1	3	—	3
Steam vessels	**16**	**16**	**32**
Screw-Mortars —	—	3	3
Total cruisers	**135**	**188**	**323**
Grand total	**183**	**230**	**413**

Appendix 5

Two tables, not in Derrick, taken from John Smith's

'A Sea-man's Grammar, With THE PLAINE Exposition of Smiths Accidence for young Sea-men, enlarged.'

(*a*) From the 1627 edition

A Table of Proportion for the weight and ſhooting of great Ordnance.

		The names of the great Peeces.	The height of the Peeces *	The weight of the peeces	The weight of the ſhot.	The weight of the powd.	The bredth of the ladle	The length of the ladle	2400li. of powder makes of ſhot in a †	Shot point blanke in ‡	Shot randome in
			Inches	Pound	Pound	Pound	Inches	Inches	Peece	Paces	Paces
TheſePeeces be moſt ſerviceable for battery, being within 80 paces to their mark, which is the chief of their forces.	1	A Canon Royall.	$8\frac{1}{2}$	8000	66	30	$13\frac{1}{4}$	$24\frac{1}{2}$	80	16	1930
	2	A Canon	8	6000	60	27	12	24	85	17	2000
	3	A Canon Serpentine	$7\frac{1}{2}$	5500	$53\frac{1}{3}$	25	$10\frac{1}{2}$	$23\frac{1}{2}$	96	20	2000
	4	A Baſtard Canon	7	4500	$41\frac{1}{4}$	20	10	$23\frac{1}{3}$	120	18	1800
	5	A demy Canon	$6\frac{1}{2}$	4000	$30\frac{1}{4}$	18	$9\frac{1}{3}$	$23\frac{1}{4}$	133	17	1700
	6	A Canon Petro	6	3000	$24\frac{1}{4}$	14	9	23	171	16	1600
Theſe Peeces be good and alſo ſerviceable to be mixt with the above Ordnance for battery to peeces being croſt with the reſt, as alſo fit for Caſtles, Forts and wals to be planted, and for defence.	7	A Culvering	$5\frac{1}{2}$	4500	$17\frac{1}{3}$	12	$8\frac{1}{2}$	$22\frac{1}{3}$	200	20	2500
	8	A Baſiliſco	5	4000	$15\frac{1}{4}$	10	$7\frac{1}{2}$	22	240	25	3000
	9	A demy Culvering	$4\frac{1}{2}$	3400	$9\frac{1}{3}$	8	$6\frac{1}{3}$	21	300	20	2500
	10	A baſtard Culvering	4	3000	7	$6\frac{1}{4}$	6	20	388	18	1800
	11	A Sacre	$3\frac{1}{2}$	1400	$5\frac{1}{3}$	$5\frac{1}{3}$	$5\frac{1}{2}$	18	490	17	1700
	12	A Minion	$3\frac{1}{4}$	1000	4	4	$4\frac{1}{2}$	17	600	16	1600
	13	A Faulcon	$2\frac{1}{2}$	660	$2\frac{1}{4}$	$2\frac{1}{4}$	$4\frac{1}{4}$	15	1087	15	1500
	14	A Faulcon	$2\frac{1}{3}$	800	3	3	$4\frac{1}{4}$	15	800	15	1500
Theſe Peeces are good and ſerviceable for the field, and moſt ready for defence.	15	A Faulconet	2	500	$1\frac{1}{4}$	$1\frac{1}{4}$	$3\frac{1}{4}$	$11\frac{1}{4}$	1950	4	1400
	16	A Sarpentine	$1\frac{1}{2}$	400	$\frac{1}{3}$	$\frac{1}{3}$	$2\frac{1}{3}$	10	7200	13	1300
	17	A Rabonet	1	300	$\frac{1}{2}$	$\frac{1}{2}$	$1\frac{1}{3}$	6	4800	12	1000

* *The height is the bore.*

† *2400 lbs represents a last of powder, which was 24 casks of a 100 lbs each, cask and all. This column tables the number of charges to be got from a last of powder for each weight of gun.*

‡ *A pace in this context is $2\frac{1}{2}$ feet, and this column and the end one show the ranges in straight trajectory and the extreme.*

(b) From the 1692 edition

86   The Sea-mans Grammar.

A Table wherein is described the *Names* of all forts of *Ordnance*, from the *Cannon* to the *Bafe*; Alſo the *Lengths, Breadths, Weights, Diameters*, &c. of Powder, Shot, Ladle, *&c.* belonging to each Peece.

The Names of the several Peeces of Ordnance now in Vſe.	Diameter at the Bore (Inch 100 parts)	Weight (pound wight)	Long (Fe 100 parts)	The Load. (poun 100 part)	Shots Diameter (Inch 100 parts)	Weight of Shot (pound 100 parts)	Length of Ladle (Inch 100 parts)	Breadth of Ladle (Inch 100 parts)
Cannon.	8.00	8000	12.00	32.50	7.50	58.00	24.00	14.75
Demi Cannon, Extra.	6.75	6000	12.00	18.00	6.62	36.00	22.75	12.0
Demi Cannon, Ordi.	6.50	5600	10.00 / 11.00	17.50	6.16	32.00	22.00	12.00
Culvering, Extraordinary	5.50	4800	10.00 / 11.00 / 13.00	12.50	5.25	20.00	16.00	10.00
Culvering, Ordinary	5.25	4500	12.00	11.37	5.00	17.31	15.00	9.50
Culvering of the leaſt ſize	5.00	4000	12.00	10.00	4.75	14.90	14.25	9.00
Demi-Culvering, Extraordinary	4.75	3000	10.00 / 12.00 / 13.00	8.50	4.50	12.69	13.50	8.50
Demi-Culvering Ordinary	4.50	2700	10.00	7.25	4.25	10.26	12.75	8.00
Demi-Culvering of the leſſer ſize	4.25	2000	9.00 / 10.00	6.25	4.00	9.00	12.00	8.00
Saker, Extraordina.	4.00	1800	9.00 / 10.00	5.00	3.75	7.31	11.00	7.25
Saker, Ordinary	3.75	1500	9.00	4.00	3.50	6.00	10.50	6.75
Saker of the leaſt ſize	3.50	1400	8.00	2.27	3.25	4.75	9.75	6.50
Minnion, Large	3.25	1000	8.00	3.25	3.00	3.75	9.00	5.00
Minnion, Ordinary	3.00	750	7.00	2.50	2.92	3.25	8.50	5.00
Faucon	2.75	750	7.00	2.25	2.58	2.50	8.25	4.50
Fauconet	2.25	400	6.00	1.25	2.01	1.31	7.50	4.00
Rabonet	1.50	300	5.50	0.75	1.28	0.50	4.25	2.50
Bale	1.25	300	4.50	0.50	1.13	0.50	4.00	2.00

whole

* The load is the weight of the charge.

Appendix 6

Flags and Pendants of Command and Distinction

The Standard

From medieval times the royal standard had been used not only to identify the presence of the sovereign, but by his commanders at sea who represented him, and who flew it at the masthead; even the ships under his command wore little banners with the royal arms along their gunwales, and this practice persisted until the end of the sixteenth century. Thereafter the standard as a flag of command was restricted to the lord high admiral until Queen Anne withdrew the privilege on her accession in 1702.

A curious anomaly occurred during the Civil War when the Earl of Warwick was appointed lord high admiral by parliament in opposition to the king's wishes, there already being a lord high admiral in the person of the nine-year-old Duke of York, though substituted for by the Earl of Northumberland. Warwick took over the fleet and flew the standard. The situation culminated in 1648 when he faced the royalist fleet off the Dutch coast, with both he and Prince Rupert, who was by that time the royalist commander, flying the same standards. Paintings showing the Duke of York at sea following the Restoration in 1660 always show a plain royal standard without the duke's label, for it was the king's standard as lord high admiral, not his own arms that he flew. Indeed when the king was present in the fleet and not actually aboard the duke's ship, the latter had to strike his standard and hoist his other badge, the admiralty flag.

The Admiralty Flag

This flag, a gold foul anchor horizontal on a red field, has hardly ever been seen at sea worn alone as a flag of command, though the sovereign flies it as well as the standard, formerly to indicate whence the board or person holding the office derived their title; though now since the formation of a unified defence council, by right of office, since the queen is again her own lord high admiral. Charles II and James II likewise held the office in their own person from 1673 until the Revolution of 1688, and James underlined the

point by putting a crown over the anchor, which for that brief reign, assumed an upright position.

Admiral's Flags

The pattern of command flags does not become really clear until the middle of the seventeenth century, but with the organisation of the squadron system in the sixteenth century determined efforts were made to create a system. Thus in 1530 it was decreed that the lord admiral should fly the standard at the main and the flag of St George at the fore, and that all his squadron should wear the St George at the main. The admiral of the van squadron should fly a St George at the main and fore and that all his squadron should wear similar flags at the fore. The admiral of the rear, or wing squadron as it was called, flew a St George at his main and mizzen, and bonaventure-mizzen if his ship had one; his squadron also wore them at their mizzens and bonaventure-mizzens. This system with variations apparently lasted until the end of the sixteenth century, and in so far as the relative dignity of the mast-heads was concerned the precedence was to be permanent.

The reign of Charles I saw the introduction of different coloured flags and ensigns to identify the three squadrons of the fleet. The commander-in-chief, if he was not the lord high admiral, flew the union at the main and his squadron had red ensigns; the admiral of the van flew a blue flag and his squadron blue ensigns, and the rear squadron had white ensigns and the admiral a white flag. There was still only one admiral to a squadron.

In 1649, after the execution of Charles I, the council of state abolished the office of lord high admiral and designed a new Commonwealth standard which was to be used by the generals at sea. This had two shields, one with a St George's cross for England and one with a harp in a blue field for Ireland. These were set in a wreath on a red field. The admirals, for by the First Dutch War in 1652 there was more than one flag-officer per squadron, had a rather similar flag, the two shields being set on a gold field with a red border, and without the wreath. In 1658 this standard was dropped and replaced by Cromwell's standard, until his death a year later. This had the St George's cross in the first and fourth cantons, the St Andrew's saltire in the second, the harp for Ireland in the third, and on a shield in the middle, an argent lion rampart on a black field.

One innovation brought in early in the Commonwealth navy was the reversal of the colours for the van and rear squadrons; the van taking the white flags and ensigns and the rear the blue. This was an arrangement which was to remain permanent.

With the restoration of the monachy in 1660 the picture becomes much clearer. The fleet was, as before, divided into three squadrons, each with three flag-officers. The senior squadron was the red squadron which was in the centre of the fleet and all the ships in it wore the red ensign which was now established as the senior colour; the private ships had red pendants. The vice and rear admirals of the squadron flew red flags on the fore and mizzen masts respectively, but the commander-in-chief, who might have been expected to fly a similar flag at the main, in fact flew a union flag, or the royal standard if he was the lord high admiral. The admiral of the van squadron flew a white flag at the main, and the flags of his two subordinates, the pendants of private ships and the ensigns were also white. In the rear squadron the same arrangement pertained but all the flags were blue. Every ship in the fleet, and indeed every ship in the service wore a union flag as a jack at her sprit-topmast.

Outside the main fleet, a private ship on independent service wore a tricolour pendant; all these pendants had a St George's cross at the head. The broad-pendant of a commodore did not come in until the late seventeenth century, before which the practice when the senior captain commanded a squadron was for the junior captains to strike their pendants leaving only the senior one flying. In the English fleet pendants were always struck in a ship wearing an admiral's flag. This contrasted with the Dutch, who didn't differentiate their squadrons with colours, but used to fly pendants at the appropriate mastheads of all the ships in a squadron and even under the admiral's flags. They also often had one squadron wearing the multi-barred flags and ensigns called the double-prince.

In English squadrons serving abroad, such as the Streights Fleet, a more liberal use was made of the union flag until the end of the century, it being flown by the flag officer present. The first difficulty arose when the English stopped fighting the Dutch and began to fight the French, all of whose ships wore the white flags of the Bourbons. These were easily confused with those of the van squadron which led to the re-introduction at the beginning of the eighteenth century, of the flag of St George for the command flags of the white squadron, a large red cross being added to the ensigns as well. The flag of St George had been for some time the perquisite of the merchant service.

The distinctive plain broad red pendant, of what after the 1690's was to be called a commodore's, dates from an order to the senior captain in the downs in 1674. The rank of commodore has always remained a temporary rank, an acting flag-officer. In 1824 the rank was divided into first- and second-class commodores according to their responsibilities, the former having red or white pendants, the latter blue. In 1864 when squadron colours disappeared leaving only white ensigns and flags, the first-class commodores flew their pendants at the main and the second-class at the fore. With the passing of the masted navy, second-class commodores used their boat pendants which had a red ball in the upper canton. In 1958 the two classes went into abeyance, so that now there are just commodores and one would have thought that the pendant retained would have been the plain St George's pendant. Not so, the commodores retain the second-class pendant with the ball of difference, though there is now no senior rank to be different from. Another anomaly is the pendant of the R.N.R. commodores, which instead of being blue, is a plain blue cross on a white field; this has no place in the heraldry of command flags. It all reflects in increasing ignorance of the meaning of symbols in the service, and a resulting carelessness in their use. R.N.R. pendants should be plain blue.

To revert to the admiral's flags, in the seventeenth-century fleet an appointment as a flag-officer was rather an office than a rank, though once an admiral always an admiral. The idea of a rigid list of seniority among flag-officers, rising through dead mens' shoes, is an eighteenth-century innovation, and affected the squadron colours of the fleet in so far as they ceased to be ruled by their position in the fleet and took instead the colour of the flag-officer in command, whatever that might be according to his position on the flag-list. This produced situations where two or more squadrons might have the same colour, but in that case they were usually changed by arbitary action of the commander-in-chief.

By 1805 there were 166 flag-officers on the active list, and in that year the rank of admiral of the red was introduced. The reasons for the abolition of the three colours in 1864 is set out in the section under ensigns; suffice to say that all flag-officers thereafter flew the flag of St George.

As with the commodores, the flag-officers in the late nineteenth century, when ships usually had only two and possibly only one mast, adopted their boat flags with enlarged balls in the cantons. These had two red balls, one in the upper and one in the lower canton for a rear-admiral, one ball in the upper canton for a vice-admiral, and none in an admiral's. The use of coloured or white balls in boat flags dates from the beginning of the eighteenth century and was designed to show a flag-officer's rank when flying his flag in the bows of his barge.

Ensigns and Jacks

The importance of the jack in the form of the union flag as being the sole perquisite of the king's ships, dates from shortly after the introduction of the sprit-topmast in the 1620's in large ships, which made it possible to rig a jack-staff on it. From that time, with a break during the Commonwealth and Protectorate, when another flag was used, the union flag at the jack-staff, and the wearing of a commissioning pendant, have denoted a naval vessel, though since the changes in design of headsails in the middle eighteenth century, which made it impracticable to wear them at sea, they are only worn in harbour or at anchor. For some reason the phrase 'union-jack' caught the public imagination and the flag is commonly known as the union-jack wherever it is found.

Ensigns were introduced into the navy in the second half of the sixteenth century and were usually striped. A painting of the return of Prince Charles with the fleet in 1623 shows the fleet with ensigns of blue, white and gold horizontal bars and with the St George's cross at the head. It was almost immediately after this, in 1625, that the navy apparently went over to red ensigns, which, being established as the first and senior ensign when squadronal colours were introduced in the middle of the seventeenth century, continues so to this day.

The three ensigns, red, white and blue, in that order, all carried a red cross of St George on a white field in the upper corner next to the staff. In 1707 the saltire of St Andrew was added after the Act of Union with Scotland so that it had the same form as the union flag of the day. Just before

this the addition of the second cross of St George across the whole of the white ensign was made, for reasons already stated.

A further change to the union flag occurred in 1801, then a red saltire was added after the Act of Union with Ireland and this was included also into the union in the ensign. They thus assumed their final form, but only in the navy until 1864, when it was decided to have one flag for the merchant service, one flag for the navy and one flag for the naval reserve and other government services. The reasons were that the navy no longer needed squadron colours; tactics had changed, and it was found inconvenient and expensive to carry round three sets of colours. It was also stated that a clear distinction should be made between merchant ships and naval ships, both of which might be wearing red ensigns. As the two junior ensigns were peculiar to the navy and regarded as tactical colours, the protection of the senior and legal ensign was assigned to the merchant service, which had worn it from its beginning anyway. The next senior, the white, was taken by the Royal Navy, and the junior one, the blue, was given to the Royal Naval Reserve and was also to be used, possible defaced, by government vessels outside the service, such as the Post Office. Merchant ships too, if they had a sufficient proportion of reserve officers in their crews, were and are entitled to wear a blue ensign.

The ensign of a naval ship was always worn on an ensign staff until the introduction of the gaff boom, which protruded over the taffrail and could not swing if the ensign staff was in place. When it was in use, and by the end of the Napoleonic Wars it was always rigged, the ensign was worn at the peak. In harbour, however, it was generally put back on the ensign staff, and the tradition remains today that when at sea the ensign is worn at the peak, and at rest on its staff. There is, of course, a modern reason for wearing it at the peak at sea, since guns or rockets fired from turrets aft would be liable to blow it off the staff.

The size and more especially the shape of flags and ensigns has changed since the seventeenth century. The early ensigns were almost square being only one-and-a-quarter times their height in the fly. In the late Stuart navy this lengthened to one-and-a-half times the height and in a first rate measured 13½ feet by 18 feet. Correctly the length of a flag should be given in breadths, a unit of 9 inches. If there was an admiral aboard his flag measured $9\frac{1}{2}$ feet by 13 feet, large by modern standards. If she was a private ship and wore a pendant; it was 96 feet long.

Early in the eighteenth the proportion of the ensigns and jacks changed again to twice the length to the height, but flags and standards remained at one-and-a-half. The increase in the size of the ships during the century was reflected in the flags, so that by 1800 the largest ships wore ensigns of 30 breadths, or $22\frac{1}{2}$ feet in the fly. Today the largest ensign issued is 22 breadths, or $16\frac{1}{2}$ feet in the fly, and in general ensigns, flags and pendants are very much smaller.

Appendix 7

Types of shot and shell in use for smooth bore muzzle-loaders in first half of the nineteenth century

1 *Solid-shot.* This was the commonest type of projectile in use from the earliest times until the middle of the nineteenth century. Originally it was usually made of dressed stone, but by the seventeenth century iron shot was preferred. It was the only type of projectile that could be fired with any degree of accuracy, except at the shortest ranges, and being also aerodynamically the most efficient, and the heaviest, it carried further and struck harder on a hull than other shot.

2 *Spherical-shell.* This type of shell was in use in mortars from the seventeenth century, but although there were experiments with it in France in ordinary cannon from the beginning of the eighteenth century, it only went into general service with the fleets in the second quarter of the nineteenth century. The shell was loaded with a special shovel which ensured that the fuse was pointing outwards. On firing the flames engulfed the shell and ignited the fuse. In the mortar shells, where a certain latitude in the time between firing and the explosion was desirable, devices for lengthening the fuse were used. One was to have a series of holes in the detonator and a covered fuse led down to one of them, the lower the hole the longer the fusing time. The normal size of shell in the mid nineteenth-century fleet was 8 inches which corresponded to the 32-pounder.

As there were no fleet actions over this period the effectiveness of this type of shell on wooden hulls was never proven, and they did not entirely take over from solid shot, which still outranged it, as it was the heavier.

3 *Fagot-shot.* A cylindrical shot made up of six pieces of iron segmented like a cake, and ingeniously fitted together and bound. This was effective against rigging or personnel.

4, 5, 6, 7 *Chain-shot.* Before steam provided propulsion, a number of types of short-range projectiles were devised to slash through a ship's rigging and disable her. A favourite was chain-shot of which four types are shown here: Nos. 4 and 7 are of the ordinary sort with the balls a good deal smaller than the bore, so that they were very inaccurate. With No. 5 an effort has been made to make a shot that, though it would divide in flight, at its initial velocity when

placed together in the barrel, would fill the bore like solid shot. The neatest one is No. 6, where the chain is housed inside the two cups which fit together. This system, however, does entail a loss of weight compared to No. 5, which would make it less effective.

8, 9, 10 *Bar-shot.* Like chain-shot, this type again was mainly effective against rigging, but because it was rigid it would strike harder on a hull if it struck end-on. The drawings show two variations of the double-headed type, Nos. 8 and 9, and a multiple bar shot, No. 10. All flailed around during trajectory, so were most inaccurate except at point-blank range. In the French service the area around the bar was sometimes filled with an inflammable composition bound with linen soaked in brimstone; this would burst into flames on discharge.

11, 12 *Elongated-shot.* This was a development of the dumbell bar-shot in that it opened to nearly twice its original length by the outward pull of the two ends as it spun in the air. This gave it more chance of hitting something if it passed through the rigging.

13 *Case-shot or Canister.* A cylindrical tin full of ball-shot which scattered on being fired, and was used for clearing the enemy's deck. Canister was particularly favoured by the French.

14, 15 *Grape-shot.* Another anti-personnel shot; this is of a rather sophisticated type. More usual was a system of cording the balls together and putting the whole thing into a canvas bag, No. 15. It is not clear whether the tiered type also went into a bag.

Two types of shot which were seldom used in the service, but which were apparently used in the Merchant Service and by privateersmen, were langrage, which covered any old collection of bits of iron put in a bag, and star-shot which was formed by a number of hooked arms from a ring which splayed out on being fired. It was close to multiple bar-shot, but lighter.

164

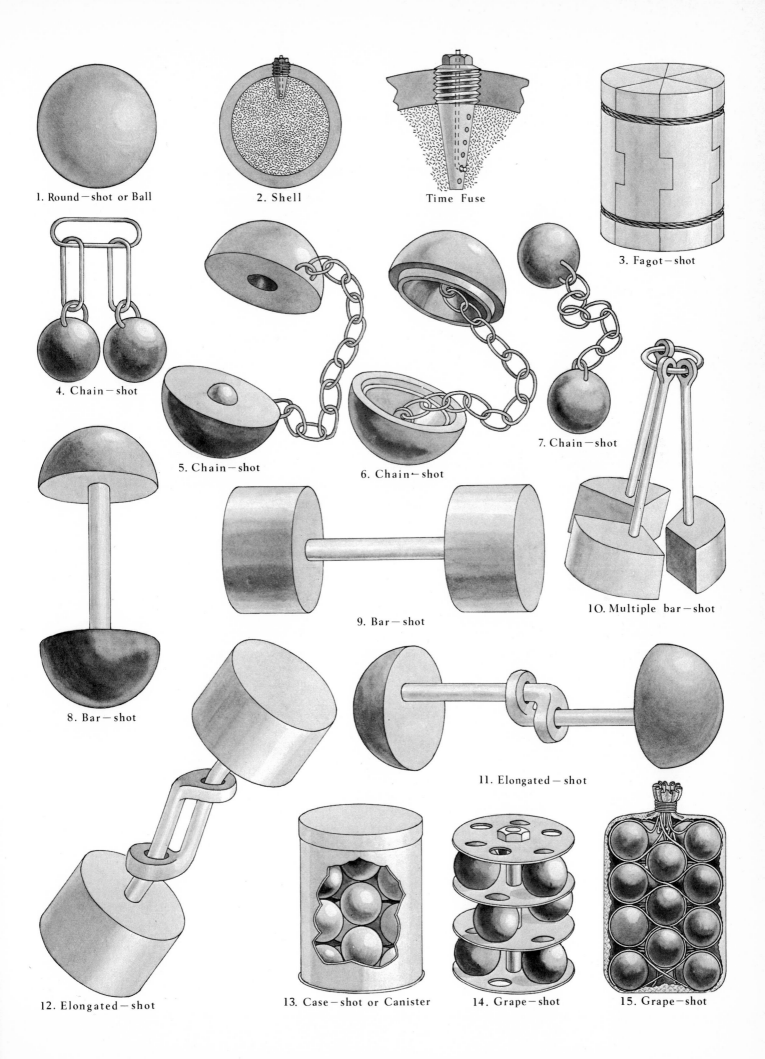

1. Round—shot or Ball

2. Shell

Time Fuse

3. Fagot—shot

4. Chain—shot

5. Chain—shot

6. Chain—shot

7. Chain—shot

8. Bar—shot

9. Bar—shot

10. Multiple bar—shot

11. Elongated—shot

12. Elongated—shot

13. Case—shot or Canister

14. Grape—shot

15. Grape—shot

Appendix 8

Glossary of Nautical Terms

Amidships — The middle of a ship between her stem and stern, or the middle between the sides when applied to the wheel.

Balinger — A large double-ended open boat with banks of oars, built as a fighting vessel in the Middle Ages.

Beam — The greatest breadth of a ship; but also, and originally, the name of the timber joining the sides of a ship and supporting her decks.

Beat to quarters — Until warships became too big for it to be practical, the men were called to action stations by a drum.

Bend — To knot one rope to another; also to bend a sail is to fasten it to its yard.

Board — Originally the moment of impact of one ship beside another, but later it meant to board and enter a ship, i.e. for men to go aboard.

Bonaventure-mizzen — The fourth mast abaft the mizzen found in some of the biggest late sixteenth- and early seventeenth-century ships.

Bowsprit — A large spar which points forwards, and in large vessels always upwards, from the bow over the ship's head.

Brig and brig-sloop — In nineteenth-century naval parlance a two-masted vessel square-rigged to topgallants on both.

Brigantine — In the same context as the brigs, a two-masted vessel square-rigged to topgallants on the fore, but fore-and-aft rigged on the main with a topmast.

Broadside — A ship's broadside was all the guns she could mount on one side or the other; also the discharge of the same.

Bulkhead — Vertical internal partitions between decks.

Bulwark — The side of ship from the deck to the gunwale.

Cable — The anchor rope or chain.

Cannon — The largest type of muzzle-loader, throwing a ball of about 30 to 60 pounds.

Cannon-drakes — A gun throwing a ball of cannon weight, but lighter and shorter in the barrel than a full cannon.

Cannon-perier — A chambered cannon throwing a stone shot of about 14 pounds in the late sixteenth century.

Carrack — The largest type of round-ship developed by the Portuguese in the fifteenth and sixteenth centuries, but also built in Northern Europe.

Carriage — (See Gun carriage.)

Carronade — (See page 63.)

Chambered gun — A gun-barrel in which the powder-chamber is of a different width to the ball or, in a breach-loader, was separate from the barrel.

Channel — Derives from chain-wale—broad, thick planks on a ship's sides down to which the shrouds are brought.

Clinker-built — Formerly called clincher-work, whereby a boat is planked so that the upper planks slightly overlay the ones below them.

Coach — In the seventeenth century the anteroom to the great cabin at upper-deck level, but in the eighteenth century an alternative name for the roundhouse, or the cabins at the after end of the quarter-deck.

Cog — A medieval double-ended round ship with a steering oar, thirteenth to late fourteenth century.

Counter — Just above the tuck and across the stern, it curves outwards under the stern-galleries.

Crank — Tender sided, incapable of carrying sail without the danger of over-turning.

Crossjack-yard — Usually abbreviated to cro'jack, it was really the mizzen yard to which the mizzen topsail was brought down. It rarely had a sail bent to it.

Culverin A gun as long as a cannon but firing a lighter ball; a smaller version was called a demi-culverin.

Cutter A single-masted gaff-rigged vessel with more than one head-sail.

Deck-head The ceiling between decks, usually consisting of the underside of the deck above.

Demi-cannon A smaller cannon throwing an iron shot of 18 pounds (late sixteenth century).

Dogger A two-masted vessel, square-rigged on the mainmast, a lateen-sail on the mizzen, and with a stay-foresail and jib.

Dolphin-striker A spreader jutting downwards from the end of the bowsprit to provide a fulcrum for stays to the jibboom and flying-jibboom.

Draught A drawing of a ship's lines for building her.

Driver (See page 55.)

Falcon A small carriage gun throwing a ball of about 5 pounds.

Falls The stepped down decks aft in Elizabethan and early Jacobean warships.

Fastening The method by which the timbers in a ship are joined together.

Filling A method of giving a ship protection against the toredines (see page 59).

Floor The inside of a ship's bottom next to her keel for as wide as it is reasonably flat.

Flush-decked A vessel whose deck or decks run continuously from stem to stern without falls.

Fly The breadth of a flag from the staff to the end.

Fo'c'sle A shortened form of forecastle, which is the fore-deck and the area immediately beneath it at the forward end of the upper-deck.

Frame The ribs making the outer shape of a ship.

Freeboard The distance from the waterline to the lowest port-sill.

Galleass A type of galley with the addition of a broadside armament over or under her oars.

Galleon (See page 11.)

Galley A large-oared vessel.

Grapple An instrument for attaching one ship to another in action, it was a

kind of hook; also the act of attacking.

Great ship The development of the carrack type of large broad vessel with large superstructures.

Gun carriage A wooden structure on which rested the trunnions and breech of the gun barrel and which could be moved on four wooden trucks, or sometimes a slide.

Gun-deck The lowest deck above the orlop on which, in ships of the line, the heaviest battery was placed.

Gunnade A type of short barrelled cannon that replaced the carronade.

Gunwale The timbers along the tops of the bulwarks.

Half-deck The deck from the break of the waist aft; it came in the late seventeenth century to be called the quarter-deck, which formerly was the deck above and abaft it.

Hermaphrodite brig A name used in the first half of the nineteenth century for what was later known as a brigantine.

Hold The space between the floor and the lower-deck.

Hoy A single-masted vessel not unlike a cutter but lacking her long gaff and bowsprit.

Jackstay A rope or rod running along a mast or yard to which a sail can be bent.

Jib-boom An extension to the bowsprit.

Jury The word is put before any part of a ship's fittings which is doing temporary duty for the real article which has been carried away or damaged.

Knee A heavy angled piece of timber connecting a ship's side timbers with her beams, latterly made of iron.

Liner A mid nineteenth-century word for a ship of the line.

Minion A small carriage gun throwing a ball of about 4 pounds.

Murderers The smallest type of carriage gun throwing a ball of about 2 pounds.

Nef The development of the cog, having a hinged rudder instead of a steering oar.

Oar-ports Small square holes in the sides of the ship for the oars or sweeps. If located on the lower deck they were fitted with hinged port lids.

Orlop A series of platforms in the hold, developing in big ships to a light deck which carried the cable, cabins for some junior officers and the surgeons operating table.

Paid off The act of de-commissioning a ship is known as paying off, because it used to entail paying the men and dismissing them. It also means when a ship's head has fallen off to leeward.

Pay An alternative to painting a ship was to coat it with a type of varnish; this was called paying.

Peak The upper corner of mizzen - sail supported by a lateen yard or a gaff.

Pivot-gun A small gun mounted in the jaws of a metal shaft set in the gunwale so that it could be freely elevated or traversed.

Primer A wafer containing gunpowder used at the touch-hole to fire the main charge.

Private ship A ship in commission but not carrying a flag-officer.

Quarters A ship's sides near her stern.

Quarter-deck Originally the deck above and abaft the half-deck, but by the end of the seventeenth century it took the place of the half-deck and became the deck running from the after-end of the waist, and above it, to the stern.

Race-built A sixteenth-century phrase for a low built galleon with very little superstructure.

Raking Bringing a ship's broadside to bear on the bow or stern of another ship.

Razee A ship that has had her hull altered by the removal of her upper decks is a razee.

Recoil The backward movement of a gun resultant on the force of its discharge.

Rifled Spiral grooving inside a gun barrel so that the bullet or shot leaves spinning, which keeps it pointing in the direction it is going.

Roundhouse The cabin space at the after end of the quarter-deck, in naval parlance also called the coach.

Royals The square sails above the topgallants used in light weather.

Rudder A flat framework hinged to the sternpost for steering the ship.

Saker A small carriage gun throwing a ball of $5\frac{1}{2}$ pounds.

Scuttles The naval term for porthole, which is used in the merchant service for the round glazed holes in a ship's sides and superstructures.

Sheathing Protective layers over the main timbers of a ship's bottom below the waterline (see page 59).

Sheer The longitudinal curve of a ship's decks or sides.

Shipwright A man physically involved with the building or repairing of ships. In naval dockyards a senior one might also be a designer.

Shrouds The standing rigging running from the mast-heads down and back to the channels on the ship's sides.

Spanker The loose footed mizzen-sail that replaced the full lateen sail, being laced to the mast.

Spar-deck A light deck in the form of a wooden grill supported on a stanchion above the upper, half and fo'c'sle decks, early seventeenth century.

Sprit-topmast A small vertical mast stepped on the end of bowsprit, carrying a square sail, seventeenth century.

Stay-sails Fore and aft sails bent to the stays.

Step A block of wood with a hole in the top to take the heel of a mast. Hence a mast is stepped into its place.

Stern-gallery A loggia at the after-end of the coach, and also of the great cabin in three-deckers, with a balustrade across the stern.

Stern-walk An iron or steel structure, usually canopied, round the stern of a ship, the successor to the stern-gallery.

Strike To remove or take down any part of the ship or her fittings.

Sweep A large type of oar.

Tackle A device of blocks and ropes for raising or securing heavy objects, or controlling guns, sails and yards.

Taffrail Old spelling tafferel, the uppermost part of the stern between the two gunwales.

Tender-sided A ship that heels over too easily and too far in a breeze.

Tier The collective name for all the cannon mounted on one side of a ship's deck.

Topgallant Used with the words masts, yards, sails, etc., denotes those

	immediately above the topmasts, and below the royals, if any.	**Tumblehome**	To reduce the weight of a ship's topsides her beam was reduced from the gun-deck upwards.
Transoms	The beams across the stern-post supporting the stern.	**Weather gage**	To be to windward of another ship.
Trebuchet	A medieval machine for throwing stones, etc. A spar on a pivot was winched back against a heavy counter-weight.	**Waist**	That part of the upper-deck between the quarter-deck and fo'c'sle.
		Wales	Extra planking at certain levels of a ship's sides above the waterline.
Troopers	Ships adapted or designed for the conveyance of troops.	**Whip-staff**	A stave attached to the tiller on a fulcrum for steering a ship (see page 58).
Tuck	The stern below the counter: in the seventeenth century round in English ships, square in Dutch and French Ships.	**Wolding**	The binding at intervals round a made-mast to hold it together (see page 56).

Bibliography

Charnock, John. *A History of Marine Architecture*. London, 1800–1802.

Clowes, William Laird. *The Royal Navy, a History from the Earliest Times to the Present Day*. 7 vols. London, 1897–1903.

Derrick, Charles. *Memoirs of the Rise and Progress of the Royal Navy*. London, 1806.

Douglas, Sir Howard. *Naval Gunnery*. London, 1821 and 1860.

Ffoulkes, Charles. *The Gun Founders of England*. Cambridge, 1937.

James, William. *Abstracts of the Royal Navy; showing how it stood, in Ships, Tons, and Classification at the commencement of every Year, from 1793 inclusive*. London, 1820.

James, William. *The Naval History of Great Britain*. London, 1822.

Morgan, William and Creuze, Augustin. *Naval Science*. London, vol. I, 1827; vol. II, 1829; vol. III, 1831.

Oppenheim, H. *A History of the Administration of the Royal Navy and of Merchant Shipping in Relation to the Navy 1509–1660*. London, 1896.

Raleigh, Sir Walter. *Excellent Observations and Notes, Concerning the Royal Navy and Sea-Service*. London, 1650.

Robertson, F. L. *The Evolution of Naval Armament*. London, 1921.

Schomberg, Captain Isaac, R.N. *Naval Chronology; or a Historical Summary of Naval and Maritime Events, from the Time of the Romans, to the Treaty of Peace 1802*. London, 1802.

Smith, John. *The Sea-man's Grammar and Dictionary*. London, 1692.

Index

Numbers in bold refer to illustrations.

Commissioning Budgee Pendant eighteenth century

2nd Class Commodore's Pendant
1824 to 1864

Commodore's Broad Pendant 1697 to 1864
1st Class from 1824 to 1864

2nd Class Commodore's Pendant 1864 to 1958
Commodore's Pendant from 1958

1st Class Commodore's Pendant
1864 to 1958

RNR Commodore's Pendant in
World War II, and since 1959

Ensign of c. 1623